What's the Best Way to Review a Resume?

Start at the bottom, where most candidates put the least flattering information, says personnel expert Robert Half, author of *The ___ ___ Get Hired in Today's Job Mar___*

Signs of weakness: 1) A la___ favorite technique of job-hoppe___ ___ ___ use of phrases such as knowledge of or assisted with or had exposure to. These are weak substitutes for hands-on experience. 3) A lengthy recital of seminars and special courses. It is a common ploy by those who lack the appropriate basic education. 4) Lots of trivia.

Source: Boardroom

The Evaluation Interview

The Evaluation Interview

Richard A. Fear
Personnel Consultant, Interviewer Training Services
Former Vice President of The Psychological Corporation

Revised Second Edition

McGRAW-HILL BOOK COMPANY
*New York   St. Louis   San Francisco   Auckland   Bogotá   Düsseldorf
Johannesburg   London   Madrid   Mexico   Montreal   New Delhi
Panama   Paris   São Paulo   Singapore   Sydney   Tokyo   Toronto*

Library of Congress Cataloging in Publication Data

Fear, Richard A.
   The evaluation interview.

   Includes index.
   1. Employment interviewing.   I.   Title.
HF5549.5.I6F4   1978   658.31′12   77-28019
ISBN 0-07-020201-X

   78910   MUBP   8987654321

*The editors for this book were W. Hodson Mogan and Joan Zseleczky,
the designer was Naomi Auerbach, and the production supervisor
was Teresa F. Leaden. It was set in Linotype by Monotype Composition Co., Inc.
Printed by The Murray Printing Company and bound by The Book Press.*

Contents

Part Two   Mechanics

Chapter Four   Helping the Applicant to Talk Spontaneously ...   59

Chapter Five   Exploratory Questions   82

Chapter Six   Guiding and Controlling the Interview   105

Part Three   Interpretation

Chapter Seven   General Factors of Interpretation 125

Chapter Eight   Interpreting Work History 163

Chapter Nine   Interpreting Education 194

Preface

The decision to write the second edition of *The Evaluation Interview* was based on continuing interest in the first edition, an interest that appears to be as strong today, after nineteen years, as it was during the first few years after its publication. During these nineteen years, moreover, the author has personally trained more than one thousand interviewers and, as a consequence, has acquired additional knowledge of interviewing techniques and interpretation of interview data.

This second edition, therefore, is a more sophisticated version than its predecessor. Chapter 4 has been rewritten with a view to encouraging the interviewee to become a partner in the interview. A completely new chapter, "Mental Ability, Motivation, and Maturity above All Else," has been added to the section on Interpretation in order to place greater emphasis on the importance of these three factors. And new material has been woven into almost all the original chapters.

The current volume provides a revised Interview Guide and a new Interview Rating Form. In place of the original chapter that included illustrative case studies, the new book provides three actual case write-ups, utilizing the new Interview Rating Form.

Many new time-tested questions have been added to several of the chapters, and the most important of these now appear for the first time on the Interview Guide. Comprehensive questions designed for the purpose of launching the discussion in each of the major areas are also included in this new edition. In short, *The Evaluation Interview* now includes *all* the source material the author currently draws upon in his own interviewer training.

This book is still an essentially practical how-to-do-it work—one that spells out detailed procedures for handling the applicant from the time he walks into the room until the interview is terminated. The reader is provided with a "track to run on" which guides him step by step through a discussion of the applicant's work history, education, early home background, present social adjustment, and self-evaluation. Comprehensive instructions for writing the report of interview findings appear in the final chapter.

As in the case of the first edition, this book is intended as an aid not only to personnel people but also to business and industrial managers who find it necessary to select new people from time to time. It should also prove useful to the colleges and universities in connection with courses in applied psychology, personnel management, and industrial relations.

In revising the second edition of this book, the author has tried in his examples to give equal emphasis to both sexes. And, when he has used *he* and *him* to refer back to such nouns as *interviewer, applicant, candidate, person,* or *individual,* these pronouns are meant to include both sexes. Finally, certain words in the business and industrial vocabulary such as *man specification* and *salesman* have such a traditional meaning that attempts to modify them can seem contrived. In any case, such words are meant to include both sexes.

This revised second edition includes suggestions for interviewing and interpreting data on minorities. However, the treatment here is confined to *major* considerations only. This book is primarily concerned with *methodology*—how to carry out a particular style of interviewing and how to interpret the ensuing information. Hence a comprehensive or extensive discussion of the interviewing of minorities would detract from the major purpose of the book.

In arriving at the philosophy and techniques here expressed, the author has drawn upon his practical experience as the principal source. At the same time, his thinking has naturally been influenced by the literature in the field which extends over a period of years and represents references too numerous to acknowledge individually. The author is also deeply indebted to colleagues past and present who have contributed valuable ideas along the way.

In the preparation of this second edition, the author wishes to express his particular appreciation to Dr. Henry H. Morgan of The Psychological Corporation for his critical reading of much of the new material and for many helpful suggestions. And, of course, he continues to be grateful for the immense assistance of other former colleagues at The Psychological Corporation for their many contributions to the original version. Dr. George K. Bennett, former president, edited the first manuscript and Dr. Rose G. Anderson, Dr. Theodore Haritan, Dr. William W. Wilkinson, Dr. Andrew Hilton, and Dr. Homer Figler provided many important suggestions.

Richard A. Fear

The Evaluation Interview

PART ONE

Orientation

CHAPTER ONE

Introduction

Since the first edition of this book appeared a number of years ago, great advances in industrial technology have taken place. In fact, it is estimated that scientific knowledge, accumulated since the beginning of recorded history, has more than doubled during the past ten years. Unfortunately, progress in the field of personnel has not kept pace. True, there has been notable progress achieved in the area of management training; but the vast majority of industrial concerns have not markedly improved their hiring and upgrading techniques—this in spite of the fact that excellent tools to do a truly effective job in these areas now exist.

That more attention is not being given to selection and promotion seems almost unbelievable, particularly in light of the fact that costs have been increasing steadily year by year. And, there seems every likelihood that this trend will continue. Much of this apparent lack of concern about selecting the right man for the right job stems, of course, from a lack of appreciation of the tremendous costs involved. Actually, the potential cost of hiring a technically trained man or woman right out of college can conceivably run into well over a million dollars. If this person stays with the organization for the rest of his working days—as many such newly hired people certainly do—he will earn an average salary of $25,000 a year and this extended over a period of forty years amounts to $1,000,000 alone. His fringe benefits and the overhead costs that must be attributed to him will amount to several hundred thousand dollars more. Yet the important hiring decision is too often made by managers who have had no formal training at all in the evaluation of people.

Happily, the more sophisticated companies are training their managers and employment staff in modern interviewing techniques. But the number of such companies is still relatively small. There is a big job to be done and, unfortunately, there is a serious shortage of really well-qualified instructors equipped to do the job. There is a great need to acquaint management with the complexity of the problem and with some of the modern tools that can be brought to bear on it.

The human being is a complex organism and as such is not at all subject to easy evaluation. The more we learn about people, the more we realize how complicated this business of selection and placement really is. We have learned, too, that there is no such thing as a "good applicant." An applicant is "good" only when placed in a job that makes maximum utilization of his abilities, satisfies his level of aspiration, stimulates his interests, and provides for his social needs. It has become equally apparent that people differ markedly with respect to these factors.

HUMAN BEHAVIOR AND
INDIVIDUAL DIFFERENCES

If we are to understand a given individual, we must have some knowledge of *how he came to be what he is today*. This presupposes some awareness of human behavior in terms of cause-and-effect relationships. For example, much of applicant A's current poise and social understanding may have been *caused* by the fact that he was brought up in high-level socioeconomic circumstances, where the parents made every effort to expose him to rich cultural influences. In our study of people we start out with one fundamental assumption: *all behavior is caused*. The behavior of a person at any given moment is a function of what he is like as an individual and the situation in which he happens to be.

If we accept the viewpoint that behavior is not accidental but arises from the interplay of the person and the external circumstances, we will be motivated to look for causes and hence to acquire a better understanding of the person. In subsequent chapters of this book, we will discuss techniques for exploring an individual's history so that these causes will become quite evident. At this point, however, it is important to know something about the factors that influence a person's development.

Psychological Growth

It is a generally accepted fact that heredity is responsible for much of our physical make-up, such as height, color of eyes, bodily structure, and glandular activity. Heredity also has a great deal to do with what we call native intelligence, energy output, and with the special talents that people exhibit in greater or lesser degree.

Environment, by which we mean the people, institutions, and situations with which the individual is in contact, represents a force of extreme importance in his psychological growth. In fact, many psychologists say that the first five years of life are critical in the development of basic personality and character traits. As a child grows older, he is subjected to many influences outside the home. These include friends in the neighborhood, school, and various groups to which the individual belongs. Generally speaking, we develop patterns of behavior which satisfy our needs, and because they do so, they tend to persist over a long period of time.

We must recognize, however, that almost without exception human traits are the products of both heredity and environment. Thus, while a single trait may be largely determined by one or the other, the influence of both must be taken into consideration.

It follows logically then that the development of the person is determined by both physiological and social factors. The individual is not a sum of these factors, but rather a product of their interaction. For example, in evaluating mental ability we must not only consider basic intelligence but also weigh the functional utility of the talent to the individual. Or, to put it another way, we must try to determine what kind of use the person makes of the talents he possesses.

By considering the relative degree of contribution to a given trait made by heredity and environment, we can determine the amount of change a person is likely to be able to effect in his behavior. There is little a person can do, for example, to change those traits largely determined by heredity, traits such as physical make-up and basic intelligence. And such traits of course represent limiting factors as far as achievement is concerned. Studies have shown, for example, that a child with an IQ under 90 has relatively little chance of graduating from high school.

On the other hand the evidence indicates that certain traits of motivation, character, and personality—traits chiefly due to environment, with heredity playing a secondary role— can be modified by varying the situations in which the individual finds himself and by exposing him to additional training. Hence, by manipulating his environment, the individual can often reduce the effects of his liabilities and in turn capitalize on his strengths.

Range of Individual Differences

We can evaluate a given person only by comparing him with a large number of other people—only by establishing a *frame of reference*. Therefore, it is important to have some idea of the ways in which people differ, as well as the range and scope of these differences. Actually, people do *not* fall into sharply divided types. Rather, individual differences are more a matter of degree than of kind. We can take almost any trait, such as height, weight, or native intelligence, and find that most people lie between the two extremes. The general pattern or distribution of many traits appears to conform to a curve that is shaped like a bell.

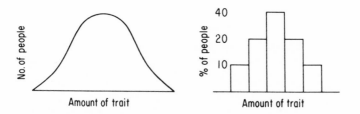

Experiment has shown that whatever the human trait or characteristic under consideration, measurement of it generally yields a distribution similar in form to that given above. We can thus think of people in terms of having more or less of a given attribute, rather than in terms of their not having it at all. Even an insecure individual has some degree of self-confidence. In our attempts to evaluate the individual and assess his growth potential, then, we must think in terms of those traits largely determined by heredity, which are primarily outside of his control, and those traits largely determined by environment and learning, which are primarily within his control. Such classification helps us to assess his growth possibilities and enables us to help him maximize his achievement within the limits of his potential.

Nature of Individual Differences

For purposes of evaluation in the business and industrial setting, it is important to realize that people differ with respect to at least four broad categories: *aptitudes, personality, character,* and *motivation.* Later on, we will discuss techniques for appraising the person in terms of these categories. First of all, let us look at each category in terms of definition and description.

Aptitudes. We all know that people differ with respect to intelligence, or their level of mental alertness and their ability to learn. Studies have shown that low-level mental ability represents the single most important reason why adolescents leave high school without graduating. On the other hand, those who attain academic honors generally rank in the upper part of the mental scale. People also vary considerably in such specialized abilities and skills as mechanical aptitude, eye-hand coordination, finger dexterity, and spatial visualization. As already noted, we are born with varying amounts of many aptitudes. At the same time, although training will not substitute for talent, an individual can be helped to capitalize on the gifts he *does* possess. There is a ray of hope for all of us here, therefore, since relatively few of us make maximum utilization of the abilities we have.

Personality. The term personality is used so loosely in our everyday language that its meaning has become somewhat obscured. When some psychologists refer to personality they mean the unique combination of traits, the sum total of which describe any one individual, dictate his reaction to stimuli, account for his adjustment to his environment, and determine the things that he can be trained to do. The category is, of course, very broad, being made up of such traits as intelligence, tact, social sensitivity, honesty, self-confidence, emotional control, and maturity, to mention but a few. For the sake of clarity and simplicity, however, the term personality as it is used in subsequent chapters of this book will be defined as those traits which are *not* included in the definitions of aptitudes, motivation, and character.

It becomes readily apparent, of course, that people differ widely with respect to any given trait of personality. Most people, however, fall between the high and low extremes of the distribution. Hence, we do not classify people as definite types, or attach labels to them. Furthermore, no one individual can be expected to have only favorable traits; each of us has both strengths and shortcomings. In our appraisal of an applicant, it is our task to decide whether or not his assets outweigh his liabilities in terms of the demands of a given job situation.

Although there are obviously wide variations in personality among people in general, and equally wide variations in specific characteristics within a given individual, it is fortunate that each of our personalities remains relatively constant. As mentioned earlier, the general personality pattern evolves during the early years. Naturally, the personality structure becomes *modified* as the individual encounters new situations and new learning experiences. But the general structure usually maintains its early form. Thus, we seldom see a person who in his younger years exhibited those traits usually associated with the extroverted personality change into an introvert during the later years of his life.

This is not to say, however, that one cannot improve the effectiveness of his personality, since these traits are potentially within his control. He can—if placed in the right situation and appropriately stimulated—develop a higher degree of a favorable trait and, at the same time, overcome to some extent certain personality shortcomings. This kind of growth we have all observed in some people who are suddenly catapulted into more demanding jobs. As a result of increased authority, greater job demands, and exposure to other people at high levels, they often acquire greater poise, become more decisive, and develop a higher degree of self-confidence.

Character. Here we are dealing with the person's moral code and ethical standards. In any given population, we find the immoral and the highly moral, the irresponsible and the highly responsible. As in the case of other human characteristics, however, most people's ethical standards fall in the middle, between the two extremes. If we study a single trait, such as honesty, we learn that people are not always consistent within themselves. That is, a person may be honest in most situations, but still he may behave in a somewhat underhanded fashion in others. It is our job as appraisers of people to know when a man will cut corners and when he will not, in order to judge the amount of responsibility he can be given.

It is fairly well accepted that the individual's basic predispositions with respect to character are molded during the early years in much the same fashion as his basic personality. Although character traits are potentially within the individual's control, in the sense that he can modify them in the right situation, these traits are perhaps more difficult to change than many others. Certainly, by the time a person is old enough to apply for a responsible job, his character will have become so firmly set that marked change is not likely.

Motivation. In this area we are concerned with the driving forces behind people's actions. We have seen that environmental and hereditary factors determine what the individual is basically like. His motivation, in turn, determines what he will do with his native talents and with his acquired skills. This relationship is often described by the formula:

$$\text{Ability} \times \text{motivation} = \text{achievement}$$

All humans possess certain common-denominator or primary drives, such as hunger, thirst, and self-preservation. The people with whom we are to deal as applicants, however, will normally have achieved a sufficiently high standard of living that their fundamental drives operate only rarely as the direct cause of behavior. The people with whom we are to be concerned will vary widely with respect to *secondary* motives such as the desire for prestige, recognition, approval, security, and money. Such forces as these, coupled with the individual's basic energy and vitality, largely determine the amount of effort he is willing to put forth in a work situation. When we probe for the person's motivation, then, we are actually trying to find out what makes him tick. This is not an easy task at best, particularly since we tend to attribute to others our own values and motives. In approaching the evaluation situation, we must strive to be as objective as possible, realizing that our own values and motives may not correspond to those held by others.

THE APPLICANT AS A HUMAN BEING

We have seen that fitting the right man to the right job is not an easy task, that there are many facets of the individual to be explored. We have also noted earlier that companies suffer tremendous losses because the hiring function is frequently executed so haphazardly.

But what about the applicant himself? He too has a very real stake in this business of selection. He is not like a commodity or a piece of machinery that can be purchased on an entirely impersonal basis. In many cases, his whole future may be involved. When any assessor of men and women makes the decision as to whether or not a given person should be hired for an important job or upgraded to a higher level position, he is assuming a grave responsibility. He had better be right in his decision, *equally for the good of the company and for the good of the individual.*

All too many people have been placed in positions that, on the one hand, make relatively little use of their real aptitudes and interests and, on the other hand, make demands upon them in areas where they are weakest. Thus, it is not uncommon to find a person with high verbal skills and low numerical skills eking out his life in some low-level accounting position. Such a person, if correctly placed and trained, might well have developed real proficiency in some job that would utilize his verbal assets, a job such as marketing or employee relations. In the employment situation, then, we must give equal attention to the individual's best interests as well as to those of the company. Normally, the two should not be in conflict, for what is best for the man is usually best for the employer. The basic objective of any personnel program is to maximize the effectiveness of all company employees.

The employment interviewer who adopts the above philosophy finds it easier to live with himself. When, after exploring all facets of a given applicant's qualifications, he is forced to make a negative decision, he does so with the realization that he is turning the applicant down for his own good as well as for the good of the company. It is more than likely that the same applicant may find a job elsewhere that is much more in accord with his abilities and interests. In fact, the decision to which we refer might well be a blessing in disguise.

If hired and inappropriately placed, the person might never realize his full potential and, what is even more serious, might develop into a frustrated, unhappy individual. In due time, of course, the employee or the company might make the decision to sever the relationship. In all too many cases, however, this does not happen; the inappropriately placed worker carries on for years as a marginal employee when he might very well have been an above-average producer in a better job climate.

The philosophy discussed above has other important consequences. When the interviewer is concerned with the applicant's best interests, this is normally conveyed to the person in some subtle fashion. As a result, the applicant becomes more cooperative than might otherwise have been the case. This is of vital importance, since *only rarely can we get the best possible picture of an individual in relation to the requirements of a job without his cooperation.*

CHAPTER TWO

Nature of the Evaluation Interview and Its Place in the Selection Program

Although this book is primarily concerned with interviewing techniques, some discussion of other commonly used selection devices helps to place the interview in its proper perspective. Since the final interview is a time-consuming and hence relatively expensive procedure, it should be used only with those candidates who satisfy the minimum job requirements. Most companies, therefore, utilize a series of screening techniques designed to eliminate rather quickly those applicants whose qualifications are inappropriate for the job or jobs to be filled. Such devices, when properly used, are of value to the candidate as well as to the company. The overall hiring procedure normally consumes several hours, and no applicant wants to waste his time being processed for a job that he has little chance of getting. An employment setup that does not allow for reasonably quick screening is not only inefficient but also unfair to the individual.

Many organizations today utilize a number of screening devices, such as preliminary interview, the application form, aptitude tests, and the reference check. All too frequently, however, these procedures are not appropriately integrated and are not given proper weighting in the final hiring decision. In some instances, for example, too much emphasis has been placed on the role of aptitude tests, with the expectation that such tests should be able to carry most of the hiring burden. Tests, of course, can make a valuable contribution in selecting people for many types of work, but at best they represent only one selection step and certainly cannot be expected to do the entire job. At some point, the all-important hiring decision must be made, and that normally occurs at the end of the final interview. Hence, the final interview represents the solid core of any good selection program.

The early selection steps then have two functions: (1) to eliminate those applicants whose qualifications can be determined as inappropriate at that stage and (2) to provide information that will be helpful to the interviewer at the time he makes his final decision. In effect, these selection steps represent a series of screens through which the successful applicant must pass, each screen being constructed of finer mesh than the previous one so that only the most appropriately qualified candidates will survive all of the screening. This means that the final interviewer sees only a fraction of the number of people who apply for jobs and thus is able to spend as much time as he needs with each surviving candidate.

TECHNIQUES OF SELECTION

Recruiting

It is axiomatic that no hiring program can be effective unless the number of applicants for a given type of work is substantially greater than the number of jobs to be filled. The very word "selection" implies the choice, for any given task, of the one best qualified individual from among a number of available candidates. Wherever careful selection is applied, it is of paramount importance that there be a relatively large reservoir of candidates from which the final selectees are chosen. This is what is known as the *selection ratio*. Ordinarily this ratio should be at least four or five candidates for each person finally selected.

We are always faced with the law of demand and supply in so far as the labor population is concerned, and the available pool of candidates for jobs requiring highly developed skills and long years of training is always limited. At the same time, it is important to choose the best people obtainable. In times of great industrial activity, many companies take a defeatist attitude toward the recruiting problem. They give up too easily, without having tapped all possible sources of supply. More alert organizations, on the other hand, maintain an aggressive recruiting policy. This often involves sending recruiters to neighboring communities, establishing company bus transportation to these communities, and contacting technical students in their junior year in college. One large chemical company has established the policy of hiring students for summer jobs at the end of their junior year in college. This not only permits a thorough evaluation of the student in the job situation but enables the company to *sell* the best-qualified students on the organization as a desirable place to work. This company's recruiting record is very impressive; it succeeds in getting a relatively high percentage of its summer-employed students at the time of their graduation from college.

Man Specifications

It is surprising that so few people recognize the seemingly obvious fact that intelligent selection is predicated on the knowledge of *what to look for* in the applicant. How indeed can we evaluate a person for a job if we do not know just what abilities and personality traits are necessary for success? Yet so many company employment departments are "playing by ear" in this respect. Now it is true that many companies have developed job descriptions as a result of their job evaluation programs. But most job descriptions tell what must be done rather than what ability and personality traits are required. Thus the job description, while certainly very helpful, is not wholly satisfactory for hiring purposes. In addition to these job descriptions, we need *man specifications.* The latter provide a list of those traits and abilities required for successful job performance, thus enabling the employment interviewer to compare the applicant's qualifications with the specific demands of the job. Without such man specifications good selection is difficult indeed. Suggestions for preparing man specifications will be found in Chapter 3.

Preliminary Interview

This represents the first screening stage. Within a period of five to ten minutes, those applicants who are obviously unqualified can be eliminated. This quickly clears the employment office and provides a means of scheduling the surviving applicants for subsequent tests and interview sessions.

The person who conducts the preliminary interview must be well trained and highly skilled. Within a short space of time, he must be able to identify obvious liabilities for the job in question and, at the same time, give the applicant the feeling that his qualifications have been given proper consideration. The latter is important in terms of the company's public relations policy and in terms of the applicant's feeling of self-worth.

Factors on which persons are normally eliminated during the preliminary interview include (1) inadequate experience and training, (2) age, (3) marked physical disabilities, and (4) completely inappropriate personality pattern for the job in question. The individual with a withdrawn, introverted personality, for example, cannot be expected to make the best use of his abilities in a pressure sales job. It should be emphasized, though, that only those applicants who are clearly lacking in necessary qualifications should be eliminated at this stage. Doubtful cases should be screened *in*.

In the case of those applicants who are *screened in* and are thus deemed qualified for further processing, the preliminary interviewer must make note of relevant points that should be followed up in the final interview. Remember, the function of the early selection steps is not only to eliminate but also to provide clues that will be helpful to the final interviewer in making his hiring decision. Thus the preliminary interviewer may get the feeling that an applicant is a "smooth operator" but, lacking sufficient time, may not be able to tell whether this will be an asset or a liability. Or he may be dissatisfied with a candidate's reasons for leaving his last job, even though his general impressions of the applicant are favorable.

Application Blank

Once the candidate has survived the preliminary interview, he is usually required to complete an application form that includes from one to four full pages of questions. Every company uses an application blank, but many such blanks fall far short of what they might be. Relatively few application blanks provide for all the information they should in terms of job and man specifications. Many application blanks for use with technical personnel, for example, fail to provide space for the applicant's publications, patents, dissertation title, and the specific nature of his previous jobs. Still fewer application blanks ask for information which might provide clues to be followed up in the final interview. For example, the inclusion of such items as (1) likes and dislikes on previous jobs, (2) age of applicant at graduation, and (3) estimate of expected earnings five and ten years hence, frequently provides clues to interests and personality traits that can be evaluated later in the selection process.

Experience has shown that it is possible, at least for some jobs, to weight certain items of experience, education, and personal history in a way that can contribute appreciably to the prediction of success during and after training. But the preparation of weighted application blanks requires a considerable amount of study, standardization groups of appreciable size, and the assistance of experts who are highly trained in their field.

Aptitude Tests

Aptitude tests provide a far more accurate tool for measuring certain ability factors than any other known device. For example, tests of mental ability, verbal ability, numerical ability, mechanical comprehension, and clerical aptitude provide more valid results than can be obtained by means of the interview. As will be shown later, however, the trained interviewer can make quite a good estimate of various aptitudes where test results are not available, drawing upon such factors as subject preferences, college-board scores, grades, effort expended, and academic standard of schools attended. This valuable function of the interview has become increasingly important, since many companies have eliminated aptitude tests because of Equal Employment Opportunity guidelines— guidelines that make it illegal to use tests that have not been validated in the specific work situation.

Aptitude tests can often make a substantial contribution to a selection program if they are carefully chosen, adequately validated, carefully administered and, finally, if the test results are closely integrated with findings brought to light through other techniques of the selection program. Aptitude tests can perform two important functions: (1) they can be used to eliminate applicants whose particular abilities do not meet the minimum job requirements and (2) they can provide valuable leads to be followed up in a subsequent interview. Let us say, for example, that as a result of careful investigation it has been shown that persons obtaining a score of less than 60 on a given test have very little chance of success on a particular job. This score of 60 then becomes a "cut-off score," and applicants whose test results fall below this point may be eliminated at this selection stage. As pointed out earlier, such elimination is in the applicant's own best interest; it is certainly not to his advantage to be placed in a job with critical demands in his weakest areas.

Tests can also provide valuable clues for the final interviewer. Such clues frequently stem from the applicant's behavior in the test situation as well as from the test results themselves. Thus the test administrator may notice that an applicant "'jumps the gun,'" beginning the test before the starting signal has actually been given and continuing to work after the stopping signal has been indicated. Such behavior might represent a possible clue to dishonesty in certain situations or might indicate that the applicant has a strong need to be competitive. Forewarned, the final interviewer is therefore in a position to follow up in an area that might otherwise have escaped his attention.

The test results themselves can often provide an alert interviewer with clues to the individual's motivation. Let us take the example of a woman whose mental test score is exceedingly high. This means of course that she is potentially capable of outstanding academic performance. If in the final interview this individual admits that her grades in school were mediocre, it becomes apparent to the interviewer that she did not apply herself in school. This alerts the interviewer to the possible finding that she may be lazy. If he can bring to light other clues pointing in the same direction, the interviewer is in possession of valuable information concerning the individual's motivation. On the other hand, the applicant with a mediocre mental score who claims to have made outstanding grades in school is either lying or, if she is telling the truth, must have worked so hard to get these grades that she has developed great application, perseverance, and self-discipline. The latter finding would indicate the so-called "overachiever," one who manages to surpass the level denoted by her basic abilities. Having discovered that he is appraising an overachiever, the interviewer would naturally want to know what prompted the applicant's needs in this direction. His subsequent findings might conceivably play an important part in his understanding of the woman's basic personality structure.

As indicated earlier, however, aptitude tests alone cannot be expected to do the entire selection job. To understand this, one has only to look at a typical man specification, one that lists factors favorable to success in any job. Now it is true that such a man specification will include factors that *can* be measured by aptitude tests. But it will also include numerous factors that do not lend themselves to test analysis. Let us take a man specification that might have been developed for a hypothetical sales job, for example. The nature and degree of favorable characteristics will obviously vary with the type of sales job under consideration, but it is safe to assume that the following abilities and traits would be found in many man specifications for sales positions: mental ability, verbal ability, social sensitivity, tact, desire to make money, willingness to work hard, self-discipline, ability to work without close supervision, extroversion, self-confidence, unobtrusive aggressiveness, sense of humor, persuasive ability, honesty, and dependability. Unfortunately, only the first two of these traits can be identified with any high degree of accuracy by means of tests; in the case of three or four of the other traits, tests can be helpful but the results must be confirmed by the clinical judgment of the interviewer in the final-interview situation. How, then, can tests alone be expected to do the entire selection job?

It is in the areas of personality and motivation that tests leave the most to be desired. The tests that have been built to measure various aspects of personality and motivation have proven least valid and reliable among all psychological tests so far developed. This is why their use is limited as an aid to selection in the average office or industrial employment situation. We should mention in passing, however, that certain personality tests—the so-called projective tests in particular—have shown promising results in the hands of the highly trained clinical psychologist. Even in this case, the projective tests are used primarily as a means of providing clues that can be followed up in the interview. Most industrial organizations are not fortunate enough to have a clinical psychologist as a member of their employment staffs. In the average company, then, means other than tests must be used to assess personality and motivation. As we shall later see, this is one of the most important functions of the evaluation interview.

Reference Checkup

In the case of applicants whose test scores satisfy the minimum job requirements, a reference check of previous employment is normally carried out. Reference checks by mail are seldom fruitful, since many employers are reluctant to commit themselves on paper with respect to an employee's deficiencies. Hence, reference checks should be made either in person or by telephone. The latter normally represents the most feasible means because the former is too time-consuming. In any event, this procedure is actually an interview situation. Only by utilizing such accepted interview techniques as establishing rapport, asking open-end questions, and getting information before giving information can one expect to get a reasonably true picture of the applicant's performance in previous jobs. These techniques will be discussed thoroughly in a subsequent chapter.

In fairness to the applicant, checks should be made with three previous employers, wherever possible. It is conceivable that one previous employer's evaluation might be emotionally toned and completely nonobjective. To take such findings at face value from a single source is both unfair and poor employment practice.

When unfavorable findings of a very serious nature are consistently obtained from two or three different sources, the applicant may be eliminated at this stage, even though he may have done well on his tests and successfully survived the other screening steps. There would be no point, for example, in spending valuable time interviewing a person who had been judged definitely dishonest by two or three former employers. For the most part, though, reference checks are principally useful as aids to the final interview. If at all feasible, then, they should be carried out before the applicant reaches the final selection stage. This permits the interviewer to check reference material with the statements the applicant makes during the interview or with the information he has supplied on the application blank. Where checks with previous employers draw attention to certain personality factors, moreover, the interviewer will be alerted to the possible existence of such traits and will make every effort to confirm them. In a sense, then, reference information provides the interviewer with a "head start." This is, of course, true with respect to all other information that stems from the early screening stages. Such "leads" help to establish hypotheses which can subsequently be examined.

NATURE OF THE EVALUATION INTERVIEW

Once the applicant has survived the early screening selection steps, he approaches the most critical aspect of the selection program, the final interview. It is in this interview that all the information obtained from the preliminary interview, the application blank, the aptitude tests, and the reference checkup is integrated with other factors of the individual's background, and the final decision is made. Too, we rely on the interview for appraisal of those traits which are impossible to assess by any other means.

Function of the Interview

The interview is designed to perform three basic functions: (1) to determine the relevance of the applicant's experience and training to the demands of a specific job, (2) to appraise his personality, motivation, and character, and (3) to evaluate his intellectual functioning, in terms of both *quantity* and *quality*. Where aptitude tests are not available, we must utilize the interview to determine how much basic intelligence we think the applicant has. And we must appraise the quality of the intellect—how much analytical power the individual has, how insightful he is, and how much intellectual depth and breadth he possesses. Suggestions for making these determinations appear in later chapters of this book. Suffice it to say here that, once all these factors have been assessed, the interviewer is in a position to make the final hiring decision. This is of necessity a subjective decision, a decision based upon the interviewer's experience and judgment. It is his task at this point to evaluate the candidate's assets and liabilities in terms of the demands of the given job. He must also judge the *extent* to which the assets outweigh the liabilities or vice versa. Only thus can he rate the applicant excellent, above average, average, below average, or poor.

Types of Interviews

For all practical purposes, interviews may be divided into three types: the direct interview, the indirect interview, and the patterned or evaluation interview. The direct interview

—perhaps best illustrated by the kind of exchange that takes place between a prosecuting lawyer and a witness in a courtroom setting—is one in which the interviewer maintains tight control, generally firing a barrage of limited and specific questions at the interviewee. This is often referred to as the "question-and-answer approach." The technique enables one to amass a large body of factual data in a short period of time but falls far short of the mark in getting at the candidate's generalized attitudes, traits, and habit patterns. In the direct interview, the applicant is on his guard and hence usually screens his remarks, giving answers that are calculated in his opinion to place him in the best possible light. Since we are looking for *true* responses rather than *screened* responses, the direct interview alone is entirely unsatisfactory for our purposes. This is primarily because this type of interview normally results in very little *spontaneous information*—information that bubbles to the surface without any conscious restrictions on the part of the applicant. Such spontaneous responses are of course likely to be much more genuine and usually provide many clues to the individual's assets and shortcomings.

The indirect interview—perhaps best illustrated by the exchange that takes place between a psychiatrist and his patient—is one in which there is usually very little control on the part of the interviewer. He permits the individual to "run with the ball" as the latter sees fit, interjecting only such questions and comments as may be necessary to keep the person on the track. Importantly, this type of interview is often completely spontaneous and, in that aspect, is highly desirable for our purposes. But, since the individual is permitted to talk about anything or everything that comes to mind, the discussion is almost completely unstructured and without any kind of system. This means that it is often quite impossible to cover all the important areas of the applicant's background within a reasonable period of time. Hence, the interviewer faces the task of making his decision on the basis of inadequate and incomplete information.

To our way of thinking, neither of the above two methods is appropriate to the business and industrial situation. Consequently, we favor the patterned interview which is actually a merger of both techniques. Here the conversation is guided adroitly by the interviewer, but the interviewee is encouraged to speak freely and at length about *relevant* topics. Control of the interview is maintained so that all important areas of the applicant's background can be covered systematically, but the information is obtained in an *indirect* manner. By adroit wording of comments and questions, and by reflecting the applicant's feelings, *spontaneous information* can be obtained without having to ask direct or pointed questions and without giving the applicant the feeling that he is being grilled or cross-examined. The patterned interview discussed in this book is referred to as the *evaluation interview* to distinguish it from other types of patterned interviews.

Basic Philosophy of the
Evaluation Interview

The evaluation interview as presented here is based on the assumption that the best indication of what an individual will do in the future stems from what he has done in the past. Past performance is not to be considered in terms of a single factor, such as work experience, but rather from the standpoint of the person as a whole. Thus, the interviewer is called upon to explore all important areas of the individual's background—his work experience, education and training, early home background, and present social adjustment. The philosophy of this interview, and indeed the philosophy of the entire selection program, is based on the principle that the more relevant information it is possible to obtain about the applicant, the better the basis for an intelligent employment decision.

Although the interview is patterned, in the sense that it follows a logical sequence and covers certain broad areas rather thoroughly, it is not at all mechanical or stereotyped. Within each interview area, in fact, the candidate is encouraged to tell his own story, the interviewer interrupting only to obtain more specific information or to direct the discourse into channels that lend sequence to the talk in accordance with the general plan of the interview. The less talking the interviewer has to do to maintain this pattern, the more successful the interview is likely to be. When thoroughly trained in these methods, the interviewer does only 15 to 20 per cent of the talking, for the most part permitting the candidate to take the center of the stage. This has the obvious advantage of enabling the interviewer to sit back and analyze the import of the applicant's remarks. If the interviewer does 50 per cent of the talking—as too many interviewers do—he has relatively little opportunity to evaluate the applicant during that half of the interview session. In an interview that lasts 1½ hours, then, the interviewer has only forty-five minutes to interpret the candidate's entire background.

We have already discussed the candidate's stake in the over-all hiring decision. And we have pointed out that it is to his advantage that the interviewer obtain a clear picture of his shortcomings as well as his assets. This objective is seldom achieved, however, unless the interviewer succeeds in getting *spontaneous information*. This, as we shall later see, is accomplished by creating a friendly, permissive, and sympathetic atmosphere and by making certain that the discussion takes the form of a pleasant conversation. In such a setting, the applicant's remarks usually become so spontaneous that he does relatively little screening of his words. Such remarks are therefore more likely to include clues to both assets and shortcomings.

Since most applicants approach the interview with the objective of putting their best foot forward, the interviewer must be motivated from the very beginning to search for unfavorable information. Otherwise, he is likely to be taken in by surface appearances and behavior. Interviewers are human and thus, despite their efforts to maintain objectivity, react more favorably to some persons than they do to others. When the initial reaction is favorable, the interviewer has a natural tendency to look only for those clues that will confirm his original impression. It must be remembered, though, that no one of us is perfect; we all have shortcomings. *The interview that results in no unfavorable information is inescapably a poor interview.*

The interview has been described as getting information, giving information, and making a friend. Although we agree with this general definition, we would reverse the order somewhat. In our scheme of things, we first concentrate on *making a friend,* then *getting the information,* and finally *giving the information* concerning the job for which the man is applying. Our rationale is that the interviewer does not get evaluative information unless he first establishes rapport with the applicant. Next we get the information about the man before we give the information about the job. Otherwise, we would tip our hand and thus make our problem of evaluation more difficult. The alert individual who is given a full description of the job at the very beginning of the discussion is in a position to color his story in such a way as to make his qualifications appear to be more relevant than they may actually be. Consequently, we make every effort not to tip our hand, either by prematurely divulging job information or by the wording of our questions. A question such as, "Did you get good grades in college?" alerts the applicant to the fact that we regard high college grades as important. In an effort to obviate such a giveaway, we try to keep our questions open-end and relatively unstructured. The question, "What about the level of your college grades?" encourages a person to talk about this subject without any knowledge of the importance we may attach to it.

Actually, this interview is an exercise in indirection. By means of adroit suggestions, comments, and questions, we try to elicit spontaneous information without having to ask direct or pointed questions. Obviously, if we are unable to get the desired information by means of indirection, our questions must become gradually more direct. Even so, we try to soften such questions by the use of appropriately worded introductory phrases and qualifying adjectives. Specific techniques for accomplishing this objective will be found in a later chapter.

SELECTING APPLICANTS FOR LOWER-LEVEL JOBS

The selection techniques described above are primarily designed for the evaluation of candidates for higher-level positions. This will represent our major emphasis throughout the remainder of the book. But the same general approach may also be used in processing applicants for lower-level jobs, the principal difference being the amount of time required. Thus, in selecting a file clerk—in contrast to a general office manager—we would normally use a shorter application form, fewer tests, and a much briefer interview. The difference in time required to process applicants for the two jobs is based on the fact that the file clerk's job is much less demanding. There would be no need, for example, to look for leadership ability and administrative skills—

abilities that would represent important requisites in the selection of a general office manager. In selecting candidates for the job of file clerk, therefore, the interview can frequently be completed within a period of twenty-five to thirty-five minutes. This is not only because the file clerk's job is less demanding but because most applicants for these positions are young people just out of high school, with relatively little experience and education to be evaluated.

In selecting applicants for lower-level jobs, the interviewer nevertheless explores all the major areas of the individual's background. And he uses the same information-getting techniques he employs in his interview with candidates for more important positions.

Interviewing in any case is truly an art and as such requires careful study and frequent practice. Mastery of this art will come only as a result of consistent, conscious application of techniques such as those discussed in later chapters of this book. Because indirection involves logical, step-by-step planning—in contrast to the impulsiveness of the direct approach—the process fortunately lends itself to a readily understood formula. Before we launch into a discussion of the recommended techniques, however, it seems appropriate to set forth some general suggestions on preparing oneself to become a good interviewer.

CHAPTER THREE

How to Become a Good Interviewer

An analysis of the interviewer's job reveals that he is called upon to perform two major functions. He must be able to acquire relevant information, and he must know how to interpret the data he has obtained.

Since it is not always easy to elicit information of a somewhat delicate and personal nature, *the interviewer must be a good salesman.* This statement may be surprising to some, but it is nevertheless true. The interviewer must be able to sell the applicant on "opening up and telling his story," even though some of the information developed may be of an unfavorable nature. Hence, it is exceedingly important that the interviewer possess the type of personality that will enable him to do a good selling job. Only by successful use of indirection and other techniques for setting the stage will the interviewer be able to get the real story.

Having obtained the appropriate information, the interviewer is then confronted with the second major function, that of interpretation. We might say in passing that interviewers in general do a better job of getting the story than they do of interpreting their findings. The latter is the more difficult function, quite probably because it places heavy demands on intellectual capacity and interviewing experience. But skill in either one of these functions alone is obviously insufficient. If the interviewer is unable to get all the relevant information, he has no real basis for evaluation no matter how good his interpretive skills. If he is successful in getting the data but unsuccessful in evaluating it, he is in equally difficult straits.

To carry out these two functions with any genuine degree of competence, the individual should possess a number of specific qualifications. Although many different qualities may contribute to the interviewer's success, the following are of paramount importance:

1. He should have a *warm, engaging manner.* Since the very essence of his job involves social contact, he must be the sort of person who meets others easily and to whom people react favorably upon first acquaintance. This quality of personality helps him to establish quick rapport and set the stage for a friendly, pleasant discussion.

2. He must be *sensitive in social situations*—quick to perceive implications in the remarks of others and sensitive to the slightest nuances of expression, vocal intonation, hesitation in responses, and other clues which may come to light in the interview situation.

3. The interviewer must be *reasonably intelligent.* His mental level should be as high as or higher than that of most of the applicants he sees, so that he will always be able to cope with the situation. Otherwise, there may be a question of who is interviewing whom.

4. *Analytical thinking* and *critical judgment* play a major role in the interpretation of data. Without these abilities the individual cannot be expected to evaluate properly all the positive as well as the negative factors and to arrive at a sound decision.

5. He must be *adaptable*. The good interviewer must keep an open mind and must be able to adjust his approach and his thought processes to a variety of applicants.

6. The interviewer must be *mature* as a person. Otherwise, he cannot be expected to show good sense or sound practical judgment.

In the light of these qualifications, it is quite apparent that not everyone can be expected to become a good interviewer. It is equally apparent that many companies fail to evaluate properly the interviewer's job. As we have already seen, the interviewer's day-to-day decisions may largely determine the organization's competitive position in the years ahead. Consequently, the interviewer should be carefully selected and well compensated. All too many companies assign inappropriately qualified persons to this function, give them very little training, and pay them far too low a salary.

IMPORTANCE OF TRAINING

It stands to reason that appropriate job qualifications are not in themselves sufficient to ensure successful interviewing performance. *A good interviewer must be carefully trained.* Interviewing is an art that involves a number of specific skills. Hence, the individual *must learn by doing.* Competence can be achieved only by practice under the supervision of an expert.

True, there are some persons who learn to play golf on their own by the trial-and-error method. But most people require the tutelage of a professional, one who can put them on the right track at the very beginning. So it is with interviewing. Like any other function involving skills, interviewing cannot be learned by reading a book, no matter how comprehensive the book may be. The book can, of course, define the skills, provide the appropriate rationale, and lay out the proper course. But practice under the supervision of an expert is the best means of acquiring a high degree of skill.

Some people regard themselves as expert merely because they have been interviewing applicants in an employment office over a period of years. But practice makes imperfect as well as perfect, and if the person has started out with an erroneous or incomplete approach to the interview situation, he may have spent much of this time simply practicing his own mistakes.

The method of interviewer training recommended here follows the classic teaching pattern. The trainer discusses the philosophy of the interview and *tells* the trainees how to perform the skills. He then *demonstrates* these skills by conducting regular interviews with bona fide applicants and permitting the trainees to observe his performance. Subsequently, the trainees do the interviewing with the trainer observing. Thus, they get *supervised practice*—practice that represents such an important element in the acquisition of a new skill. Their mistakes are corrected and they start out on the right track at the beginning. Because of his experience and greater frame of reference, moreover, the trainer can *establish standards of evaluation,* thus enabling the trainee to give proper weight to the various findings that come to light in his interview. The trainees thus learn to make sound over-all decisions with respect to the applicant's qualifications for a given job.

MAJOR INTERVIEWING ERRORS

One of the functions of a book such as this is to point out errors that inevitably creep into interviewing practices. Such errors are quite easily recognizable, and many interviewers may see some of their own tendencies highlighted in the section that follows. A frank admission of the existence of these tendencies together with a sustained effort to eliminate them should result in a much better performance.

The Unsupported Hunch

Perhaps because of the pressure of having to see a number of people in too short a time, many interviewers rely upon so-called "hunches," jumping to conclusions which have little or no basis in fact. Many of us, for example, have a temptation to classify people according to physical appearance. We may jump to the conclusion that the man with a square jaw is a person with great determination, or that the person with red hair has a hot temper, or that the individual with eyes set rather close together is not to be trusted. Many studies, of course, have shown that such conclusions have not the slightest validity.

It can be emphasized, too, that there is little truth in the adage that neatness of dress indicates careful job performance. Investigations have shown that the carelessly dressed die maker may very well be a meticulous workman. The most fastidiously dressed employee may have slovenly work-habits.

The evidence indicates that some judgments developed in the course of an interview may be affected by factors of which the interviewer is unaware. All of us are undoubtedly influenced—often without recognizing the fact—by our conceptions of what a criminal, a dilettante, or an honest man really looks like. We build up stereotypes of such people over a period of years on the basis of our personal experiences, movies, radio, newspaper cartoons, and the like. If we are not constantly on the alert, we may base an important interview decision on the resemblance of an applicant to some preconceived stereotype.

The Halo Effect

It is also a human tendency to permit a single prominent characteristic to overshadow all others. Thus, we may become so favorably impressed with a man because of his outstanding habits of hard work that we tend to rate him higher than he should be rated on other traits. This error has been called the "halo effect," since the interviewer reacts as if the one outstanding trait had cast a halo around the applicant, making all his other characteristics appear correspondingly better.

The halo effect also operates in the opposite direction. If a man rates below average in mental ability, for example, we may have a tendency to write him off, without taking the trouble to explore fully his real assets. It is conceivable that he may work so hard and may make such extensive utilization of the abilities he does have that he compensates in large measure for his below-average mental level. Remember, we are not being fair to the man if we permit one shortcoming to influence judgment of his other traits disproportionately.

If one is to avoid the halo effect, he needs to think in terms of specific traits and to strive for objectivity in his judgments. We once knew a college professor who scored an examination in essay form by reading question number one as answered by each student in the class, then reading the second question, and so on until he had completed all the papers. He admittedly did this so that he would not be unduly influenced by a given student's performance on a single question.

Now *some* initial impressions are very valuable to an interviewer, *but only if he is able to obtain subsequent information that supports these impressions.* We may see that a given applicant is very strongly aggressive, for example, and hence may get the impression that he might not be very tactful. In a sense, this gives us a head start since we can look specifically for the possible existence of tactlessness. But we can only appraise him as tactless in our final evaluation if we find good and sufficient evidence of this trait, as a result of our exploration of the man's work history, education, and present social behavior. In all cases, we must think in terms of the individual applicant, base our judgments on concrete observations and inferences, and be specific in our evaluations.

BUILDING MAN SPECIFICATIONS

To become a good interviewer, one must acquire a thorough knowledge of the jobs for which he is selecting applicants. As we have pointed out in a previous chapter, far too little attention has been given to this important factor. The interviewer must not only know what the man is to do in a given job, but must also have a knowledge of the specific traits and abilities necessary for success in that job. Otherwise, he finds it impossible to match the applicant's qualifications with the job demands.

As a first step in acquiring an understanding of job requirements, the interviewer should spend a considerable amount of time in the plant or office, familiarizing himself with working conditions, physical demands, promotional possibilities, occupational hazards, and other factors of the work setting. Next, he should give his attention to specific job requirements in each department. In this connection, he will want to become acquainted with the supervisor as a person, for the purpose of developing a cooperative working relationship with the individual and getting his views on what he regards as important for success in the various jobs under his direction. In the course of his discussions with the supervisor, the interviewer, if appropriately observant, will learn something about the man's personality make-up and will get some definite impressions as to the type of applicant he prefers. He may find that a given supervisor is unusually hard-boiled, for example, the kind of man who would quickly break the spirit of an overly sensitive, soft employee. Or he may find that one supervisor is prejudiced against individuals with higher education or those who have "weak chins." On the basis of these findings, the interviewer learns whom to refer to a particular supervisor and whom not to refer. We all know that an employee has two strikes against him if he happens to be the type of person against whom his immediate superior is prejudiced, even though he may be a perfectly good worker.

In his investigation of job requirements, the interviewer should chat with various persons on the job in each department. These are the people who are actually performing the job duties and are, therefore, in a position to provide salient information. It is important not only to get their ideas of trait and ability requirements but also to find out what aspects of the job give them greatest satisfaction. In this way, the interviewer builds up a body of information concerning the job climate. In talking with subsequent applicants, he will be in a better position to know whether or not the candidate's likes and dislikes fit the pattern of the workers in a given department.

On the basis of his observations, his discussions with supervisors, and his visits with people on the job, the interviewer is in a position to write down a list of *man specifications,* those traits and abilities which appear to be most important for successful performance on the important jobs in each department. This list should include such factors as general mental level, any specific aptitudes such as mathematical ability or mechanical comprehension, personality requirements, physical demands, and general attitudes. And the interviewer should check his observations by every means possible. Thus, he may be able to test current employees as a means of establishing the optimal level of mental ability and other specific aptitudes. He can also make a study of job failures by carrying out a thorough discussion in an exit interview at the time the employee leaves the company. This permits him to modify his man specifications in accordance with subsequent experience. It is vitally important that the man specifications be kept up-to-date. In some of the younger, more dynamic industries, such as the aviation industry, the job content changes rather frequently. This occurs at the upper levels as well as at the rank-and-file level.

If the interviewer's function extends to the employment of clerical people or sales personnel, he should make a similar study of those jobs. In acquiring familiarity with the requirements of sales positions, it is advisable not only to talk with the sales manager but actually to accompany a number of the salesmen on their regular rounds. As a result of the latter, the interviewer gets a first-hand picture of the problems that confront the salesman. In this way, he can get a far more accurate estimate of the degree to which various personality traits and abilities are required.

The resulting man specifications for any job will be composed of a list of *favorable factors,* those qualifications that play the biggest part in successful job performance. In appraising applicants for a specific job, one will, of course, seldom find a man or woman who possesses *all* the favorable factors; the employment decision will have to be made by selecting the person who possesses more of these qualifications than his competitors.

Before embarking on the task of developing man specifications, the interviewer should have in mind a *general idea* of the qualifications normally found in successful employees on a wide variety of jobs. This permits him to ask about the relevance of a given trait, should the supervisor or subordinate fail to include it. If the interviewer is able to give the impression of having some understanding of certain jobs, he will gain quicker rapport with supervisors and subordinates alike. They will get the feeling that he knows his business and can be helpful in adding good workers to their unit. They will be correspondingly more cooperative and will do a better job of supplying the needed information.

With these objectives in mind, we have prepared a series of general man specifications for a number of key jobs, based on knowledge gained from evaluating candidates for these jobs over a period of many years. It should be emphasized that the specifications that follow are *general* rather than *specific.* Hence, they cannot be expected to represent the requirements for any one job in any given organization. On the contrary, they are designed to give the interviewer a general overview and are to be used primarily as background information. Specific job demands vary widely from company to company, depending upon job content, organizational setup, and company atmosphere. In developing the following man specifications, we have omitted certain common-denominator traits that are important in practically all jobs, traits such as honesty, loyalty, willingness to work hard, and ability to get along with people. In other words, these specifications are limited to those traits and abilities which are most likely to vary from job to job. Abilities preceded by a bullet are those which can be best determined by means of aptitude tests.

MANAGEMENT

Qualifications for executive positions vary with respect to level of responsibility and the kind of people to be supervised. The chief accountant, for example, need not have the same degree of dynamic, tough-minded leadership normally required in the plant superintendent. In general, however, the qualifications for the executive may be broken down into two categories: leadership and administrative ability.

Leadership	*Administrative Ability*
Aggressiveness	■ High-level mental ability
Production-mindedness	■ Good verbal ability
Tough-mindedness	■ Good numerical ability
Self-confidence	Ability to think analytically
Courage of convictions	and critically
Ability to take charge	Good judgment
Ability to organize	Long-range planning ability
Decisiveness	Good cultural background
Ability to inspire others	Breadth and perspective
Tact and social sensitivity	Ability to see the broad,
	over-all picture

Rationale

The ideal executive is a happy blend of the leader and the administrator. To make these terms more meaningful, let us take an example from the military establishment. Leadership is best personified in the second lieutenant operating on the front lines who personally influences his subordinates into carrying out his commands. Administrative ability is represented by the critical job demands found in headquarters staff assignments, where officers operate behind the lines planning the logistics, working out the strategies of battle, and making the all-important decisions.

As a leader, the executive must be able to influence his subordinates so that they willingly carry out his wishes. On the one hand, he must be forceful, dynamic, and willing to take charge. Since he is dealing with the human element, he must at the same time use tact and social sensitivity in his general approach. Social sensitivity, or awareness of the reactions of others, plays a big part in the development of good human relations. The leader who understands his subordinates and senses their reactions knows which one needs forceful direction and which one needs a "pat on the back" in order to obtain optimal job performance.

A true leader must have the decisiveness born of self-confidence and the courage of his convictions. He must believe implicitly in his own abilities and, once he has set his course, he must follow through without any wavering of purpose. In this connection, too, he should be tough-minded, in the sense that he is willing to make difficult decisions that tread on the toes of the few but work for the good of the many.

In the final analysis, industry rewards the one who is able to get things accomplished. Thus, the leader must be able to organize and inspire his men so that he accomplishes his purpose in the shortest possible period of time. This ability is often referred to as production-mindedness.

As the behind-the-scenes administrator, the executive is faced with day-to-day as well as long-range planning. Since this is an intellectual function, it requires a rather high degree of mental ability. The individual is called upon to think in the abstract and to integrate a large number of complex factors. To do a top job as an executive, then, the individual's mental level should be appreciably above the average of college graduates. This also holds for verbal and numerical abilities. The former play a big part in one's ability to communicate, to express oneself well orally and on paper. The executive who cannot establish good lines of communication is handicapped indeed. Although numerical ability may not be quite so important as verbal ability in many executive positions, it nevertheless plays an important role in such job functions as setting up budgets, analyzing statistical reports, and the like. The administrator is constantly faced with the task of analyzing various problems, breaking them down into their component parts. In working out solutions to these problems, he cannot afford to take things at face value. He must examine each factor critically, looking beneath the surface to explore any possible hidden meaning.

If he is to exercise good judgment, it logically follows that the administrator must have breadth and perspective. He must see every item in relation to the whole picture. Otherwise, he will find himself in the place of the man who cannot see the forest for the trees. Experience has shown that a good cultural background adds appreciably to one's ability to see the over-all picture. Some knowledge of the arts and some understanding of the cultures of other peoples normally produce a body of knowledge that contributes to intellectual maturity and judgment. This is the factor to which many industrial leaders refer when they characterize someone as "broad-gauged."

The executive qualifications discussed above are, of course, not all inclusive; there obviously are many other traits and abilities that make a contribution. The discussion of every conceivable contributing trait, however, would undoubtedly complicate the presentation in such a way that attention might be diverted from the most important prerequisites. We should like to emphasize again that no single executive is likely to possess *all* the above qualifications. None of us is perfect; we all have some shortcomings. For the most part we carry out our jobs as well as we do because certain of our assets are strong enough to compensate for our shortcomings. So it is with the executive; he may possess certain traits in such abundance that they largely make up for what he may lack in other areas.

RESEARCH AND DEVELOPMENT

Jobs in this category spread over a wide scale as far as job content is concerned. At one end of the scale we have the "long haired" research worker who is searching for truth for truth's sake. At the other end of the scale we find the practical pilot-plant operator who is principally concerned with getting the "bugs" out of some process that others have conceived and developed. The vast majority of research and development people, however, fall somewhere between the two extremes of the scale. Their general qualifications can be summarized as follows:

- Superior mental capacity
- Superior numerical ability
- Good verbal ability
- Good mechanical comprehension
- Good spatial visualization

Ability to think analytically and critically

Tendency to be reflective
Intellectual curiosity
Creativity
Carefulness
Methodicalness
Ability to handle details
Patience
Good academic training

Rationale

There can be no substitute for top-level mental and mathematical abilities if one is to operate with a high degree of productiveness in a research and development job. In fact, this type of a position probably places more demands on intellect than any other industrial assignment. Much of the work involves thinking in the abstract and using current knowledge as a springboard to new and uncharted fields. In many technical jobs, moreover, mathematics and physics are requisite to obtaining the desired objectives. Thus, the best people invariably possess numerical facility, an understanding of mechanical principles, and an ability to perceive spatial relationships. As a group, they are also remarkably analytical and critical in their thinking.

The ability to conceive new ideas is, of course, an important requirement in a research and development person. Here again intellect plays an important part. Although all brilliant people are not necessarily creative, one seldom finds a real "idea man" who does not have a relatively high degree of intelligence. Such a person is usually reflective, in the sense that he has a strong theoretical drive. He is the kind of person who has so much intellectual curiosity that he is motivated to dig to the bottom of a problem and find out what makes things tick. His curiosity leads him to forsake the *status quo* in quest of new and better ways of doing things.

Because the job requires a reflective person and one who can adjust to a somewhat confined work situation, the research and development person usually displays some degree of introversion. For the most part, he is not the kind of a person who requires contact with large numbers of people in order to find satisfaction on the job. On the contrary, he is usually content to work by himself or as a member of a small group.

Technical experiments are of such a precise nature that one minor slip may completely invalidate the results. Consequently, the research and development person learns as a result of sad experience that his approach to problems must be carried out methodically, systematically, and with painfully accurate attention to detail. Nor can he afford to be impatient if his first hypothesis proves to be inadequate. The majority of new developments come only as a result of attacking a problem over and over again.

In view of the high technical demands and the unusual complexity of the work, extensive academic training is naturally an important prerequisite. Whether the person be a chemist, a chemical engineer, or a mechanical engineer, he must have taken full advantage of his educational opportunities and acquired a tremendous body of knowledge and skills before he arrives on the industrial scene. Ordinarily, then, our top research and development people will have obtained high academic grades in college and in graduate school.

PRODUCTION SUPERVISION

The people who oversee the manufacture of the final product include foremen, general foremen, and plant superintendents. Hence, job requirements will vary with respect to the level of responsibility. The differences between foremen on the one hand and plant superintendents on the other are those of *degree* rather than *kind,* however. We expect the plant superintendent to have a higher degree of the essential qualifications than that possessed by the general foreman. Presumably this was the reason he was promoted to his job. In turn, the general foreman rose from the foreman rank because he had a little more of what it takes. Experience has shown that the following qualifications are generally basic for production supervision:

- Good mental ability
- Good verbal ability
- Average numerical ability
- Good mechanical comprehension

Ability to see the over-all picture
Ability to plan and organize
Strong practical interests

Production-mindedness
Ability to improvise
Aggressiveness
Tough-mindedness
Self-confidence
Ability to take charge
Tact
Social sensitivity

Rationale

Production supervisors are a special breed. They are the people who devote most of their attention to putting out day-to-day fires, eliminating production bottlenecks. It is their prime function to get the final product "out the door." Consequently, they must have exceedingly strong practical interests and must be unusually production-minded. The foreman, general foreman, or plant superintendent who is not highly motivated to get things done in a hurry is not worth his salt. Since production bottlenecks may occur in the most unexpected places, the production man must be a good improviser, one who can solve problems for which there has been no time to prepare. On the basis of his ingenuity and past experience, he must somehow make the thing work, even though a better solution to the problem may subsequently be found.

Anyone who is called upon to solve problems must, of course, have a certain degree of mental ability. Because the production supervisor's job is so much concerned with ability to communicate to others, verbal ability represents an important requisite. Although numerical ability perhaps plays less of a role than verbal ability in this type of work, a certain degree of number facility is involved in such job functions as scheduling, preparing time sheets, and in analyzing statistical reports. More often than not, the manufacturing process has to do with making "hardware," objects such as appliances, airplanes, automobiles, and furnishings. Such an activity, therefore, requires mechanical know-how and understanding. As indicated by the bullets above, mental, verbal, numerical, and mechanical aptitudes can be validly determined by means of tests. In considering an applicant's test results in the light of the demands of various production jobs, different normative data for tests will usually be used. In other words, the plant superintendent's tested abilities will usually be compared with those of college graduates, whereas the tested abilities of the foreman and general foreman will be compared with those of high school graduates.

Although the production supervisor is first and foremost a leader, he must also have some traits of the administrator in his make-up. He is faced with the problem of planning and organizing his work, and he must be able to see the broad picture. If he gives an inordinate amount of attention to one specific aspect of the work, the manufacturing process as a whole will suffer.

This type of work places unusually heavy demands on the leadership function. The production supervisor must have those qualities that enable him to inspire his people, motivating them to get out the production in the shortest period of time. Confronted with the task of supervising some employees who may be hard to handle, the supervisor must be particularly tough-minded, aggressive, and self-confident. At the same time, he cannot afford to ride roughshod over his subordinates. A certain amount of tact and social sensitivity is important here, as it is in all supervisory positions.

SALES

There is perhaps more variation in sales jobs than in any other single business function. They range all the way from high-pressure, foot-in-the-door selling to low-pressure, technical sales service. Hence, some of the traits listed below will loom more important in some sales jobs than in others. But all salesmen have two important functions in common: they are required to contact people and they are called upon to persuade others to their point of view. These functions inevitably demand the following qualifications:

- Good verbal ability
  Good self-expression
  Extroversion

  Strong desire to make money
  Aggressiveness
  Tough-mindedness

Color	Self-confidence
Infectious enthusiasm	Tact
Sense of humor	Social sensitivity
Persuasiveness	Self-discipline
Practical interests	Perseverance

Rationale

The best salesmen are normally those who need the stimulation that comes from dealing with people in order to find job satisfaction. Quite the opposite of the reflective individual, they tend to be extroverted, outgoing, colorful, and infectiously enthusiastic. They call upon these traits in their efforts to persuade others to buy their product. Competition being what it is, the sales job is not an easy one. The better people are highly articulate, possess good basic verbal ability, and know how to handle themselves adroitly in face-to-face situations. The latter ability, of course, involves tact and social sensitivity. The salesman must know when to talk and when to keep still, and he must be continually alert to the customer's reactions. This permits him to take a different tack if he notes that his first approach is not getting across. A good sense of humor is indispensable in many types of sales jobs.

The salesman's lot can be quite an arduous one. He lives out of a suitcase and often spends days at a time on the road away from his family. There must be some motivation, then, that attracts him to this field, in addition to the one of having a chance to deal with people. That motivation is usually compensation. Most salesmen are extremely practical and have a strong desire to make money. Many of them find that they can make more money in sales than in any other type of work for which they might qualify. It is true that sales jobs as a whole pay better than many other types of work.

The task of getting a hearing demands certain traits of personality. Busy executives often feel that they do not have time to see the salesman and instruct their secretaries accordingly. In order to gain a hearing, then, the salesman must be unobtrusively aggressive and self-confident. Too, he must be sufficiently tough-minded to take rebuffs in his stride.

Many salesmen work largely on their own, with very little supervision from their immediate superiors. This calls for a good bit of self-discipline. The one who goes to the movies in the afternoon just because he has made a big sale during the morning seldom turns out to be a top producer. He must be constantly aware of the law of averages, that the more calls he makes the more sales he is likely to get. In going after big accounts, moreover, he cannot become discouraged. He must persevere, calling on that account again and again until he finally makes the sale.

PURCHASING

The purchasing agent has often been called a salesman in reverse. Although he is on the other end in the sales situation, it is nevertheless his job to bargain with the salesman in an effort to get the lowest possible price for his company. In a sense, then, he performs the same functions as the salesman. He deals with people and he has to sell the salesman on getting the best price.

Although the purchasing agent need not be as extroverted as the average salesman, he should have many of the traits listed above under the sales category. Certainly, he must be aggressive, self-confident, and tough-minded in his bargaining activity. And he must utilize all the various traits that contribute to persuasiveness.

There is at least one important difference between the purchasing agent and the salesman. That difference is cost-consciousness. The purchasing agent has a big responsibility for his company's cost of operation. A quarter of a cent a pound in the price of some raw material used in tremendous quantity may result in the saving of hundreds of thousands of dollars in a large corporate enterprise.

FINANCE

This category includes a series of jobs ranging from the accounting clerk to the company comptroller. Again, although there is a marked similarity in the traits required in all of these jobs, the degree of each trait required will vary in accordance with level of responsibility. The lower-level jobs, of course, do not make as much demand on the intellectual and administrative factors. In practically all financial jobs, however, the following traits and abilities play an important role:

- High-level mental ability
- High-level numerical ability
- Good verbal ability
- Good clerical aptitude

Ability to think analytically and critically

Ability to plan and organize

Good judgment

Ability to see the over-all picture

Carefulness

Methodicalness

Orderliness

Attention to detail

Rationale

Although employees in the financial field naturally deal with people, they are principally concerned with figures and with things. Their work is likely to be rather confining, and the people who adjust most easily to this type of work are, therefore, inclined to be somewhat introverted. Since even the smallest error must be found before reports are submitted, financial people place great stress on accuracy and close attention to detail. As a group, they are very careful, methodical, and systematic.

High-level intelligence is combined with superior numerical facility as prime requisites in financial jobs. Arithmetical computation is not in itself sufficient. Practically all of these jobs require a high degree of mathematical reasoning. Statistical data must be *interpreted* in the light of the facts and in the light of the company's needs. Clerical detail must be handled quickly and accurately. This is why the better people tend to have high clerical aptitude. At some point, financial statements and other reports have to be prepared for top management. Hence a degree of verbal ability is necessary.

At the upper levels, the finance person is required to supervise relatively large groups of people. Since the majority of his subordinates are likely to be somewhat introverted, however, he is normally not required to exert dynamic, tough-minded leadership. Rather, his leadership is of an administrative character. Principal emphasis here is placed upon good judgment, ability to plan and organize, and ability to see the broad picture. The comptroller must be able to watch all the company operations and must be able to assimilate and integrate his findings so that he can keep his finger on the financial pulse of the entire enterprise. Above all, he must be analytical and critical. The comptroller takes nothing for granted; he is accountable to top management and therefore must not only be in possession of the facts but must be aware of the underlying reasons.

Modern industry is showing an increasing tendency to diversify and to develop multiple products. Multiplant operations make the financial job all the more complex. To qualify for top-level positions in this field, then, the individual should have sound academic training. Today, many of the better young candidates have a master's degree in business administration, with a major in finance.

EMPLOYEE RELATIONS

There was a time when little thought was given to the demands of employee relations work. For this reason, the personnel staff in many companies was not carefully selected or trained in their specialty. Nor were these people given the chance to develop the skills with which to do their job—at least to the same degree as personnel in other jobs.

It is is good to be able to report, however, that the situation is gradually changing and that employee relations is finally emerging as a profession. This happy development is due primarily to two factors: the labor unions and management's final awakening to the need for stimulating the growth and development of all personnel. Because their tactics have been so effective, labor unions have literally forced management to staff its employee relations department with more competent people, men and women who can meet with labor leaders on an equal footing. After many years of neglecting the human element in an industry, management has at long last discovered that its work force represents its greatest single asset. Today, many progressive organizations sponsor comprehensive programs designed to help each individual realize his greatest potential. These programs include more effective selection and placement procedures, better-designed merit-rating procedures, and a wide variety of employee-training procedures. Such activities obviously require able people at the helm.

The employee relations function, as it now exists in the more progressive organization, may be divided into two categories: personnel services and labor relations. The former include recruiting, selection, placement, wage and salary evaluation, employee benefits, and training. As might be expected in view of the differences between these two functions, the qualifications necessary for success in the personnel services end of the business vary somewhat from those required in labor relations work. There are many individuals capable of doing a bang-up job in personnel services who are completely incapable of bargaining with unions. The best qualified employee relations person, of course, will possess qualifications for both types of jobs. These are the people who have the best chance eventually of heading up the employee relations department. In order to clarify the difference between the two major employee relations functions, requisite traits are listed separately below:

Personnel Services	*Labor Relations*
■ Good mental ability	■ Good mental ability
■ Good verbal ability	■ Good verbal ability
Good self-expression	Good self-expression
Ability to think analytically and critically	Ability to think analytically and critically
Good judgment	Judgment
Ability to plan and organize	Shrewdness
Social drive (desire to help others)	Aggressiveness
Genuine liking for people	Tough-mindedness
Extroversion	Courage of one's convictions
Friendliness	Self-confidence
Warmth	Fortitude
Tact	Perseverance
Social sensitivity	Fair-mindedness
	Ability to improvise

Rationale

Many persons are initially attracted to personnel services because they have a genuine liking for people and are strongly motivated to help others. This is all to the good because these qualities play an important part in such activities as placement, training, and employee benefits. Individuals who carry out these duties are usually extroverted, friendly, and the kind of people to whom others like to take their problems. To help others with their problems, a personnel employee must be able to approach the individual and win his confidence. This obviously takes an abundance of tact and social sensitivity.

But people in personnel must not be so highly motivated to help others that they permit their hearts to run away with their heads. Many of their duties—particularly that of employment interviewing—call for mature, objective decisions. Because these decisions involve people rather than things or ideas, they should be none the less objective or impartial. Practically every personnel function involves the evaluation of people in one way or another. Hence, the job requires intelligence, judgment, and good powers of analysis. Personnel people work largely through the verbal medium, moreover, and should be able to communicate effectively.

Although people in the labor relations field need many of the traits and abilities required by people in personnel services, their job demands an additional constellation of personality characteristics. They have to deal with representatives of labor, many of whom are aggressive, hard-boiled, and able strategists. Thus labor negotiators have to be exceedingly tough-minded, so that they will be able to take it when the going gets rough. They must be self-confident, aggressive, and have the courage of their convictions. A good labor negotiator is also a shrewd individual, one who has a little of the "Yankee horse-trader" in his make-up. At the same time, he must develop a reputation for being completely fair; otherwise, he will never be able to win the confidence of labor representatives or develop a working relationship with them.

Bargaining sessions consume long, weary hours during which each side jockeys for position. Company representatives at the bargaining table must learn to meet fire with fire, match persistence with persistence, and maintain their position without getting discouraged. They also have to be good improvisers, in the sense that they can cope with unanticipated developments. All of this takes its toll of many individuals. As pointed out above, there are numerous people in personnel services who simply do not have the resilience and mental toughness to stand the gaff in labor relations.

MATCHING THE APPLICANT WITH THE JOB

We have discussed at length the need for acquiring a complete understanding of the jobs for which applicants are to be selected. Remember, though, that the man specifications outlined above, while not all-inclusive, nevertheless represent the *ideal* worker. In our appraisal of candidates, we are unlikely to find any one individual who possesses all the favorable factors for any given job. All of us have our shortcomings, and it has already been pointed out that the interview that brings to light no unfavorable information is a poor interview. Almost every candidate will therefore lack some of the desirable factors. But the best of these people will have assets in such abundance that they compensate for their liabilities. The interviewer's job, then, is to find the applicant who has the most desirable qualifications for a specific job.

At this point, it is only fair to ask the question, "How do we go about determining whether or not an applicant actually possesses the appropriate qualifications?" Well, we have already noted that a few of these qualifications can be determined by means of aptitude tests. But tests are primarily useful in measuring *abilities alone*. We must therefore rely upon the interview as a means of appraising *personality, motivation, interests, character,* and the *nature of intellectual functioning*. Subsequent chapters of this book show how the patterned interview may be used to accomplish this task.

Mechanics

CHAPTER FOUR

Helping the Applicant to Talk Spontaneously

In a previous chapter we discussed the applicant's stake in the selection process. It is his life with which we are concerning ourselves. We must keep in mind, however, that we can be of maximum assistance to him—and to our company—only if we succeed in helping him to talk *spontaneously*. In an interview where there is no genuine rapport, many of the applicant's responses are screened, in the sense that they reveal only those facts and attitudes calculated to put him in the best possible light. If we are to do a successful selection and placement job, however, we need to know his *entire* story—his shortcomings as well as his assets. And we can only accomplish this by helping him talk spontaneously, without screening his discussion.

Appropriate job placement means the kind of work situation where the individual is not only able to draw upon his greatest strengths but where his shortcomings will handicap him the least. The latter concept has received far too little attention. This is why we sometimes find personnel employees with below average verbal skills and labor relations people who lack patience or find it difficult to control their tempers. If we are to place the applicant in the kind of a job where he will have the best chance for success, then, we need to know about all his traits and abilities. The rapport-getting techniques presented in this chapter represent nothing radically new. Actually, they are techniques which are used automatically by almost every person who has mastered the art of effective interpersonal relations. As the reader studies these techniques, he should think about some of his friends and associates who are skillful in their interpersonal relationships. He will immediately conclude that they draw upon many if not all these techniques.

In our effort to help the applicant "open up" and tell his entire story, we utilize a number of techniques which have been clinically tested over the years. If we do this successfully, the applicant gradually develops confidence in us and realizes that it is to his advantage to disclose not only his assets but also those areas in which he needs further improvement. He thus becomes a partner in the interview, assumes the center of the stage, and spontaneously discusses his life story.

PHYSICAL SET-UP

If we are to gain the applicant's complete confidence and establish appropriate rapport with him, the interview must be conducted in *private*. Unfortunately, this consideration has not received enough attention in many companies. Many interviewers work in offices where the walls do not extend to the ceiling and clear glass windows permit observation by passers-by. Such a setting is not at all conducive to the task of getting the applicant to talk freely about the details of his background. The interviewer's office need not be large or handsomely furnished but it must be private!

Privacy is more than four walls. The word implies *lack of interruptions of any kind*. Thus, the telephone should be cut off during the discussion and other persons in the organization should be discouraged from breaking in. True, this kind of privacy may be difficult to achieve in a situation where the reverse has been true. It is, nevertheless, the interviewer's task to educate his associates in this regard. Since the interviewer makes decisions that have far-reaching effects on the organization, he must be given the best possible physical set-up for achieving his objectives.

The reasons for interviewing privacy are manifold. In the first place, the applicant must be made to feel that the consideration of his qualifications is so important that he merits the interviewer's undivided attention. Such attention impresses him favorably and helps to gain his confidence. In addition, it automatically raises his opinion of his prospective employer. He says to himself, "Here is a company that is seriously interested in getting the right person for the right job. It must be a good company to work for." Remember, the applicant's first impressions of an organization stem from his reactions to the hiring situation, and his first impressions are important.

When interruptions do occur, the interviewer's job is made more difficult. He not only risks loss of rapport but frequently finds that the interruption has fractured his train of thought and stopped the process of analysis, the analysis of the applicant's qualifications that had been going on since the latter entered the room. Thus, when the interview is resumed, the interviewer finds it more difficult to pick up the threads of his interpretation.

GREET THE
APPLICANT PLEASANTLY

Most applicants approach the interview situation with a certain amount of tension. Because they feel that their future may be at stake, they are anxious to make a good first impression. The interviewer, of course, must do everything he can to ease this tension, for in so doing he removes the barrier that separates him from the applicant's innermost thoughts. If he fails to relieve the tension and establish rapport, his interview will inescapably be a poor one. It is axiomatic that confidence does not flourish where tension prevails. If rapport cannot be established, little in the way of spontaneous information results. And, if spontaneous information is not forthcoming, the interviewer will learn little about the applicant that does not already appear on the employment form.

Most of us, of course, try to be pleasant when we meet another person for the first time. But in a busy day when an interviewer is seeing a number of people one after the other, he may forget about the importance of warmth and friendliness unless he thinks of this as a conscious technique. The interviewer should greet the applicant warmly, introduce himself, shake his hand firmly, and do everything possible to put the individual at ease. Among other things, he should, of course, invite the applicant to have a chair and allow him to smoke. The interviewer should adopt a generally relaxed, disarming manner. Just sitting back in one's chair will in itself give a relaxed, informal touch. In short, he should handle the first few minutes of the interview in such a way that the applicant gets the distinct impression that the interviewer is an easy person with whom to talk.

FACIAL EXPRESSIONS

Few of us stop to realize how limited are our means of getting through to another person in a face-to-face situation. Actually, there are only three such means: facial expressions, voice, and gestures. The last is perhaps the least important of the three and thus does not merit major consideration here. In fact, too frequent use of gestures can be a distracting influence. This means, then, that we must concentrate primarily on facial expressions and vocal intonations. Experience in training interviewers reveals, however, that few of us utilize our full potential in this respect.

If the reader has any question about the importance of facial expressions, he should think for the moment of those persons in his acquaintance who are most effective in interpersonal relationships. Almost invariably, they will be people who are *facially responsive*—people who react facially as well as verbally to another individual's comments.

Anyone can improve his facial expressions by doing two things: (1) raising his eyebrows from time to time and (2) smiling more frequently. Raising of the eyebrows, in particular, should take place whenever important questions are posed and whenever the applicant has told of a particularly impressive achievement. The ensuing expression gives the interviewer the appearance of being *receptive* and serves as a powerful tool in getting the subject to open up.

It is not expected, of course, that anyone can go through an entire interview with a smile on his face. At the same time, it is extremely important that a half-smile be permitted to play about the lips, particularly when asking somewhat personal or delicate questions. The edge is taken off a delicate or personal question when it is posed with a half-smile and with the eyebrows raised.

None of us finds it pleasant to talk to a stone-faced individual. On the other hand, we enjoy talking with someone who reflects our views in his countenance and gives the appearance of understanding and appreciating what we are saying. In an interview situation it is vital that we give the appearance of being understanding, sympathetic, and receptive. Some interviewers are so accomplished in this regard, in fact, that they are able to keep the subject talking almost by facial expressions alone. Unfortunately those of us who tend to be less animated are not always aware of the impression we make on others. It is for this reason that interviewer trainees are encouraged to practice some of their questions in front of a mirror, so that they may learn to use the full potential of their facial expression.

It stands to reason, of course, that the business of facial expression can be overdone. When any of the techniques are used to the extreme, they give the appearance of being artificial and insincere. This is to be avoided at all costs. Facial expressions are not to be regarded as an ingenious expedient but rather as an overt manifestation of warmth and geniality. Experience has shown that few people have to be concerned about using too much facial expressions. In fact, most of us tend to *underplay* rather than *overplay* facial expressions. Hence, conscious attention to this important technique can often pay big dividends.

VOCAL EXPRESSION

Just as most people fail to make full use of appropriate facial expressions, so do they overlook the effective use of the voice in an interview situation. Many men, in particular, tend to use only the lower register of the voice, with the result that the vocal intonation lacks variety and becomes monotonous. We have already indicated that voice and facial expression represent the two most important means of getting through to the other person in a face-to-face situation. Yet few of us stop to realize how important a tool the voice really is. Certainly though, the art of persuading others relies heavily upon the voice as the most important instrument for obtaining the desired objective. We have only to think of some of the great persuaders in history to realize the truth of this statement. For example, President Franklin D. Roosevelt owed much of his following to the magnetic quality of his voice. He used his vocal apparatus with such consummate skill in his radio broadcasts that people were drawn to him by the millions. We have only to look around us in our own companies to become aware of the fact that the persuasive power of many of our associates is directly related to effective use of vocal equipment.

Since the interviewer faces the rather formidable task of persuading the candidate to divulge *all* important aspects of his background, he must give special attention to the most effective employment of his vocal powers. In fact, he must be constantly aware of proper vocal inflection as a conscious interview technique. What, we may ask ourselves, can we do as interviewers to improve our vocal effectiveness? Well, there are two main points that we must keep in mind. We must keep the volume of the voice down to a conversational level and, at the same time, we must strive to use the complete vocal range.

Some interviewers tend to talk too loudly. This often has the effect of threatening the applicant and pushing him off the center of the stage. Remember, we want the applicant to do some 80 to 90 per cent of the talking. He must therefore become the "leading man" of our interview production. When interviewers talk too loudly they tend to relegate the candidate to a minor role. It stands to reason that we must keep our own voices at a rather low conversational level, in this way encouraging the candidate to assume the center of the stage.

Even if we control the volume of the voice, we nevertheless must make certain that we are utilizing the entire vocal range. In particular, when we ask a question or give the subject a compliment, we must use the upper ranges of the voice. This has the effect of making us sound more interested in what the other individual may have to say. In turn, he becomes more highly motivated to give us the answer we seek and does a more complete job of revealing his innermost thoughts. A highly skilled interviewer learns to use his voice in much the same way that the musician plays a pipe organ. The latter pulls out various stops to get certain effects. In like manner the interviewer learns to shade and color his voice in drawing out the applicant's story. For example, if the latter reveals something unfortunate or tragic about his background, the interviewer's voice takes on a sympathetic tone. When the candidate divulges something of a highly personal nature, the interviewer's voice reflects an understanding quality. Complete *responsiveness* on the part of the interviewer has an unusually powerful effect upon the other person, making him not only willing but often actually anxious to talk about the things that are uppermost in his mind.

As in the case of facial expressions, however, vocal inflections and colorations can be overdone. Obviously, we must avoid any intonation that borders on the unctuous. This gives the impression of insincerity and may have the effect of alienating the individual rather than attracting him. Again, though, the tendency is to *underuse* rather than *overuse* vocal inflections. Consequently, most of us will benefit from more rather than less use of the vocal powers. At the very least, we must learn to listen to our own vocal presentation, as a means of making the corrections that may be indicated.

SMALL TALK

Since the interview takes the form of a pleasant conversation, the same amenities observed in any similar conversation are observed here. Once the applicant has been greeted appropriately and seated comfortably, a few minutes of so-called "small talk" normally proves most effective in developing initial rapport. Actually, this initial discussion represents a critical part of the interview, since it sets the stage for the interview proper. This is the interviewer's first opportunity to get the applicant to assume the major portion of the conversational load. If he can be helped to do most of the talking during the early discussion, he naturally assumes this to be his role throughout the interview and often falls into this role without any difficulty at all. On the other hand, if the small talk involves a series of short, direct questions, such as, "What do you think of this weather?" it usually leads to a "question and answer" approach where the interviewer does at least 50 per cent of the talking. In that case, the applicant has a right to assume that his role is the one of simply answering any question that may be addressed to him, rather than talking spontaneously.

An appropriate topic for small talk represents the best means of getting the applicant off to a spontaneous start. During his preparation for the interview, the interviewer should study available application data, in an effort to come up with a topic on which the applicant might be expected to talk freely and perhaps even enthusiastically. Such a topic might consist of some esoteric interest found on the application blank. Or it could conceivably be concerned with differences the applicant may have noted living in two or more different parts of the country. At any rate, the interviewer should go into the discussion with one or two topics for small talk already in mind.

The way in which the small talk question is asked represents the key to getting early spontaneity. This question should be phrased in such a way that the applicant cannot answer "yes" or "no." Rather, the question must be sufficiently complex that the applicant will be required to talk perhaps two or three minutes in order to answer it. Thus, the interviewer may say: "I was very interested in looking over your application blank to note that you list deep sea diving as an avocation. Tell me how you happened to get into that activity, what you actually do, and what kinds of satisfactions it provides." Or, the interviewer may start the discussion with such a question as: "I noticed from your application blank that you grew up and went to school in Tennessee. How would you contrast life in Tennessee with your existence here in Boston—with respect to such factors as cost of living, educational opportunities, attitude of the people, or cultural differences?" Both of these questions are sufficiently complex that the applicant should be required to talk for several minutes in order to answer them. If he stops after a few sentences, simply "wait him out" utilizing the technique discussed later on—the "calculated pause."

Encouraging the candidate to do much of the talking is just as important here as it is in the subsequent discussion. The sound of his own voice in a strange situation gives him confidence, eases his initial tension, and helps to develop rapport. Because he is not immediately put on the spot by being asked to tell about some aspect of his background, he does not feel the immediate need to sell himself and thus has a chance to relax and to chat informally about matters which are of no great concern. In a sense, too, he has a chance to become acquainted with the interviewer and to establish a friendly, easy relationship.

The duration of the small talk normally ranges from two to five minutes, depending upon how nervous and ill-at-ease the candidate may be at the start of the session. If he happens to be an extroverted, poised, and confident individual, the small talk may be terminated after a very brief period. On the other hand, if he is a withdrawn, inhibited, and shy person, the small talk should be carried on until he settles down and seems more at ease. In any event, this early discussion helps enormously to break the ice and establishes a friendly, informal interviewing climate.

As in the case of all other recommended techniques, however, the small talk should not be overdone. Care must be taken not to become overfriendly, patronizing, or too enthusiastic. Nor should the small talk become so extended that the applicant begins to wonder whether he was invited in to talk about himself or to discuss deep sea diving. Hence, as soon as he begins to talk freely and naturally, he should be encouraged to launch into a discussion of his own background.

THE COMPREHENSIVE
INTRODUCTORY QUESTIONS

In moving from small talk to the interview proper, the interviewer should bridge the gap with such a comment as: "Let me tell you a little bit about our discussion this morning." He then directs the conversation to the real purpose of the session by making an appropriate opening remark. This general opening remark should include a statement of the company's sincere interest in placing new employees on jobs that make the best use of their abilities. In these remarks, the interviewer must also get across the idea that he is truly interested in learning as much as possible about the applicant's background so that the latter's qualifications can be matched with job demands. It is also well to present an *overview of the interview* by pointing out that the discussion will include as much relevant information as possible about work experience, education, and present interests. Thus, the candidate should be given a preview of all the major topics included on the Interview Guide that will be found at the end of this book. A comprehensive introductory question such as the following will usually suffice: "In this company we make every possible effort to place people in jobs that will draw upon their best abilities. We know from experience that properly placed new workers make more progress, eventually earn more money, and are more useful to the company. In order to make the right kind of job placement, I need to know as much about you as I possibly can—your work experience, education and training, and present interests."

In his opening remarks, the interviewer will use every means at his disposal to *sell* the candidate on the desirability of providing the necessary information. In particular, he will consciously use the appropriate facial expressions and vocal intonations and, by his very manner, he will *assume consent.* Just as the skillful salesman assumes that the customer wants to buy, so does the interviewer assume that the applicant is desirous of providing all the necessary information. He therefore phrases his questions *positively* in such a way that there is no alternative but to answer them. The phrase, "Suppose you tell me" is practically always more effective than the phrase, "I wonder if you would be willing to tell me." The latter choice of words provides the alternative of answering or not and thus fails to assume consent. Moreover, it gives the impression that the interviewer is not sure of his ground and may not be certain whether he should ask the question.

Having provided the applicant with a discussion of the purpose of the interview and having given him an overview of the general topics to be considered, the interviewer launches immediately into a discussion of previous work experience, the first topic that appears on the Interview

Guide. In so doing, he uses a *comprehensive introductory question*. The very comprehensiveness of this question invites the subject to assume the center of the stage and is the *single most important factor* in getting the applicant to carry the burden of the conversation. The comprehensive introductory question should be almost all-inclusive, in the sense that it should spell out most of the main factors which the interviewer needs to know about the subject's work experience. It should include many of the items listed under work history on the Interview Guide. And it should give direction to the discussion by indicating appropriate chronology. Thus the applicant should be asked to start with his first job and work up to his present position, supplying information as to duties, likes and dislikes, special achievements, and earnings. The following question will accomplish all these objectives: "Suppose you begin by telling me about your previous jobs, starting in with the first job and working up to the present. I would be interested in your duties and responsibilities, the level of earnings, any duties you particularly liked or disliked, and any special achievements along the way."

Based upon other items listed on the Interview Guide, a similar approach can be used to open the discussion in each of the other major interviewing areas. For example, the following question could conceivably be used to launch the discussion of education, "Suppose you tell me now about your education, starting with high school and going on to college. I'd be interested in your subject preferences, grades, special academic achievements, extracurricular activities, and the like."

The average applicant will, of course, forget to cover every aspect included in the comprehensive introductory question. For example, he will often have to be reminded to discuss subject preferences and to talk at greater length about his academic achievements. The important thing to remember, though, is that such follow-up questions are simply *reminders* of some of the things he has initially been asked to relate. As such, they do not represent new questions and hence do not require quite so much concentration on the applicant's part.

As already implied, the question or statement that launches the discussion in each new interviewing area should be so comprehensive and should give the applicant such a clear picture of what he is expected to relate that he is normally able to talk several minutes without further prompting. This permits the interviewer to sit back and concentrate exclusively on the applicant's story. He is thus in a good position to pick up significant clues in the applicant's remarks and analyze their meaning. He can also make a mental note of any inconsistencies in the subject's story and can sift the content with respect to topics that might prove fruitful for further exploration in follow-up questions.

Many interviewers unconsciously raise their voices and become more serious and intent when they embark upon a new interviewing area. This behavior is, of course, just the reverse of what should be done. The comprehensive introductory question should be injected into the discussion naturally and adroitly, in such a way that it seems to flow logically from what has gone before. Thus a connecting clause or complete sentence can be very helpful at this stage. For example, when the discussion of the work experience has been concluded, the interviewer can say, "That gives me a very good picture of your work experience; suppose you now tell me a little bit about your education." Or, in proceeding from education to early home background, the interviewer can make this transition by such a comment as, "Suppose we talk a little now about your early life." These transitional comments help to avoid the impression that the interview is segmented and give it much more of a pleasant, conversational tone.

Additional discussion of the comprehensive introductory question will be found in Part III of this book where a full chapter is devoted to each of the major areas found on the Interview Guide. Because of the tremendous importance of these questions as a means of getting spontaneous information, however, it has been necessary to touch briefly upon them in this chapter as a conscious technique.

ASSUME A PERMISSIVE GENERAL MANNER

Once the candidate launches his discussion in response to the comprehensive introductory question, the interviewer uses a number of additional techniques to encourage complete responsiveness. Thus, the interviewer listens intently to all the applicant says and encourages him to expand his discussion by frequent nodding of the head and by making such short comments as: "I see," or "I can understand that," or "uh-huh." These comments are so short that they do not interrupt the applicant's story, and yet they do give the impression of responsiveness. Certainly, the applicant should not get the feeling that he is talking in a vacuum.

A skillful interviewer never shows surprise at anything the subject may say, never openly disagrees with an applicant on any point, and never gives the appearance of cross-examining the individual. To do otherwise often causes the subject to freeze up. When this happens, rapport suffers, and the candidate begins to screen his responses in such a way that he does not reveal the complete story of his background.

Even when the applicant relates attitudes and ideas with which the interviewer does not agree, the latter should not interrupt to argue the case. Rather, he should hear the person out, making every effort to analyze the import of what he is saying.

Obviously, if an applicant relates past behavior which he

now recognizes as having been quite undesirable, the interviewer should not give him the impression of supporting such behavior. Rather, he should show understanding and sympathy by such a remark as, "I can understand how that might have happened under those particular circumstances." This kind of reaction is reassuring to the applicant and often encourages him to discuss additional information—information which he might not otherwise have felt free to bring to light.

GIVE FREQUENT PATS
ON THE BACK

Although a permissive interview climate is extremely helpful and very necessary, it is not, in itself, sufficient. We must go a step further to encourage the individual to tell his full story. This step takes the form of supportive behavior on the part of the interviewer. Comments such as "That's fine!" or "You deserve a lot of credit for that!" or "Very good!" give the applicant the feeling that his achievements are being appropriately recognized. Everyone has some things of which he is very proud. These may include (1) hard effort expended on a job, (2) high academic standing in high school or college, (3) promotion to higher-level job assignments, (4) election to class offices in school, and the like. When achievements of this kind are recognized by the interviewer in the form of a compliment, the applicant often visibly warms to the discussion and becomes increasingly expansive and spontaneous in his ensuing remarks. To be appreciated is a human need, and the job applicant is no exception in this respect.

Supportive comments should be distributed throughout the interview. In a sense, they serve as a kind of *lubrication,* frequently motivating the applicant to go into more detail than he might otherwise have done. Once he becomes aware of the interviewer's real interest—as reflected in his supportive comments—the applicant usually warms to his task and willingly provides all the information required of him.

In making use of supportive comments, particular attention should be devoted to inflection of the voice. When the voice is consciously placed in the upper register, the comment takes on greater significance. In other words, it sounds more enthusiastic and more as though the interviewer is really impressed. This is of special importance for, if the applicant gets the feeling that the interviewer fully recognizes his achievements, he will subsequently be more willing to discuss some of his shortcomings. A person does not mind telling about a few of his problems if he is absolutely certain that the listener is completely aware of his successes.

In complimenting an applicant, we must be sure that we do not go too far, to the extent that our remarks sound over-enthusiastic and even a bit artificial. Here again, however, most people are unaccustomed to giving compliments and hence there is a natural tendency not to use enough such remarks rather than to overdo them.

PLAY DOWN
UNFAVORABLE INFORMATION

In accordance with the general interviewing philosophy, the applicant must be encouraged to impart *unfavorable* as well as *favorable* information. One of the most effective means of accomplishing this objective is to make it as easy as possible for him to talk about the negative aspects of his background. Whenever he does divulge unfavorable information, therefore, we *play down* the importance of that information by some casual, understanding remark. If, for example, the candidate tells about a difficulty he has experienced with some supervisor, we encourage him to describe the experience in some detail and then play down the importance of the experience by such a remark as, "I guess a good many people run across a boss like that somewhere along the line." Or, if a woman indicates that her grades in high school were below average, we hear her out and then help her to save face by saying, "A good many high school students are more interested in athletics or other extracurricular pursuits than in strictly academic affairs." When a man discusses difficulty with some subject matter such as mathematics, this can be played down by saying, "We all have different aptitude patterns, and very few of us have high aptitudes in all areas. If you had trouble with math, the chances are that you were able to do substantially better in some other subject."

Sometimes failure can be played down by complimenting a man for having been able to recognize his difficulty and face up to it. For example, if he reveals that he was a failure as a supervisor because he was too soft and let his subordinates run all over him, the comment might be, "It is to your credit that you were able to analyze yourself and recognize the problem. Recognition of the problem is the first step in self-development." Occasionally someone will openly admit that he was guilty of being lazy in his response to the demands of a given job. Obviously, we cannot condone this type of behavior but we *can* show that our attitude toward the person has not been seriously affected by saying, "You know, the fact that you were able to recognize this and talk about it today indicates that you have been trying to improve yourself in this respect and have already made some progress."

The interviewer who gives the slightest indication that judgment is being adversely influenced by unfavorable information will get no further information of this kind. Once he reacts negatively—either verbally or facially—he disqualifies himself as a sympathetic listener. And no man willingly and spontaneously talks about his difficulties and failures in a climate where the listener does not give the appearance of being understanding. On the other hand, when such information is not only accepted without surprise or disapproval but is also played down, the applicant is permitted to *save face* and hence usually finds it easy to discuss additional negative data as it subsequently occurs in the unfolding of his life story.

As in the case of all the other techniques discussed in this chapter, it is possible to go too far in playing down unfavorable information. The interviewer when confronted with genuinely unfavorable data should never say, "That is not important; think no more about it." Such dismissal of behavior that the candidate knows to have been wrong is far too glib and gives the impression of hollow insincerity. It is better not to play down at all than to do this in such an obvious manner.

THE CALCULATED PAUSE

Inexperienced interviewers have a tendency to become uncomfortable whenever a slight pause in the conversation occurs. Hence, they are likely to break in prematurely with unnecessary comments or questions.

Experienced interviewers, on the other hand, tend to wait the applicant out, purposely permitting a pause to occur from time to time. They do this as a *conscious technique,* knowing full well that the applicant will frequently elaborate on a previous point rather than allow the discussion to come to a standstill. The latter often senses that the interviewer by his very silence expects a fuller treatment of the topic under consideration.

The calculated pause is one of the most powerful techniques that the interviewer can draw upon in terms of developing spontaneous information. Such pauses are not only remarkably effective in drawing out the applicant but they also enable the interviewer to do less talking himself and help him to perfect the art of becoming a good listener.

Obviously such pauses should not be used too frequently. Nor should a pause be permitted to extend too long. If the candidate does not pick up the conversation after an eight-or ten-second break, the interviewer should come to his assistance with an appropriate question or comment.

INJECT A LITTLE HUMOR ALONG THE WAY

Because the interview takes the form of a pleasant conversation, it must, of course, include all elements of such a conversation. A discussion that lasts as long as an hour-and-a-half would normally have its lighter moments as well as its more serious episodes. As a conscious technique, therefore, the interviewer introduces a variety of moods, in such a way that the conversation gives the appearance of being completely *natural*. Since most of the discussion will inescapably be of a more serious nature, ways and means must be found to lighten the mood from time to time in such a way that the conversation does not bog down into a ponderous, deadly serious affair. This is normally accomplished by turning one of the applicant's phrases a bit facetiously so that he immediately sees the humor of it and gets a little laugh out of it himself.

The interviewer should *not* try to lighten the conversational mood by telling jokes or by telling amusing incidents in which he has participated. This is not only maladroit and obvious but consumes valuable interviewing time. If he is to tell a story, moreover, the interviewer must assume the center of the stage, and this is exactly what he should not do.

Whenever the interviewer assumes the center of the stage, he breaks the threads of the applicant's story and interrupts his own continuing analysis of the candidate's qualifications.

SEQUENCE OF THE INTERVIEW

A glance at the appended Interview Guide will reveal the proper sequence in which the applicant's background is to be considered. This sequence is important in maintaining control of the interview, as discussed in Chapter 6, but it is also designed as an aid in getting spontaneous information.

That *work experience* appears on the Interview Guide as the first area for discussion is not a matter of chance. There are a number of good reasons for beginning the conversation with a discussion of the candidate's work history. In the first place, the work experience represents a topic which is normally easier to discuss than any other area of a person's background. An applicant is familiar with what he has done on each job and he usually finds some satisfaction in talking about his past work achievements. Secondly, he expects to be asked about his previous jobs and this, therefore, comes as no surprise to him. Usually, too, this area can be discussed in a matter-of-fact way without many highly personal overtones.

The area of *education* is the next item on the Interview Guide because this, too, usually lends itself to easy discussion. Every applicant expects to be invited to talk about his high school and college experiences and, because these experiences meant a great deal to him, he can frequently talk about them with considerable relish. Even if some aspects of his educational background, such as below-average grades, are a bit painful in retrospect, he can usually wax enthusiastic about other more pleasant items such as athletic prowess, fraternity life, or participation in clubs and musical organizations.

Discussion of work and educational background normally

requires approximately seventy minutes. This gives the interviewer ample opportunity to establish rapport and gain the applicant's confidence by encouraging discussion in areas that are primarily factual rather than personal. In this time the interviewer has had a chance to prove his worth as a sympathetic listener and to demonstrate his sincere interest in appropriate job placement. By the time he has completed the discussion of his work history and educational background, the applicant will have discovered that he is being given a complete opportunity to discuss *all* important aspects of his past experience, as a basis for the decision of matching his qualifications with the job that best uses his abilities. And he has had a chance to react to the interviewer as a person. Because of the relationship established between the interviewer and the interviewee, moreover, the applicant will normally be talking freely and spontaneously by the end of the first hour—in most cases long before that time.

It becomes apparent, then, that the applicant is far more ready to discuss the more delicate and sensitive aspects of his personal history after he has talked about his work experience and education. Confronted with the necessity of disclosing personal information at the beginning of the interview, applicants have a tendency to resist or, at best, to be somewhat perfunctory and guarded in their disclosures. By delaying the personal history discussion, however, the interviewer is in a much better position to obtain truly significant data about the applicant's personal life. And by treating the various areas in proper *sequence,* the interviewer has a chance to stimulate spontaneity of response and to maintain this spontaneity throughout the discussion.

IMPORTANCE OF SUBTLETY
AND FINESSE

The fact that some people use the techniques discussed here easily and naturally does not mean that everyone can acquire them overnight. The techniques of indirection as a means of drawing out the applicant's spontaneous response rest almost entirely upon subtlety and finesse. Unless they are artfully employed, they defeat their own ends. In fact, the art of indirection is a relatively fragile thing, in the sense that it does not take much to destroy it. For this reason most interviewers require specific training if they are to master it in all its complexities.

CHAPTER FIVE

Exploratory Questions

Almost all the books currently available on interviewing tell *about* interviewing; very few provide specific help in terms of how to accomplish this rather complicated task. In rather sharp contrast, the *Evaluation Interview* provides a detailed description of a complete interviewing technique. The reader is supplied with an Interview Guide which outlines areas of the interview to be explored and items to be covered in each of these areas. In Chapter 4 of this book, moreover, the author has supplied comprehensive introductory questions designed to *launch* the discussion in each area.

Now in Chapter 5, we concern ourselves with exploratory questions—questions that help to *keep the applicant talking* in such a way that he is encouraged to divulge the important aspects of his previous experiences. The questions and comments discussed in this chapter have been developed and tested over a lifetime of interviewing. And, in this second edition of the book, a number of valuable questions have been added to those which appeared in the first edition. Several of these questions have been written on the Interview Guide which appears at the back of this book. The comprehensive introductory questions discussed in Chapter 4 and the exploratory questions discussed here in Chapter 5 have worked so well over the years that almost anyone using them conscientiously will inevitably develop an appreciable amount of evaluative information concerning the applicant's general behavior.

With practice, the interviewer will learn to formulate many of his own exploratory questions. Until such skill has been developed, however, he can rely on many of the questions suggested in this chapter and included on the Interview Guide. In the long run, though, much of the interviewer's success will depend upon the skill he develops in the phrasing of exploratory questions. The questions must be so phrased that they penetrate to the heart of a given matter and yet they must not give the appearance of being barbed, too direct, or "investigative" in nature. And they must be worded so that they sustain the interview as a pleasant conversation.

The interviewer cannot anticipate all the questions that may be necessary to draw out the full story of any given applicant. Each applicant is a unique human being and has a unique background of personal experiences. Hence, the applicant's response to one question frequently dictates the nature of the subsequent question. Thus, a general knowledge and understanding of the nature and function of the exploratory question is of paramount importance in successful interviewing.

NATURE OF
EXPLORATORY QUESTIONS

In general, the exploratory question represents an extension of the comprehensive introductory question. It is used to prod the applicant from time to time, in this way helping him to reveal his life's story to the fullest extent and to become more definitive concerning its important aspects. Actually, the interviewer's remarks should be interjected so artfully that he seldom if ever assumes the center of the stage. Rather, he darts in and out with such facility that the applicant seldom becomes aware of the fact that his discourse is being directed. The ability to keep the interview going in this fashion requires consummate skill—skill that accrues only as a result of considerable practice and a thorough understanding of the basic principles of good interviewing. In achieving this skill, a number of factors must be kept in mind.

Comments Are Usually More Adroit Than Questions

A normal conversation between two people consists principally of comments that *anticipate a response.* When two people meet at a cocktail party, for example, the conversation usually begins with such a comment as, "This is quite a party" or "Everyone seems to be having a very good time tonight" or "We are certainly having a stretch of wonderful weather." Comments such as these are just as effective in stimulating conversation as questions, and they are far more adroit.

So it is with interviewing. Whenever a comment can be substituted for a question, the conversation flows more naturally and the interviewer gives the appearance of being *less investigative* in his approach. If he wants more information on a given subject, he can frequently get such information by the simple comment, "That sounds very interesting." So encouraged, the applicant is quite likely to provide further elaboration, without having been specifically asked to do so. The comment, "Tell me a little more about that," is usually more effective than the question, "What else did you find of interest in that situation?"

When comments fail to produce the specific information the interviewer desires, his remarks must, of course, take the form of questions. But these questions should be used sparingly and, in so far as possible, interspersed with comments. A series of questions one after another gives the effect of cross-examining the applicant, and this must be avoided at all costs.

Exploratory Remarks Should Encourage Elaboration

Since the interviewer tries to confine his participation to 15 or 20 per cent of the total conversation, his exploratory remarks must be so phrased that they elicit a considerable amount of discussion on the part of the applicant. Hence, he seldom asks questions which can be answered by a simple "yes" or "no." He would not say, for example, "Did you like that job?" He should say instead, "Tell me some of the things that you liked best about that job." The latter comment gives the applicant a chance to be *definitive* and frequently results in as much as five minutes of spontaneous response.

Keep Questions and Comments Open-End

Many interviewers put words in the applicant's mouth by asking *leading* questions or making leading comments. By so doing, they unintentionally structure their remarks so that a favorable response is strongly suggested. Remarks of this kind are a great waste of time since they seldom result in meaningful information. They make it too easy for the applicant to conceal something that might have an important bearing on his qualifications for a given job. Furthermore, leading comments make the applicant immediately aware of what the interviewer considers a favorable response. The comment, 'I suppose you had a pretty happy early childhood," encourages the applicant to answer in the affirmative, even though this may not have been the case. By putting words in the applicant's mouth the interviewer has tipped his hand, thereby precluding information that might have made a valuable contribution to understanding the candidate's behavior.

A leading question such as, "Did you get pretty good grades in high school?" makes it very difficult for the applicant to give a negative response. Since the interviewer has put the words in his mouth, he is greatly tempted to say "Yes." If his grades were poor and he honestly admits this, he realizes at once that this may count against him, and he may become uncomfortable in the interview situation.

In order to avoid leading comments, remarks should be kept open-end. This means that they should be unstructured, in the sense that they do not suggest the most desirable response. The comment, "Tell me a little more about that," is completely unstructured, leaving the applicant free to discuss favorable or unfavorable information. In like manner, the question, "What about grades in high school?" gives no clue at all as to the weight which the interviewer may place on grades. A question that includes all ranges of the scale can also be classified as open-end, since it gives the applicant the opportunity to *select* a point on the scale that applies to his own situation. The following question illustrates this point: "What about grades? Were they average, above average, or perhaps somewhat below average?" It is abundantly clear that such a question is much more likely to elicit a true response than the leading question concerning grades that was discussed above.

Leading questions can also be avoided by suggesting possible alternative responses—responses which are more or less equated with respect to social desirability. The question, "Did you concentrate on grades in school or were you more active in extracurricular affairs?" provides alternatives which seem fairly equal in acceptability to many applicants. Thus, the applicant who has attained mediocre grades but who has been quite successful in extracurricular activities can use the latter as the basis for his response. In so doing, he often makes a parenthetical remark about his poor grades. This gives the interviewer an opportunity to discuss the grade situation in greater detail *because the door has been left ajar*. In other words, he can explore the grade situation quite naturally, at the same time giving the applicant an "out" by complimenting him on his success in extracurricular affairs.

Talk the Applicant's Language

As the discussion progresses, the interviewer makes mental notes concerning such factors as the applicant's vocabulary, level of sophistication, and tendency to be formal or more informal. He then uses this newly found knowledge in the phrasing of his follow-up remarks, in order to maintain rapport and to encourage spontaneous response. There is no quicker way to lose rapport than to use words which are outside the applicant's vocabulary. In talking with a person of limited education and low-level verbal ability, one would never say, "Was your father extroverted or introverted?" Rather, he would paraphrase these terms by saying: "Was your father outgoing in the sense that he had a lot of friends or was he more inclined to be reserved and to spend more time by himself?" A bright, highly sophisticated applicant, on the other hand, would lose respect for the interviewer who did not talk his language. Hence, the interviewer must be quite flexible in adapting his approach to the various applicants with whom he talks.

Never Ask a Question without a Clear Purpose in Mind

The interviewer must strive to keep one mental step ahead of the applicant. Because the phrasing of follow-up questions and comments is so important, he must phrase these questions mentally while the applicant is still responding to the previous question. This enables the interviewer to "interject" the new question without any perceptible pause in the discussion. If he is to avoid a meaningless conversation, moreover, the interviewer must select follow-up remarks that are consistently designed to produce evaluative information—information that contributes to his understanding of the applicant's behavior.

FUNCTION OF EXPLORATORY QUESTIONS

As we have already seen, the function of follow-up remarks is essentially that of helping the applicant present a clear picture of his qualifications. By means of adroit questioning, the interviewer must be able to draw out the applicant so that the latter can present his real assets. Equally important, the interviewer must be able to structure the discussion in such a way that he gets an equally clear picture of the candidate's shortcomings. Within this broad framework of objectives, however, follow-up remarks serve a number of specific functions.

Reminding Applicant of Omitted Parts of Comprehensive Introductory Questions

The questions that are used to introduce the discussion in each of the major interviewing areas are so comprehensive that the typical candidate will forget to discuss some of the items in response to the comprehensive introductory question alone. Usually he will have to be *reminded* to discuss such job factors as likes, dislikes, earnings, and accomplishments. And he may have to be reminded to discuss such things as subject preferences, grades, and extracurricular activities. Then, there are other items listed under each interviewing area on the Interview Guide that may have to be brought to the applicant's attention in follow-up questions. For example, if the applicant fails to tell why he left a certain job, the interviewer will have to bring this up in the form of a casual follow-up question.

Getting Further Work and Education Information Relevant to the Job

We have already noted that the interviewer must have a clear mental picture of job and man specifications at the time he discusses an applicant's qualifications for a given job. As the interview progresses, he mentally checks the extent to which the applicant's work history and education measure up to these job and man specifications. Since the applicant has not been acquainted with these specifications, he will not know which aspects of his background to emphasize, in terms of establishing the relevance of what he has done to what will be expected of him. The interviewer must therefore help him with this task.

To use an example, let us assume that a technically trained person is being interviewed for a job that involves a considerable amount of report writing. In this case, the interviewer would use follow-up questions in an effort to determine the amount of report writing the candidate has done on his various jobs and the degree of writing facility he has acquired. He would, of course, try to mask the intent of his questions with appropriate phrasing and casual, offhand presentation. He might say, "In connection with your research and development work with that company, was there more emphasis placed on the actual technical experimentation or on the writing up of results?" After the discussion he might add, "How did you feel about your accomplishments there? Did you feel that you were relatively more effective in the actual experimentation or in the report writing?" Even though the applicant may have felt that he made his greatest contribution in laboratory experimental work, he will usually volunteer information concerning his report-writing ability in response to such a question. And he will often place a relatively objective value judgment on his writing ability, particularly since he probably does not know how important this may be in the job for which he is being considered.

Clarify True Meaning of Applicant's Casual Remarks

Clues to the applicant's behavior will not always be clear-cut In response to a question concerning job dislikes, for example, a candidate may say that he found detail work less satisfying. Now, the interviewer cannot assume from such a remark that the applicant cannot do detail work. He must try to pin down this clue by fixing the *degree* of dislike. In this case, he could respond to the original remark by saying, "Many people find detail work much less interesting than other aspects of their job." This kind of a sympathetic response often encourages the applicant to elaborate. In so doing, he may reveal an *intense dislike* of detail and may openly admit that he is not very proficient in the type of work that requires close attention to detail. Or he may indicate that, while he does not enjoy detail, he nevertheless finds it relatively easy to carry out when it is an important part of the job. Obviously, the interpretation of these two responses would be quite different. The first response, if supported by other clues pointing in the same direction, would lead the interviewer to the possible conclusion that the applicant was not a good detail man. The second response, on the other hand, would lead to no such conclusion.

Probing More Deeply for
Clues to Behavior

Highly skilled interviewers often pick up little clues to the applicant's possible behavior relatively early in the discussion, and these clues help them to establish a *hypothesis* with respect to the possible existence of certain assets or liabilities. They know, however, that such hypotheses must be supported by more tangible evidence; otherwise they must be rejected entirely. The interviewer therefore uses exploratory questions to probe for clues that might support his hypothesis. If none is found, he must, of course, discard that hypothesis and search for new ones.

For purposes of illustration, we will assume that the interviewer has obtained some initial impressions of the applicant that point in the direction of superficiality, lack of depth, and limited powers of analysis. As he leads the applicant from area to area, he will, of course, be on the lookout for supporting evidence or for the lack of it. From time to time, he will interject so-called "depth questions"—questions that require a fair amount of analysis. For example, he may ask the applicant what a job has to have in order to give him satisfaction. Or he may ask what gains in terms of personality development accrued to him as a result of his military experience. If the candidate's responses to a series of such questions reveal little ability to dig beneath the surface, the interviewer may rightly conclude that the individual is indeed superficial and without much ability to analyze.

Let us take another example. In this next case, we will

assume that the interviewer has formed an early hypothesis that the applicant may be somewhat lazy. Let us say that he has arrived at this tentative judgment because of the man's professed unwillingness to work overtime hours. In order to check and support this intial hypothesis, the interviewer will use follow-up questions to probe specifically for such factors as (1) how much effort the applicant may have expended on other jobs, (2) how hard he studied in school, and (3) any demonstrated willingness to carry out constructive tasks either at home or in the community after putting in a regular work day. If he finds that the candidate (1) took the easy way out to avoid tackling difficult problems, (2) studied just hard enough to get by, or (3) decided against graduate work because it would have meant going to school at night—if he is able to get consistent information of this kind—he is able to *document* his views concerning the candidate's lack of motivation. The point to remember here, though, is that this kind of information probably would not have been brought to light had it not been for the fact that the interviewer probed for the appropriate clues by means of follow-up questions.

Quantifying Information

In our effort to *document* our findings with respect to the applicant's behavior, it is important to help him become as *definitive* as possible in his responses. When he talks in general terms about his successes, failures, or even about his reactions, therefore, we must urge him to become more specific. For example, if he simply indicates that his grades in college were "above average," we must use such a follow-up question as: "Does that mean that your grades ranked you in the top ten percent of your class, the upper quarter, the upper third, or perhaps the upper half?" Or, if a candidate merely indicates that he was given a raise in salary after his first six months on a job, we must follow through with: "What did that amount to in terms of dollars?" Again, if a man indicates that he was "out of work for a while," we need to know how many months he was actually unemployed.

Controlling the Interview Conversation

As we shall see in Chapter 6, follow-up remarks are used also to *control* the interview conversation, so that the applicant is not permitted to wander off the track and the interview does not get out of hand. Since an entire chapter is devoted to this important aspect of interviewing skill, we will not concern ourselves at this point with the specific ways in which follow-up questions are used to control the interview. At the same time, we can point out here that follow-up questions and comments are used to (1) push the applicant along when he goes into too much irrelevant detail, (2) ensure intensive coverage of each interviewing area, and (3) direct the applicant's attention to those aspects of his background which give the greatest promise of providing evaluative information concerning his behavior.

KINDS OF EXPLORATORY QUESTIONS

In a previous chapter we have likened the interviewer to an actor performing a role on the stage. He does certain things to get certain effects. And this, of course, includes the manner in which he uses his exploratory remarks. The skillful interviewer knows that there are *different kinds* of exploratory questions, and he has learned that one kind of remark is likely to be more effective in a given situation than any of the other kinds. He therefore *consciously* uses the specific type of exploratory remark that he thinks might

be most productive in each interview situation with which
he is faced.

The Simple, Straightforward "Reminder" Question

As indicated previously, since the applicant will usually forget to discuss all the items included in the interviewer's comprehensive introductory question, the latter jogs his memory
with simple, straightforward "reminders." In so doing, he
makes every effort to keep these questions open-end. He
may have to say, for example, "What were some of the things
you liked best on that job?" or, in stimulating further discussion concerning the candidate's education, the interviewer
may ask, "What about the level of your grades in college?"
If the applicant does not discuss his interests in sufficient detail, the interviewer may say, "What else do you do outside
working hours for fun and relaxation?"

The Laundry-list Question

Applicants almost invariably find some areas more difficult to
discuss than others. Confronted with a question that requires
considerable analysis, they frequently "block" and find it
somewhat difficult to come up with an immediate response.
In such a situation, the interviewer comes to the applicant's
assistance with a laundry-list type of question. As the name
implies, this type of question suggests a variety of possible
responses and permits the subject to take his choice. If the
subject blocks on the question, "What are some of the things
that a job has to have is order to give you satisfaction?", the
interviewer may stimulate his thinking by such a laundry-list
comment as, "You know some people are more interested
in security; some are frankly more interested in money; some
want to manage; some want an opportunity to create; some
like a job that takes them out-of-doors a good bit of the time

—what's important to you?" Given a variety of possible responses, the applicant is normally able to marshal his thinking and supply a considerable amount of information.

The laundry-list question can also be used as a means of confirming clues to behavior that the interviewer has obtained from some previous aspects of the discussion. Let us assume, for example, that the applicant has dropped some hints that seem to indicate a dislike for detail. The interviewer can often follow up on such clues by including a reference to detail in the laundry-list question at the end of the discussion of work history. For example, the interviewer may say, "What are some of the things that a job has to have in order to give you satisfaction? Some people want to manage whereas others are more interested in an opportunity to come up with new ideas; some like to work regular hours whereas others do not mind spending additional hours on a job—hours that might interfere with family life; some like to work with details while others do not; some are quite happy working at a desk while others prefer to move around a good bit—what's important to you?"

If, in response to the above question, the candidate said, "Well, I certainly do not want anything that involves a lot of detail; actually, I'm not at all good at that type of work," the interviewer would certainly have obtained further confirmation of the subject's reaction to detail. The very fact that the individual selected this item for discussion reflects the importance he attaches to it. If the applicant were being considered for a job where attention to detail figured importantly in the man specifications, his response could be interpreted as revealing a relatively serious shortcoming.

Besides taking a candidate "off the hook" when he tends to "block," the laundry-list question has the further function of spelling out to the applicant what the interviewer specifically has in mind. By the very nature of the items he uses in his series of possible responses, the interviewer encourages the applicant to respond specifically rather than generally, and he makes certain that the responses will be helpful to him in his evaluation of the individual. Toward the end of the candidate's discussion of his work history, for example, the interviewer asks him what he has learned about his *strengths* as a result of working on his various jobs. In order to tell the applicant what the interviewer specifically has in mind, he uses such a laundry list as: "Did you find that you worked a little harder than the average individual, got along better with people, organized things better, gave better attention to detail—just what?" Such a laundry list question helps to "tie down" the person's responses, so that he talks in terms of *traits of personality, motivation, or character.*

Two-step Probing Questions

In order to probe deeply for clues to behavior that might not otherwise come to light, two separate questions are frequently required. The first question is usually more general in nature, whereas the second question is much more specific and digs more deeply. This approach is called "two-step probing," the first step involving a question which usually results in identification of a specific interest and the second step involving a question which digs for the basis of that interest.

As a means of illustrating the two-step digging technique, let us assume that the interviewer is interested in probing for the quality of the applicant's thinking and is trying to accomplish this objective by asking about the latter's subject preferences in college. He might ask a first-step question, "What subjects did you most enjoy in college?" The applicant might reply, "Mathematics was always my favorite." Now, this information is interesting but it does not tell us much about the subject's quality of thinking. Hence, a second-step question is in order, "What was there about mathematics that particularly appealed to you?" One applicant might reply, "Oh, I don't know; I just liked it, that's all." Responses of this type—particularly if they are characteristic of the candidate's responses in general—frequently indicate a lack of intellectual depth. On the other hand, another applicant might give this answer to the above question, "I liked mathematics because it provided such an intellectual challenge. Moreover, it is an exact science, where the problems result in clear-cut answers. Unlike the shades of gray you find in social studies, mathematical answers are usually black or white. Furthermore, the investigational possibilities in the field of mathematics are infinite; there is no theoretical ceiling." It will be apparent from the second applicant's response that the interviewer has uncovered an appreciable amount of information concerning the quality of the subject's thinking—information that might not have come to light at all if he had not utilized the two-step probing technique.

The two-step probing technique must, of course, be used sparingly throughout the interview. There is not sufficient time to probe for the "why" of everything the applicant says. Moreover, too-frequent use of this technique places the applicant too much on the spot and gives him the feeling that he is being *grilled*. The technique must be reserved for probing in the most fruitful areas. Only the well-trained, experienced interviewer will be able to recognize a fruitful area when he comes upon it. What might conceivably prove to be a fruitful area for investigation in one applicant's background might represent quite a barren area for exploration in another person's history. With appropriate training and experience, the interviewer senses the most fruitful areas for deeper exploration as the interview discussion progresses. His sensitivity in this respect can be compared with that of a mining engineer who uses a Geiger counter in his search for uranium. The engineer often covers a considerable amount of ground before the Geiger counter begins to tick. When this occurs, he immediately digs into the earth to ascertain the extent of the ore body.

It will be clear from the above that the two-step probing question is used primarily to bring to light the "why" of some of the actions or decisions a given candidate has made. And responses to such "why" questions frequently throw a great deal of light on the individual's personality or motivation. If, in response to an initial question as to where a woman went to college, she tells you that she went to the University of Connecticut, this response is interesting but insufficient. It is often much more meaningful to follow through with the second step of such a question with: "How did you happen to select the University of Connecticut?" If her reason turns out to be the fact that one of her close friends went there, this does not provide any real clues to judgment or maturity. But if she tells you that her choice was based upon the outcome of her investigation of four different colleges, with the result that the University of Connecticut seemed to her to have the best faculty and the most comprehensive course of study in her chosen field, a very genuine clue to maturity would seem to have been brought to light.

Double-edged Questions

This type of questioning is used to make it easy for the applicant to admit his shortcomings and to help him achieve greater self-insight. The questions are double-edged in the sense that they make it possible for the subject to choose between two possible responses. Moreover, the first alternative is usually phrased in such a way that the subject would not choose that alternative unless he really felt that he possessed the ability or personality trait in question to a fairly high degree. The second alternative is phrased so that it is easy for him to choose that alternative, even though it is the more undesirable of the two possible responses.

We will assume in this case that the interviewer has obtained several clues which seem to indicate that a given applicant tends to be too soft and unaggressive. He might then try to get further confirmation by questioning the applicant concerning his performance on a given supervisory job. He might say, "Were you usually as firm with your subordinates as you would like to have been or did this represent an area in which you could have improved to some extent?" Note that the question is so phrased that the subject is not compelled to admit that he was actually poor or deficient in the trait under consideration. He is simply asked if this might not have been an area in which he could have *improved*. When a question is so phrased, it frequently opens the door in the sense that it encourages discussion of a shortcoming that might not have been revealed otherwise. As we shall see in a subsequent chapter of this book, the double-edged question can also be effectively used to stimulate the applicant's *self-evaluation*. If, in discussing the subject's shortcomings with him, the interviewer wishes to get confirmation of previous clues indicating lack of self-confidence, he can say, "What about self-confidence? Do you think that you have as much self-confidence as you would like to have or do you think that this represents a trait that might be improved a little bit?" If the interviewer has established rapport with the applicant, the latter often finds it easy to admit that he could *improve* his self-confidence. In so doing, he admits by implication that he is somewhat deficient in this particular trait.

The question might be raised that anyone could improve in almost any given trait. Experience has shown, however, that the average applicant will not admit the need for improvement unless he recognizes some deficiency in the trait under consideration.

HOW TO SOFTEN
EXPLORATORY QUESTIONS

The evaluation interview is basically an exercise in indirection. By encouraging spontaneous response on the part of the applicant, we hope to learn as much as possible about his background. By means of indirection, moreover, we hope to get information in the more critical and sensitive areas For example, as a result of questioning a woman in detail about her dislikes on the job, she frequently tells us her reason for leaving that job, *without our having to ask for it.* If information of this kind does not come out spontaneously, however, we have to become more direct in our questions. Thus, if she does not tell us spontaneously why she left the given job, we have to ask her specifically.

When the interviewer finds it necessary to switch from the indirect to the more direct type of questioning, he must make every effort to soften such questions. If he poses his direct questions bluntly and maladroitly, he runs the risk of upsetting the applicant and losing rapport. This pitfall can be avoided by utilizing appropriate *introductory phrases* and subsequent *qualifying words or phrases.*

Introductory Phrases

Appropriately worded introductory phrases help to remove the blunt aspect of a direct question. Such phrases make the question seem *less investigative* and hence more palatable as far as the applicant is concerned. He does not feel quite so much as though he had been put on the spot.

The following introductory phrases will help to soften almost any direct question:

Is it possible that	How did you happen to
Would you say that	Has there been any opportu-
What prompted your deci-	nity to
sion to	To what do you attribute
	that

Qualifying Words or Phrases

These qualifiers help to remove the blunt edge from a direct question because they introduce the *concept of degree*. In other words, they give the implication that the situation under discussion may have been unfavorable *only to a degree* rather than wholly bad.

The following qualifying words and phrases are most effective in softening direct questions:

Might	Somewhat
Perhaps	Fairly
To some extent	A little bit
Quite	Or not so much so

Help the Applicant to "Save Face"

Direct questions can frequently be phrased in such a way that they give the applicant an out. This permits him to "save face" and gives him the feeling that his response has not seriously damaged his cause.

Examples of the Way Direct Questions Can Be Softened

Study of the two types of questions listed below will reveal the extent to which the direct question has been softened by means of (1) introductory phrases, (2) qualifying words or phrases, or (3) giving the candidate an out.

Too Direct	*More Appropriate*
1. Why did you have trouble with your boss?	1. *To what do you attribute the little* difficulties you experienced with your supervisor?
2. How much money do you have?	2. *Has there been any opportunity to* acquire a *little* financial reserve?
3. Why did you leave that job?	3. *How did you happen to* leave that job?
4. Was your father bull-headed?	4. *Is it possible that* your father *might* have been a *little* set in his ways?
5. Do you lack self-confidence?	5. *Would you say that* you *might* desirably acquire *a little more* self-confidence?
6. Were you spoiled as a youth?	6. *Would you say that* you were brought up *fairly* strictly *or not so much so?*
7. Why did you switch from mechanical to industrial engineering?	7. *What prompted your decision to* change from mechanical to industrial engineering?

NOTE TAKING

Discussion of the mechanics of the interview would not be complete without some reference to the taking of notes. This is a subject, incidentally, about which a considerable amount of controversy has taken place over the years, some authorities claiming that note taking results in a loss of rapport and others indicating that the interviewer should feel free to take as many notes as he desires.

We take the view that the decision as to whether or not to take notes should be made on the basis of the *experience and training of the interviewer.* This is another way of saying that the untrained, inexperienced interviewer should *not* take notes, while the well-trained interviewer should be able to carry out this activity without any loss of rapport.

At the time one is learning to use the recommended information-getting techniques, he is of course rather unsure of himself and a bit awkward in almost everything he does. Thus, he has his hands full in terms of his efforts to establish rapport, without attempting anything in addition. And it is true that the taking of notes does tend to diminish rapport if this is not done adroitly and unobtrusively. Moreover, the interviewer will normally have little difficulty remembering the salient aspects of the candidate's background, provided he writes up the case immediately after the discussion has been concluded. This subject is treated in greater detail in Chapter 13.

On the other hand, one who has achieved genuine skill in the use of such techniques as facial and vocal expression, pats on the back, playing down of unfavorable information, and adroit questioning should be able to take notes in such a way that the applicant becomes almost unaware of this activity. The candidate usually becomes so absorbed in the discussion that he takes little notice of the skilled interviewer's note taking.

As indicated above, however, any writing done by the interviewer should be carried out as unobtrusively as possible. Thus, he should keep a pad of paper on his knee throughout the discussion and should keep a pencil in his hand at all times. The simple movement of placing the pencil on the desk and picking it up at frequent intervals can often be distracting.

Notes should only be made when the candidate relates objective data concerning his background or when he tells about his past achievements. Whenever he imparts information of a highly personal or derogatory nature, the interviewer obviously refrains from any writing. Rather he waits until the applicant volunteers the next bit of favorable information and, at that time, records both the favorable information and the unfavorable data previously obtained.

Finally, skilled interviewers learn to record their findings without diverting their attention from the candidate or breaking eye contact for more than a few seconds at a time. This places the note taking function in its proper perspective, as a seemingly minor aspect of the interview.

CHAPTER SIX

Guiding and Controlling the Interview

In the two previous chapters devoted to the *mechanics* of the interview, emphasis has been placed primarily on ways and means of getting the applicant to talk freely. This of course represents a first objective. Unless the applicant talks spontaneously, the interviewer can learn little about him.

Spontaneous discourse in itself, however, is not sufficient. Discussion must be guided and channeled in such a way that the applicant tells what the interviewer wants to learn rather than simply what he himself wants to relate. Indeed, it is quite possible for an applicant to talk as long as three hours in an uncontrolled situation without giving as much salient and evaluative information as he could have provided in 1½ hours of guided conversation.

In an earlier chapter, we discussed the merits of three types of interviews: the direct interview, the indirect interview, and the patterned interview. The major difference in the three types of interviews is that of control. In our view, the direct interview exercises too much control and the indirect interview too little. In the evaluation interview, on the other hand, just enough control is exercised to get the kind of information wanted within a reasonable period of time. The goal is to do this without interfering with the applicant's spontaneity of response.

PROBLEMS OF CONTROL

Teaching interviewers how to exercise optimal control represents one of the most difficult—if not *the* most difficult—task in the entire training procedure. During the earlier stages of the training, the trainees invariably exercise too little control. In their desire to get spontaneous information, they are inclined to let the applicant go on and on, just so long as he talks freely. At that stage of their training, they are often afraid to direct the conversation for fear that such direction might inhibit the flow of conversation. As a result of this completely permissive approach, the applicant often is allowed to ramble excessively in discussing his background and to go into too much detail on topics that may not be particularly relevant. As a consequence, the interview suffers from lack of intensive coverage in the important areas and from lack of balance—too much emphasis on one area of the applicant's background and too little on the other areas. Also, such an interview takes far too much time.

When it is suggested to interviewer-trainees that they exercise greater control, they have a tendency to go too far in that direction. They do too much of the talking, ask too many follow-up questions, and give the appearance of grilling the applicant. That elusive quality, *spontaneity of re-*

sponse, evaporates into thin air and the interview is reduced to a question-and-answer affair.

Under the guidance of the trainer, the interviewer-trainee gradually learns to use just the right amount of guidance and control. And he learns to do this tactfully and unobtrusively. In the very early stages of the interview, he permits the applicant to talk very freely, even though some of the resulting information may not be particularly relevant. He does this to set the *pattern* of getting the candidate to carry the conversational ball. Once this pattern has been established, however, he does not hesitate to inject comments and questions at critical points, in order to ensure intensive coverage and sufficient penetration in each area of the applicant's background.

FUNCTION OF CONTROL

As implied above, measures of control are designed to (1) ensure adequate coverage of each area in the applicant's background, (2) provide proper balance in the discussion of each of these areas, (3) secure appropriate penetration into the really salient aspects of the candidate's previous experiences, and (4) utilize the interviewer's time efficiently and economically.

Coverage

When properly used, techniques designed to get spontaneous information are often so effective that the applicant takes the conversational ball and runs away with it. In so doing, he frequently skips over some important factors too quickly and leaves out other factors entirely. In launching his work-history discussion, for example, he may make no mention of part-time jobs carried on during high school and college. And he may devote only a minute or two to his first postcollege job, leaving out such factors as likes, dislikes, and reasons for leaving. Or, in telling about his education, he may go right into a discussion of college, forgetting to say anything about the high school experiences.

When the applicant begins to race over his history too rapidly, the interviewer should step in to *control the situation,* tactfully reminding the candidate to fill in the needed information. Otherwise the individual might conceivably cover an entire area such as work history in as few as ten or fifteen minutes, without providing any real clues to his behavior or any substantial information about his accumulated skills.

In his attempts to get maximum coverage, the interviewer directs the discussion with the image of the job and man specifications uppermost in his mind. And since he has by far the better knowledge of the job requirements, he is responsible for leading the discussion into the most fruitful channels of discourse. If he knows, for example, that a given job requires high mathematical facility, he will make very sure that the applicant covers such factors as math grades, amount of study time required to obtain those grades, and the extent to which mathematical facility has played an important part in job accomplishment.

Balance

During the early stages of their training, interviewers frequently fail to apportion interviewing time appropriately. They permit the candidate to spend far too much time on one area of his background and far too little on some of the other areas. Such interviews lack balance.

Problems concerned with balance usually occur as a result of allowing the applicant to provide too much irrelevant detail about his previous work experience. In an insufficiently controlled interview, some applicants find it quite easy to spend as much as an hour and a half discussing their previous jobs. In so doing, they naturally include a lot of unnecessary and irrelevant information. When this occurs, the interviewer suddenly realizes that too much time has been spent on the work area. Then, in order to complete the discussion within a reasonable period of time, he pushes the applicant through the other areas of his background too rapidly. The ensuing lack of interview balance precludes comprehensive evaluation of the individual's qualifications. In fact, lack of interview balance can frequently lead the interviewer to completely erroneous conclusions concerning the candidate's suitability. In spending too much time on the work history, he may, for example, skip over the early home background so fast that he fails to bring to light highly critical information—information that could have provided the real key to understanding the individual's behavior.

Now, it is not reasonable to expect all information supplied by the applicant to be relevant. Of necessity, much of the discussion provides little more than a framework that is used by the interviewer as a basis for probing into more fruitful areas. At the same time, the interviewer must continually guard against excessive and irrelevant detail. He must continually ask himself, "Am I learning anything about the applicant's behavior or anything about the extent to which he meets the job specifications, as a result of this particular segment of his discussion?" If the answer is "No," he must tactfully push the candidate along to another topic.

In order to achieve proper balance, the interviewer should place a clock on the table in front of him. And he should casually refer to the clock at rather frequent intervals. Time spent in the various interview areas with applicants for higher-level jobs should be apportioned roughly as indicated below. These time limits, as discussed in Chapter 2, can be appreciably shortened in interviews with candidates for lower-level positions.

Work history—40 to 50 minutes
Education—15 to 20 minutes
Early home background—10 to 15 minutes
Present social adjustment—5 to 10 minutes
Self-evaluation—10 to 15 minutes

The above timetable permits a minimum of an hour and twenty minutes and a maximum of an hour and fifty minutes. It must be emphasized, though, that these time allowances are to be used only as a rough *guide*. Since there are such marked differences between individuals, it will obviously take longer to interview one person than another. Factors that influence interviewing time requirements are primarily those of *age* and *psychological complexity of the individual*. The older applicant normally requires more time because he has more experiences to be discussed and evaluated. Regardless of age, the individual who is complex psychologically requires greater time because there are more facets of his personality to be considered.

There are cases, too, where the suggested timetable may have to be modified with respect to the amount of time required for a given interview area. If the applicant is fresh out of college, for example, and has had few summer or other part-time jobs, it will obviously be unnecessary to spend as much as forty minutes on the work history area. In evaluating such an individual, proportionately more time should be spent on his education and on the other areas of his background. In another case, the individual's current domestic situation may be such that it requires as much as twenty minutes of discussion.

The suggested timetable is therefore a very flexible one. But if an interviewer spends more than the indicated time on a given area, he should at least be aware of it and should have a good reason for so doing. As indicated above, the timetable serves as a guide or check. If, for example, the interviewer suddenly discovers that he has spent thirty minutes on work history without touching upon any of the jobs held by the applicant during the past ten years, he knows that he will have to move the individual along more rapidly if he is to have sufficient time to explore the remaining areas of the man's background.

Penetration

In general, applicants supply two types of information: *descriptive* information and *evaluative* information. If the interview is not sufficiently controlled, almost all of the information may be of a descriptive nature. The applicant may describe the companies for which he has previously worked, go into elaborate details concerning his job duties, and talk a lot about the fun he had in college. Now, some of this descriptive information serves a purpose, but it does not tell us much about the make-up of the individual himself.

Hence, the interviewer must control the discussion to get evaluative information—information that can be used as a basis for determining the applicant's personality, character, and motivation. By artful and tactful questioning, he must *penetrate* to the candidate's basic reactions to key situations, with a view to determining the possible effects of those situations on the individual's growth and development. For example, to learn that a man spent five years in the Army, attended a variety of schools, fought in the tank corps overseas, and was awarded a Bronze Star is not sufficient. We want to know, in addition, how he got along with his superior officers, how well he adjusted to military life, and how much he developed and matured as a result of the over-all experience. Normally, the average applicant will not supply answers to these questions unless his discussion is *channeled*. In other words, the interviewer must find a way to cut off descriptive information and probe more deeply for evaluative data.

Economy of the Interviewer's Time

The good interviewer is always jealous of his time. Although he must not in any way convey this fact to the applicant, he nevertheless uses control in order to complete his interviews in the shortest possible time and still get the best possible picture of the candidate's qualifications. The interview that runs for $2\frac{1}{2}$ to 3 hours is ordinarily an inefficient one. Such an interview not only consumes more time than is necessary but results in so much irrelevant detail that interpretation becomes more difficult. In other words, the interviewer has difficulty separating the wheat from the chaff primarily because there is so much chaff.

If an interviewer is to assume a normal case load of two to three comprehensive interviews per day, he cannot afford to spend much more than $1\frac{1}{2}$ hours per interview and still have time to write up his notes. Moreover, interviewing is a very fatiguing experience because of the attention factor. If the interviewer spends too much time on one interview, he will not have sufficient energy to give other applicants the attention they deserve.

The indicated case load of two to three interviews per day may strike some as a surprisingly low number. It is true, of course, that an employment interviewer can conduct a relatively large number of *preliminary interviews* in a single day. And he can carry out as many as seven or eight final interviews on applicants for lower-level plant or office assignments. But it is unreasonable to expect him to do more than three comprehensive interviews per day in the case of persons being considered for higher-level positions. Since the evaluating of key applicants represents such a critical function, it is much better to hire and train additional interviewers than to overload the interviewing staff.

TECHNIQUES OF CONTROL

Effective interview control is more than a matter of too little or too much. It is also a matter of *how it is accomplished.* And this represents one of the most important aspects of the art. It is a relatively easy task to teach interviewers the art of getting spontaneous information. The big job is to teach them how to control. For if this is poorly done, the applicant "freezes up" and rapport is lost. Description of the recommended techniques is of course no substitute for personalized training and supervised practice, but it does constitute an important first step.

Interview Guide

This provides the interviewer with a "track to run on" and, as such, represents the very foundation of control. If carefully followed, the Interview Guide can bring order, system, and intensive coverage to a discussion that might otherwise have been rambling and inconclusive.

This Interview Guide not only specifies the sequence of the discussion but lists the important factors to be taken up in each major area. The interviewer operates with this form on his lap and he constantly refers to it throughout the interview. When he completes the discussion of the educational background, he turns the form over so that he can use it as a guide through the rest of the session. The form should be turned over in an unobtrusive manner, so that the applicant does not become unduly aware of it. The interviewer does this by fixing the applicant's attention with his eyes while talking with him about some aspect of his education and training. In nine cases out of ten, the applicant will not even be aware that the form has been turned over.

After considerable practice, some interviewers feel that they no longer have a need to rely on the Interview Guide. When they put this out of sight, however, they almost invariably leave out some important aspect of the applicant's background. Hence, no matter how much experience with the form the interviewer accumulates, he should always operate with it before him.

Obviously no form—no matter how well designed—can include all the topics that might be discussed with every conceivable applicant. But if the interviewer will make certain to get thorough coverage on each point listed under each of the major areas, he should have a reasonably good basis for a hiring decision by the time he has concluded the discussion.

Follow-up Comments and Questions

As indicated in the previous chapter, one of the important functions of follow-up questions and comments is that of guiding the interview. Such remarks are used (1) to return the applicant to the subject under discussion when he wanders off the track, (2) to push him along when he begins to go into too much irrelevant detail, and (3) to shift his discussion from descriptive information to information that provides more clues to his personality, character, and motivation.

In order to control the interview unobtrusively, it is necessary to make use of two exceedingly important factors: *timing* and *lubrication*. Essentially, control means *interruption* of the applicant's remarks. But it is impolite to interrupt him in the middle of a sentence and, if we wait for him to conclude a sentence, he may already have begun a subsequent sentence before we can get around to interrupting him. In order to solve this problem, we must learn to *anticipate* the end of a sentence. With practice, one can determine that point at which the applicant is about to end a sentence. This is when the interruption should take place and this is what is meant by *timing*.

When the interruption is made, it should come in the form of a *positive* or *lubricating* comment. This tends to soften the interruption in such a way that the applicant may not even become aware of it.

Let us assume, for example, that the applicant races lightly over his first two or three jobs, apparently thinking that they are not germane to the discussion. Since this would normally occur at the very beginning of the interview and since we want to establish the pattern of having him carry the conversational ball, we would let him talk for three or four minutes. Then, just as he was about to put a period at the end of a sentence, we would inject a positive comment and redirect him to a more thorough treatment of his first job. We might say in this instance, "You have certainly had some interesting early experiences—so interesting in fact that I would like to know more about them. Suppose you tell me more about your likes, dislikes, and earnings on that first job."

To take another illustration, let us show how easy it is for an applicant to wander off the track. In answering the question as to what he liked on a given job, he might say, "That job gave me satisfaction because I like to work with my hands. I guess I get that from my father, who was a real craftsman." Already off on a tangent, the applicant may follow with a lengthy discussion of his father—information which would normally be obtained later on in the area of early home background. Now, this represents a situation which we must control if we are to prevent him from rambling. Yet, we do not want to give him the impression that he has wandered out into "left field." Hence, we *lubricate* the situation with a positive comment and then redirect him to the subject in hand. After he has talked a little about his father and just as he is about to come to the end of a sentence, we might say:

"Your father must have been a very interesting person, and I can certainly understand how you happened to acquire some of his traits. What else did you like about your job with the Superior Steel Company?" This kind of remark gets a person back on the track without any loss of face.

When an applicant goes into too much irrelevant detail, we *push him along* without trying to make this apparent to him. Again, we use timing and the positive or lubricating comment. Let us assume for purposes of illustration that, in response to a question concerning outside interests, the candidate mentions hunting and starts to give a detailed description of a moose-hunting trip he took a year ago in Canada. Now, the interviewer may himself enjoy hunting and may be very much interested in getting a complete account of this hunting trip. *But he cannot afford the interviewing time,* since this information would be unlikely to tell him very much about the man's behavior. Accordingly, he adroitly cuts off this discussion and pushes the man onto a new topic. After the candidate has talked a minute or two about his hunting trip and just as he is about to conclude a sentence, the interviewer might take over with, "That must have been a mighty fine trip; I would like to do something like that myself one of these days. What else do you like to do for fun and recreation?" This control device effectively pushes the man on, but because positive interest was expressed, does so without losing rapport.

When an applicant goes into too much detail in discussing a certain job, push him along by repeating part of the comprehensive introductory question, "Tell me briefly about your next job—what you did, your likes and dislikes, your earnings, and so forth." The words "tell me briefly" are used not because the person is expected to give a cursory account of his next job but because he is the kind of individual who will be likely to go into too much detail unless such instructions are included.

We have already noted that most applicants tend to keep their discussion on a descriptive rather than an evaluative level unless the interviewer steps in to guide the situation. In response to the comprehensive introductory question on education, for example, the candidate will probably be content with a *listing* of his subject likes and dislikes. Such a descriptive listing may be of interest but it does not contribute enough to understanding the individual. The interviewer must know *why* he disliked a subject such as mathematics. Accordingly, he cuts off the descriptive discussion in order to dig deeper for more meaningful clues to abilities or personality characteristics. In this case, he might say, "What was there about mathematics that did not appeal to you?" Such a question forces the candidate to think and often results in more significant data. In response to this question, the applicant might say, "The subject of mathematics was too abstract for me. I just could not get it through my head. Because I disliked it so, I just put in enough time to get by." This response has provided clues to possible mental limitation (inability to think in the abstract) and immaturity (unwillingness to work hard on things he dislikes). The remark also carries a possible clue to lack of motivation.

General Interviewing Manner

Even though the interviewer does only 15 or 20 per cent of the talking and seldom assumes the center of the stage, he nevertheless guides the discussion by his very manner and by the way he carries out his role. This requires poise, presence, and ability to meet unanticipated situations. Although he is friendly, disarming, and permissive, there is a point beyond which he cannot be pushed. By means of vocal and facial expressions, he *assumes consent*. In other words, he asks his questions and makes his comments in such a way that the applicant is expected to answer. This inner firmness creates an atmosphere of "remote control." Thus, the interviewer takes active control only when he has to, but he is always ready to step in when the occasion demands. Since the interviewer is already in the "power position"—it is the applicant who is seeking the job—he can usually maintain control in a very unobtrusive fashion.

One occasionally meets an applicant who is inclined to be facetious. Such a person may make light of some of the interviewer's questions or may even challenge their relevancy. This situation obviously requires firmer control. If the interviewer backs down, in fact, he might as well give up then and there. To lose the respect of the applicant is to lose control completely. When a question is challenged or treated facetiously, the interviewer simply restates the question, giving his reasons for asking it. By his manner rather than by anything he says, the interviewer underscores his seriousness of purpose. This approach almost invariably prevails, the applicant becoming very cooperative thereafter. Although they are fortunately few and far between, some applicants like to test the interviewer, just to see how far they can go. Once they determine the point beyond which they cannot go, they usually become very cooperative.

SPECIFICS OF CONTROL

Since applicants vary so widely in abilities, personality, motivation, and background experiences, it is impossible to enumerate all situations where control may be necessary. There are some general rules, however, that may be applied in almost every case.

Get Information Chronologically and Systematically

Although the applicant should be allowed considerable freedom in his choice of subject matter, he should nevertheless be encouraged to supply this information chronologically and systematically. In discussing his work experience, for example, he should be asked to start with his first job and work up to his most recent job experience. This not only gives a sense of order to this segment of the interview but also makes it easier for the interviewer to ascertain the applicant's vocational achievement over the years. In the educational area, it is always best to start with high school and go on to college. This gives the interviewer an opportunity to see how the applicant fared as he progressed to more difficult academic subject matter and came up against sterner competition. In like manner, it is best to follow the order indicated on the Interview Guide in discussion of the applicant's early home background and present social adjustment.

Exhaust Each Area before Going On to the Next One

Constant reference to the Interview Guide helps the interviewer to get all the salient information in one area before he goes on to the next. After completing the work-history discussion, for example, he may discover that he has neglected to get the applicant's pattern of earnings. He can then go back and get this before launching into education.

When the applicant is permitted to crisscross between areas, it becomes very difficult for the interviewer to evaluate total achievements in any one area. Moreover, he invariably finds that he has forgotten to get some important bit of information after the applicant has left the room.

When omissions do occur and when the interviewer does not become aware of this until he is midway in the next area, he should complete the discussion in the current area before going back to get the desired information. If, for example, he interrupts the applicant in the middle of a discussion of his education to get job earnings, not only does he interrupt the latter's train of thought, but the applicant may not be able to remember where he left off when he returns to the discussion of his education.

An attempt should also be made to keep the discussion in each area "pure." This is sometimes quite difficult, particularly when trying to separate jobs from school experiences. Obviously, chronology is of great importance in discussing jobs held at the time the applicant was going to school. Start with the jobs that he had while going to high school. Next, discuss the *jobs* he carried out while going to college. If he happened to go into the Army after finishing one year of college, encourage him to discuss his Army experience at that point, since for all practical purposes this can be considered as another job. If the man returned to college after his Army discharge, ask him about the *jobs* he may have had while completing his college education.

In keeping the record straight, it is often helpful to inquire about dates. This also gives the interviewer a chance to note any periods of unemployment.

Try to Exclude Irrelevant Detail from Discussion of Military Experiences

Unless the interviewer exercises a fair amount of control here, the applicant may easily spend twenty to twenty-five minutes discussing his Army or Navy experiences. And he may do this in such a descriptive manner that he supplies very few clues to his behavior. Consequently, he should be pushed through the descriptive aspects of this experience rather quickly— the training he received, his experiences in this country and overseas, his promotions, and his date of discharge. This can usually be accomplished in about five minutes. At this point, the interviewer begins to probe for whatever effects this experience may have had on the individual's development. He does this by getting the applicant's reactions to associates and superiors, by exploring his likes and dislikes with respect to the experience as a whole, and by asking him frankly what effects he thinks the military experience had on his growth and development.

With Older Applicants, Spend Less Time on Early Jobs and More Time on Recent Positions

When an applicant has reached the age of thirty-five or forty, there is little point in developing elaborate information concerning his early jobs. Unless an early part-time job had some unusual features, there is little need to probe for likes, dislikes, and earnings. Rather, confine that discussion to such simple facts as duration of employment, number of hours worked, and reasons for leaving.

When evaluating an older person with a long job history, there is not sufficient time to obtain complete information on every experience. Moreover, a given applicant is today more like what he has been during the past ten years than he is like what he was twenty years ago. Hence, we move through his early jobs quite rapidly and then give more exhaustive attention to his recent experiences.

Avoid Awkward Pauses

Although, as indicated in the previous chapter, pauses are sometimes consciously utilized as a means of prodding the applicant to a more elaborate explanation of a given subject, they should not be permitted to last too long. If this occurs, the applicant begins to feel uncomfortable, since he does not know quite how to extricate himself. Before this feeling is allowed to develop, the interviewer should step in with another question or comment.

The inexperienced interviewer will sometimes momentarily "block" because at that particular instant he cannot think of an appropriate question. Rather than permit an awkward pause to develop, he can always throw the conversational ball back to the interviewee by saying, "Tell me a little more about that experience." During the applicant's subsequent reply, the interviewer can gather his thoughts for the next question.

EFFECTIVE CONTROL REQUIRES JUDICIOUS PACING

Here we return to a subject discussed at the beginning of this chapter. If spontaneity of response is to be maintained, control must be exercised tactfully, unobtrusively, and *at appropriate intervals*. This means that the interviewer must never ask a series of questions one after the other. This gives the appearance of grilling the applicant and puts him on the spot. Thus, after asking a penetrating question, the interviewer must find other ways to encourage discussion before asking a second penetrating question. These other ways consist of facial expressions, verbal pats on the back, vocal intonations, and consciously designed pauses.

In a sense, the interviewer is not unlike the coachman of yesteryear. In guiding his six-horse team, the coachman learned to pace his horses so that they would cover the necessary miles without becoming too fatigued. In so doing, he would let them gallop for a while and would then pull them up to a walk. So it is with interviewing. The interviewer encourages the applicant to talk spontaneously, but every once in a while, he stops him to keep him on the track or to probe more deeply for salient information. Then he immediately gives the individual his head, encouraging him to carry on. In short, he consciously *paces* the interview in such a way that he gets all the information he desires without *pressing* the applicant and without losing rapport.

PART THREE

Interpretation

CHAPTER SEVEN

General Factors
of Interpretation

Since securing information has such a direct bearing on the evaluation of the applicant's over-all qualifications, discussion in previous chapters has already touched upon certain factors of interpretation. When, as in the case of securing and interpreting interview information, activities are performed simultaneously, it is somewhat difficult to discuss one activity without considering the other. In the remaining chapters of this book, emphasis swings from securing information to interpretation of findings. Because of the interdependence of the two, however, no effort will be made to confine the discussion to interpretation alone. In fact, subsequent chapters will be concerned with the *specifics* of exploring and interpreting each major area of the interview. Chapter 8, devoted to interpretation of work-history information, will also include further suggestions for carrying out the work-history discussion. In like manner, succeeding chapters will deal with education, early home background, present social adjustment, and self-evaluation.

Prior to any discussion of information obtained from the various interview areas, some consideration must be given to the interpretation process itself. In this present chapter we shall therefore discuss some general factors of interpretation. This material represents background information concerning the process of evaluation as a whole. These general factors must be kept in mind in evaluating all interview findings, regardless of the interview area from which such findings emerge.

COMPLEXITIES
OF INTERPRETATION

Evaluation of interview data represents an involved mental process. In the first place, interview data are not made up of hard, cold facts that can be reduced to any precise mathematical formula. For the most part, they are composed of clues that alert the interviewer to the possible existence of certain traits of personality and motivation. In the second place, the interview produces a large mass of information *only part of which is relevant in terms of interpretation.* As the discussion progresses, the interviewer must constantly separate the wheat from the chaff. In the third place, a given applicant's qualifications comprise a relatively large number of individual traits and abilities. Interview data must therefore be obtained and organized in such a way that there is sufficient supporting information for evaluating each of the requisite characteristics. It is not enough to know that the applicant has had sufficient technical training and experience; we must also decide the extent to which he possesses such characteristics as honesty, willingness to work, ability to get along with others, emotional stability, self-confidence, and ability to plan and organize.

In general, it is far easier for a novice to learn how to secure the necessary information than to learn how to interpret the findings he obtains. This is because most people respond quite readily to the information-getting techniques discussed in previous chapters. Within two or three days a novice can learn to apply these techniques so effectively that he usually experiences little or no difficulty in getting the candidate to "open up." But learning to interpret is another matter. People in general do not fall into any set pattern of traits and abilities. There are wide individual differences. In briefing a trainee for a given interview, therefore, one cannot predict the kind of information he is likely to encounter. Of course, certain broad predictions can be made on the basis of the application blank, test, and reference data, but such data usually tell relatively little about the applicant as a unique human being.

It is also difficult to teach interviewers to be objective. Unless there is an opportunity to subject the trainee to an extended period of supervised interviewing practice, he frequently drifts into such pitfalls as the "halo effect" and interviewer bias—problems discussed in an earlier chapter. In evaluating an applicant's over-all qualifications, moreover, interviewer-trainees tend to arrive at hiring decisions that place too much weight on certain factors and too little on others.

Despite the complexities of evaluation, experience has nevertheless shown that appropriately qualified individuals *can* be trained to interpret interview findings with a relatively high degree of accuracy. As noted above, such training requires extended periods of supervised practice and exposure to a variety of applicants.

INTERPRETATION AS A UNIQUE
AND SEPARATE FUNCTION

Although the information-getting and interpretation skills
are interdependent, they nevertheless occur in different di-
mensions. The information-getting skill is the "on stage" or
obvious aspect of the interview, whereas the interpretive
skill represents the "behind the scenes" aspect. As the drama
of the applicant's story unfolds, the interviewer mentally
scrutinizes each bit of information for possible clues to behavior. Yet he carries out this evaluation process in such a
way that he completely masks his true reactions and gives
the applicant not the slightest inkling of how he is interpreting the remarks. Because interpretation is a unique and
separate skill, it can be discussed here as an isolated process.
For clarity of presentation, let us analyze this process as a
separate entity.

Cataloguing Clues

As soon as the applicant enters the room, the interviewer
begins to get impressions of him in terms of his possible
effectiveness in the job for which he is being considered. The
interviewer may note, for example, that he makes a nice appearance. This may be mentally catalogued as one factor in
the individual's possible effectiveness with people. Later on,
as a result of the complete candor with which the applicant
discusses his strengths and shortcomings, the interviewer
evaluates him as sincere. The interviewer may catalogue
this as both an indication of character and a further clue to
the individual's possible effectiveness with people. So it goes
throughout the interview. Each statement the applicant
makes is carefully examined in terms of its implied as well as
its obvious meaning. Resulting clues to behavior are then
mentally catalogued as possible indications of such traits as

willingness to work hard, emotional maturity, self-confidence, and adaptability.

Acceptance or Rejection of the Applicant's Statements

The manner in which the applicant's remarks are interpreted depends in large part upon the extent to which he seems to be telling the truth. Early in the discussion, the interviewer must decide whether the applicant is telling the whole truth or whether he is coloring certain aspects of his story to make the best possible impression. If the interviewer decides that the applicant is being completely honest, he can accept his statements pretty much at face value. If, on the other hand, he decides that he is overplaying his hand or withholding important information, the interviewer mentally rejects much of the ensuing information as being not particularly indicative of the individual's true behavior.

Since the techniques described in this book normally result in spontaneous information, the vast majority of applicants will give a relatively complete and unvarnished description of their experiences, attitudes, and reactions. In fact, they realize that it is to their advantage to do so. Almost from the beginning, they discuss their unfavorable experiences as well as their achievements. In so doing, they provide clues to their shortcomings as well as documentation of their assets. In such cases, the interviewer is quick to note the obvious sincerity and decides that he can believe practically all the applicant's remarks without serious reservation. When, in addition, the applicant's story is completely consistent and fits into a general pattern, there need be no reservations.

In general, however, two factors loom most important in trying to determine whether a given applicant is "coming clean": (1) the extent to which he willingly discusses his shortcomings and (2) *internal consistency*. When an applicant openly discusses his shortcomings, the interviewer is obviously more willing to believe what he says about his strengths. And, when an applicant's remarks provide clues which are consistent with clues picked up in other interview areas they "make sense" and are readily understandable. This is what is known as *internal consistency*—the tendency of clues to behavior to emerge consistently in all the interview areas. Thus, when inconsistencies occur the interviewer should probe further in an effort to make certain that he understands completely what is being said. Obvious inconsistencies raise a question concerning basic honesty.

Even when the recommended techniques are expertly employed, the interviewer will occasionally encounter an applicant who tries to fool him. In such a case, the interviewer has the job of recognizing this at the earliest possible point in the discussion to avoid being taken in. From that point on, he takes everything that the person says with a grain of salt. Ability to spot the applicant who tends to overplay his hand or to conceal important information of course depends upon experience and training. The experienced interviewer looks constantly for certain danger signals indicating that the applicant may not be telling the whole truth. For example, the applicant who emphasizes his achievements and carefully avoids any indication of shortcomings is obviously withholding part of his story. Again, the individual who pauses perceptibly before answering key questions is more often than not screening his intended reply. In other words, he is thinking up an answer that will put him in the best possible light or will be most acceptable socially. The applicant who fences with the interviewer in order to avoid admission of shortcomings represents still another type of person toward whom the interviewer must be on guard. Finally, there is the extremely clever type of person who disarmingly admits the existence of certain minor shortcomings in order to give his over-all story more credibility. Whenever these danger signals develop, the interviewer should look further for inconsistencies in the candidate's story and should give special attention to his bodily posture and facial expression. In trying to conceal the complete truth, many persons give themselves away by unconsciously squirming in their seats and by noticeable changes in facial expression. At the risk of redundancy, it should be pointed out again that the interviewer must mask his reactions completely whenever he encounters an applicant who does not "come clean," thus giving no inkling of the fact that he is not going along with the individual's story.

Organize Mentally a List of Assets and Liabilities

As the discussion progresses, the interviewer mentally compiles a list of the applicant's strengths and shortcomings with respect to the job for which he is being considered. Although his outward manner is permissive and disarming, he nevertheless evaluates analytically and critically everything the applicant has to say. As the discussion progresses from one area to another, a general pattern of behavior normally begins to make itself evident. Thus, the interviewer may get clue after clue attesting to the candidate's forcefulness, willingness to accept responsibility, and strong drive to get things done quickly. At the same time, since a high degree of strength in certain areas may be accompanied by concomitant shortcomings in other areas, the interviewer may also pick up a series of clues indicating lack of tact, inflexibility, and even ruthlessness. As he catalogues such clues, he finds it increasingly possible to build a list of assets and liabilities. In fact, such a list of assets and liabilities should be so well documented by the end of the discussion that the interviewer can write it out immediately after the applicant leaves the room.

He then makes his hiring decision on the basis of the extent to which the assets outweigh the liabilities or vice versa.

BASIS OF INTERPRETATION

An earlier chapter called attention to the sound psychological assumption that the more we can learn about an individual's past history the better we can predict what he will do in the future. This is another way of saying that we are all inescapably the product of what has happened to us in the past. Thus, if we can establish a clear pattern of the candidate's past history, we have developed a useful basis for predicting his probable performance on the job to which he may be assigned.

Because of the importance of an individual's history, therefore, it is necessary to cover as much of this history as possible within a reasonable period of time. In order to systematize this fact finding, we have divided the history into four major areas—work history, educational background, early home experience, and present social adjustment. To these four areas we have added still another—self-evaluation. In the latter area, the candidate is encouraged to provide his own self-analysis. In so doing, he may not only confirm the interviewer's findings but also come up with a few assets or shortcomings that the interviewer may have missed. This rather exhaustive treatment of the candidate's past history is concerned with evaluating the individual as a whole. The theory here is that the more areas covered, the more likely one is to come up with all the salient information.

Importance of
Cause-and-Effect Relationships

It is important not only to get a clear picture of the candidate's pattern of personality and motivation but also to determine *why* he developed into the person he is today. If we can understand the *causes* of his current pattern of behavior, we shall have a better understanding of the resulting make-up of the individual.

In our quest of causes of behavior, we search for influences that may have contributed to the molding of the current pattern of personality, motivation, and character—influences that may have occurred in childhood, education, work experience, or in social and domestic life. When these influences are clearly defined, we are better able to judge the characteristics that resulted from such influences. We may find, for example, that much of a given applicant's shyness and oversensitivity has stemmed from the fact that he was overprotected as a child. Or we may find that another candidate's feelings of inferiority resulted in large part from the fact that he was not able to compete successfully with his classmates in school in terms of athletic prowess. With such knowledge of *causes* we can better understand the current pattern of behavior and also get some estimate of how much positive development has already taken place. If the individual has largely outgrown the shyness and oversensitivity he experienced as a child, we know that he has done much to eliminate these traits and may be expected to eliminate them to a greater extent in the future.

WHAT TO INTERPRET

As indicated previously, every interview results in *relevant* and *irrelevant* information. Much of what the applicant says is likely to be *descriptive,* providing little in the way of clues to behavior. The interviewer, of course, tries to keep such information at a minimum, controlling the discussion so that the applicant concentrates on evaluative data. Even so, a certain amount of irrelevant information is certain to ensue.

The interviewer naturally pays as little attention as possible to irrelevant discussion. He constantly sifts the wheat from the chaff and makes his interpretations accordingly.

In general, the more relevant information is likely to be found in the applicant's *attitudes and reactions.* Thus we learn much more about a woman as a result of her attitudes and reactions toward a given job than we do from a description of the job duties. Remember, too, that we are looking specifically for clues that will support a rating of the traits of personality, motivation, and character listed on the back of the Interview Guide. From the very beginning of the discussion, we must be alert to any clues that will provide supporting evidence of a person's emotional maturity, willingness to work hard, self-confidence, tact, and other such characteristics.

We also look specifically and critically at any information that will establish the relevance of the applicant's work experience and education in terms of the job for which he is being considered. This means that the interviewer must carry a mental picture of the job and man specifications into the discussion with him. As he listens to the description of previous jobs, for example, he must be quick to notice any similarity betwen previous jobs and the job for which the applicant is now being considered. And he must decide whether the candidate is capable of performing the job in question with a minimum of orientation or whether a protracted training period will be necessary to bring him to a productive level. In like manner he evaluates the candidate's education, deciding whether or not he has the kind and quality of technical training that will enable him to solve the problems with which he will be confronted.

In addition to our search for clues to personality, motivation, character, and relevance of job and work history, we must also concern ourselves with the *level of the applicant's abilities.* Obviously, aptitude tests can be of tremendous help in establishing the level of a candidate's mental ability, verbal ability, numerical ability, clerical aptitude, and mechanical comprehension. In fact, tests can do a far more accurate job of determining such abilities than the interview. But test results are not always available to the interviewer, and in such cases he must do the best he can to establish ability levels on the basis of his interview findings. Suggestions for accomplishing this task will be found in subsequent chapters of the book.

Even when test results are available, the interview can be useful in determining the *quality* of the applicant's abilities as well as the extent to which he makes use of the abilities he possesses. For example, some people of average intelligence utilize their mental ability so extensively that they actually accomplish more than brighter individuals who use only a fraction of their talent. Again, suggestions for determining the extent to which a given applicant makes use of his abilities will be found in subsequent chapters.

Although aptitude tests tell us the *degree* of a given ability possessed by the applicant, the interview goes a step further in establishing the *quality* of that ability. For example, a good intelligence test provides a measure of the ability to learn and to cope with complex problems. But such a test does not do the complete job of telling us how analytical or critical the applicant may be in his thinking. Actually, interview findings supply many clues to the latter. The manner in which the applicant responds to our depth questions and the discernment of his remarks about the people and situations he has encountered provide a great many clues to his analytical ability and his ability to think critically.

HOW TO INTERPRET

In determining the relevance of the applicant's work history and education, one has only to compare what the candidate has done in the past with what he will be expected to do on the job for which he is being considered. This is a relatively simple interpretive task, provided that the interviewer has a clear picture of the demands of the job in question. Understanding and utilizing the process described below as the *concept of contrast* will help immeasurably in carrying out this interpretive function. But the task of interpreting information with respect to personality, motivation, and ability is not quite so easy or clear-cut. For this more complex assignment we use two principal methods: *direct observation* and *inference*.

Concept of Contrast

Used primarily to establish the relevance of the candidate's work experience and education, this process involves the continual contrasting of each aspect of the applicant's job and school history with the specifications of the job for which he is being considered. In those areas where little or no contrast is involved—or where the difference is in the positive direction —no real adjustment problem exists. And this of course represents a favorable finding. On the other hand, a contrast in a negative direction may point to the fact that the candidate might experience a very real adjustment problem in acclimating himself to the new job situation. Although the difference may be insufficient to exclude the applicant from further consideration, nevertheless it represents an *unfavorable factor*.

An engineer who has occupied himself primarily with trouble-shooting assignments in the production situation, for example, might experience a real adjustment problem in taking over a new job primarily concerned with design work. Not only is he without solid design experience but he might also find design work too confining in the light of his previous history. At the very least, it will take him some time to become oriented to his new duties, even though he may have been trained for such duties in college. The interviewer thus recognizes this particular situation as representing an unfavorable contrast and considers this as one of the factors that must be weighed in making his employment decision.

Another unfavorable contrast would be encountered in an applicant who is already earning more money on his present job than he would be paid as a starting salary on his new job. He might express a willingness to take the new job at a lower salary because it may offer greater long-range opportunities. Once he takes the new job, however, a certain amount of dissatisfaction is likely to develop. This dissatisfaction, moreover, may be stimulated further by a spouse who finds it necessary to make ends meet on a smaller budget. If, on the other hand, the applicant is to be paid a starting salary in excess of his present earnings, he can be expected to be more satisfied with his new lot, other things being equal. This of course represents a difference in a positive direction and is evaluated by the interviewer as a *favorable factor*.

The degree of supervision involved in previous jobs and in a proposed new assignment may also provide an unfavorable contrast. An applicant who has grown accustomed to jobs involving relatively little supervision normally takes satisfaction in being his own boss and in ordering his own life. Technical service and applications-engineering personnel usually fall into this category. When such individuals take new positions involving much closer supervision, they ordinarily find adjustment somewhat difficult. In fact, they often have the feeling that the supervisors are breathing down their necks, and this of course makes them unhappy, at least in so far as initial adjustment to the new job is concerned. The alert interviewer recognizes the potentially unfavorable contrast and adds this to his list of negative factors.

Interpretation by Direct Observation

Certain of the more obvious characteristics such as appearance, grooming, self-expression, poise, and presence can be evaluated by direct observation during the interview. In other words, the interviewer simply observes the applicant's outward or surface behavior during the discussion and makes his evaluation of certain characteristics accordingly. If he spends as much as an hour or an hour and a half with a given individual, he can certainly size up the latter's general manner and appearance.

By direct observation the interviewer may also be able to obtain at least partial evaluation of such personality traits as aggressiveness, social sensitivity, and tact. He may note, for example, that a given candidate's personality has considerable impact and that the individual is exceedingly forceful and dynamic in relating his story. Such observable behavior provides considerable support for rating that individual as aggressive. That same individual may frequently interrupt the interviewer in the middle of a sentence, or may talk disparagingly about certain minority groups without any knowledge as to whether or not the interviewer may be a member of such a group. Directly observable behavior of this kind obviously provides documentary evidence of tactlessness and lack of social sensitivity.

Interpretation by Inference

Although a limited number of characteristics can be evaluated by direct observation, the vast majority of traits concerned with personality motivation and character must be appraised by inference. This applies also to the determination of abilities. It is not possible, for example, to rate the applicant on *willingness to work hard, emotional maturity,* or *intelligence* simply by observing his behavior during the discussion. In order to determine the degree to which a given applicant possesses characteristics such as these, the interviewer must develop an inference based upon a *series* of clues pointing in the same direction. Moreover, clues pointing to the existence of a given trait will normally appear in each of several interview areas, rather than being confined to a single area such as work history alone, thus establishing a pattern of internal consistency.

It stands to reason that we cannot base an inference on one or two isolated clues. Because a given applicant may have had difficulty with his superior and may have been fired from one job, we cannot automatically assume that he does not have the ability to get along with people. It is quite possible in such a case that the problem was due almost entirely to the supervisor rather than to his subordinate. On the other hand, if it develops that the applicant has had trouble with supervisors and subordinates on several jobs, has had difficulty with his teachers in school, and was a problem child during adolescence, the interviewer would be quite safe in concluding that the individual does not get along well with people. Having developed *a series of clues* pointing in the same direction, he is in a position to *document* his evaluation. In like manner, we cannot categorize an applicant as emotionally immature simply because he refused to apply himself to those subjects which he disliked in school. But if we can develop evidence that he rationalizes his failures on his jobs, has unrealistically high vocational aspirations, and consistently insists on doing everything his own way, there is ample support for a finding of some degree of emotional immaturity.

Not infrequently the interviewer will come up with a single clue that is not subsequently supported by clues pointing in the same direction. In some cases, subsequent clues may point in the opposite direction. Hence, the interviewer must make his judgment on the over-all weight of the evidence. To illustrate this point, let us take the case of a woman who was admittedly shy and withdrawn as an adolescent, who refrained from participation in extracurricular activities in school, and who was reluctant to assume additional responsibilities in connection with her early jobs. Among other things, the interviewer would be justified in forming an *initial hypothesis* that she may lack initiative. In talking with her about her more recent experiences, however, the interviewer may find that she has overcome many of her inhibitions, has shown a tendency to carry out current tasks in new and novel ways, and is presently reaching out for ever-increasing responsibility. This means of course that the interviewer would have to discard his original hypothesis and conclude that the applicant has developed to the extent that she now possesses an appreciable degree of initiative.

We have already indicated that clues must be interpreted as soon as they become evident. This provides the interviewer with a beginning or starting point upon which he can build later on. Using such a clue as a temporary supposition, he mentally catalogues the clue as a possible indication of a given trait. With this supposition as a foundation, he subsequently probes at appropriate intervals throughout the discussion for additional specific clues to support his suppositions. Let us assume for purposes of illustration that an applicant has expressed a strong dislike for detail in connection with an early clerical job. The interviewer catalogues this appropriately and wisely decides to wait, listen, and not *prejudge*. At the same time, he actively probes for further evidence. But he probes only in those areas which would be most likely to provide such evidence. Thus, when the applicant tells him about a subsequent job as a drafter, the interviewer—knowing that a drafting job involves a great amount of detail—will try to get further evidence of this trait by stimulating the applicant's spontaneous recital of his likes and dislikes on that job. If the applicant does not mention attention to detail as either a like or a dislike, the interviewer may specifically ask him how he felt about the detail involved. Later on, the interviewer may probe in like manner for the candidate's reactions to a design engineering course in college, again knowing full well that such a course involves a great amount of detail. Toward the end of the discussion, the interviewer may try to get further confirmation for possible dislike and inability to carry out detailed work by bringing this up under self-evaluation as a possible shortcoming.

We therefore see that interpretation by inference goes on throughout the interview, the interviewer making tentative hypotheses and probing specifically for confirming evidence. If his task were confined to the development of clues to a single characteristic, his diagnostic function would be relatively easy. The truth of the matter is, however, that he is required to develop clues to as many as fifteen or twenty characteristics, and he does much of this simultaneously. It is even possible that a single statement made by the applicant may provide clues to as many as three or four characteristics. Hence, the interviewer is confronted with a mentally demanding assignment. This is the primary reason why he must become so skilled in the mechanics of the interview that they become almost second nature. Once this has been accomplished, he can devote the major portion of his attention to the process of evaluation.

HYPOTHESES BASED ON LEADS
FROM PREVIOUS SELECTION STEPS

In an earlier chapter, it was suggested that the interview should ideally represent the last step in the employment process—after the candidate has completed the application form and the aptitude tests and after the reference checkups have been completed. This is because these earlier selection steps frequently supply leads that can be followed up in the interview situation. Such leads often give the interviewer a tremendous head start as far as the interpretive process is concerned. Even before the interview begins, for example, the interviewer may have a lead to possible emotional instability, as a result of having noted rather frequent job changes on the application blank. Or if the test of mental ability reflects a high level of intelligence, the interviewer will expect to see this reflected in above-average grades in school. If the latter does not turn out to be the case, he will immediately probe for the reason why, suspecting low level of application or disorganized study habits. Thus, by studying information available to him before the interview, the interviewer can frequently develop usable hypotheses which he carries into the discussion and seeks to support or reject on the basis of the evidence presented. It must be emphasized, however, that a lead is just that and nothing more. If it cannot be supported by tangible interview evidence, it must be discarded. The manner in which leads supplied by the early selection steps can be specifically used to advantage in the interpretation process will be discussed in subsequent chapters.

TRAIT CONSTELLATIONS

Experience has shown that certain traits tend to be related to each other and hence *may* be found in a single grouping or constellation within one individual. Thus, if it is possible to identify the *key trait* of a given constellation, it is more than possible that certain related traits may also be found in the individual's make-up.

In three of the five trait constellations discussed below, the key trait frequently becomes evident within the first five or ten minutes of the interview. A knowledge of the constellation permits the interviewer to probe specically for the possible existence of related traits as soon as the key trait has been identified. This, again, gives the interviewer an initial advantage in terms of diagnosing traits of personality and motivation. In other words, he can form his hypotheses more quickly and can specifically direct his probing in a more meaningful manner.

Familiarity with trait constellations may represent a real danger in the hands of the inexperienced interviewer. Such a person may be tempted to assume too much and may even attempt to type individuals. Nothing could be further from our purpose. Just because the interviewer identifies a key trait, he *cannot automatically assume* that the individual possesses the related assets and liabilities. In fact, it would be the unusual individual indeed who possessed all the suggested related traits. Moreover, some individuals possess the assets related to the key trait but have few if any of the liabilities. Once the key trait has been identified, the interviewer simply looks for the *possible existence* of the related characteristics. True, he probes specifically for the possible existence of these traits, but he discards the hypothesis if he is not able to come up with substantial supporting evidence.

The interviewer should familiarize himself thoroughly with the five trait constellations outlined below. A knowledge of these possible relationships can be of tremendous help to him in probing for clues to behavior. Whenever he is able to identify the *key trait* of a given constellation, he *may—but not invariably*—find subsequently that the applicant possesses some of the related assets and liabilities that go with that key trait.

Once again, it must be emphasized that the knowledge of

possible trait constellations should be used solely as a means of developing initial hypotheses. If the hypothesis cannot be supported by subsequent documentary evidence, it must be discarded completely.

Key Trait: Strongly extroverted

Assets	Shortcomings
Warmth	Impatience
Friendliness	Impulsiveness
Enthusiasm	Tendency to make snap
Aggressiveness	decisions
Self-confidence	Inability to think analyti-
Persuasiveness	cally
Seldom worries	Little organizing and plan-
Ability to improvise	ning ability
	Carelessness
	Lack of thoroughness
	Disregard of detail

Rationale

As indicated above, the strongly extroverted individual is frequently a good improviser, in the sense that he is able to think quickly on his feet and can normally rise to the occasion by acceptably handling situations for which he has had no opportunity to prepare. This particular ability, by the way, is often found in the top-flight salesman who is continually called upon to handle customer objections that cannot be anticipated. Now, ability to improvise represents an obvious asset but, at the same time, this ability often leads to the development of certain shortcomings. The strongly extroverted individual, for example, sometimes depends too much upon his ability to improvise. As a result, he becomes a "seat of the pants" operator, confident of his ability to handle any situation that may arise. By temperament, too, he likes to get one thing out of the way quickly so that he can go on to the next. As a consequence of his proven ability to improvise, he is not inclined to let problems worry him, and he often does not take sufficient time to prepare for his various assignments. Thus, he does not take time to think things through beforehand. This means, of course, that he does not cultivate the habit of analyzing a situation, or organizing and planning for it in advance. Hence, he tends to skim over the surface of matters and does not always dig deeply enough to investigate the heart of the problem. Because he operates so much on the spur of the moment, he frequently makes snap decisions —decisions too often born of impatience and impulsiveness. Hence, he is often careless, lacking in thoroughness, and not inclined to give appropriate attention to detail.

The extrovert often compensates for his shortcomings through the development of a very effective approach to people. Thus he cultivates warmth, friendliness, enthusiasm, forcefulness, and persuasive ability. Incidentally, these traits are normally prominent among the assets of the successful salesman. They enable the salesman to win others to his point of view. At the same time, any sales manager will be quick to admit that some of his best salesmen turn in the poorest reports, because of their impatience and dislike for detail. In an attempt to reward their best salesmen, moreover, many companies elevate such individuals to sales management. And, if the promoted individual has many of the shortcomings of the extrovert, he is not likely to be able to turn in a top performance as a manager. For as a manager he must be able to plan, organize, analyze, and give attention to detail. Many companies are discovering that their best salesmen do not necessarily make their best sales managers.

Of course, many extroverts succeed in modifying their behavior. Confronted with tasks that demand attention to detail, ability to analyze, and ability to plan and organize, they sometimes acquire a reasonable degree of facility in these areas. This is one reason why it is dangerous to assume that an extrovert necessarily possesses the shortcomings listed above.

After the interviewer has identified an applicant as an extrovert during the first few minutes of the discussion, he should probe specifically for the possible existence of the above-mentioned shortcomings. An out-and-out extrovert can of course be quickly identified by his outgoing manner, his gregariousness, and his warm, friendly affability. As soon as this identification is made, the interviewer should say to himself, "I wonder if this person is impatient and impulsive? I wonder how analytical he is? I wonder to what extent he gives appropriate attention to detail? I wonder how well he plans and organizes?" Having raised these questions, he should then proceed to try to find the answers by probing specifically for the possible existence of these traits. As a matter of fact, it is well to go through these mental steps even in cases where the applicant may be only somewhat extroverted. It is quite possible that such a person may have one or two of these related shortcomings. Suggestions on how to probe for suspected shortcomings will be found in subsequent chapters.

Key Trait: Strongly introverted

Assets	Shortcomings
Reflectiveness	Shyness
Analytical thinking	Self-consciousness
Imagination	Lack of confidence
Good attention to detail	Undue sensitiveness
Carefulness	Tendency to worry
Meticulousness	Poor improvisation
Methodicalness	Lack of poise
Orderliness	Tendency to be inhibited
Patience	Lack of mental toughness
	Lack of aggressiveness

Rationale

At the outset, it must be pointed out that introversion does not necessarily represent a shortcoming. In fact, introversion is a decided asset in certain positions where a fair amount of confinement is involved—in such positions as drafting, design, and certain types of research work. Because strongly extroverted individuals find it very difficult to adjust to jobs of a confining nature, they are seldom found in the positions enumerated above. Hence, in selecting an applicant for a given job, appropriate attention must be given to the type of temperament which is likely to be most appropriate for the position in question.

Although the introvert frequently possesses many important assets, he is likely to be unsure of himself in social situations. Unlike the extrovert, therefore, he is inclined to take great pains in preparing for a given assignment. In so doing, he takes plenty of time to reflect about the task at hand and usually analyzes it from every conceivable angle. He is sometimes so concerned that he may not measure up that he documents his thinking in great detail being very careful that his approach is logically planned and systematically organized. Since he gives a great amount of thought to his approach, he is often able to come up with a number of new and original ideas.

But the introvert's lack of confidence is often outwardly reflected in a series of concomitant shortcomings. Many of these shortcomings limit his facility for dealing with people effectively. Thus he is often shy, self-conscious, inhibited, unaggressive, and lacking in poise and presence. Some introverts are so insecure, moreover, that they tend to worry unduly and become oversensitive to criticism.

As noted above the assets of this particular trait constellation provide a rather good description of the qualifications of the successful research and development person. This perhaps represents one reason why so many good research and development people tend to be on the introverted side. It is equally true, moreover, that many research people have a problem selling their ideas and often find it difficult to assume responsibility for the direction of others.

Again, the pronounced introvert may be quickly identified in the early part of the discussion by means of direct observation. Such a person is often ill at ease in talking with a stranger, his shyness, self-consciousness, and inhibited nature becoming noticeably apparent within the first five or ten minutes of conversation. As soon as identification of the introvert takes place, the interviewer should ask himself, "I wonder if this person lacks confidence? I wonder if he is oversensitive? I wonder if he has a tendency to worry unduly? Having set up these tentative hypotheses, he then tries to document them by probing for tangible evidence.

In making use of trait constellations as a basis for further probing, it is well to remember the tentative aspect of the hypothesis. Certainly, all insecure people are not introverts. Moreover, many introverted individuals attain a high degree of emotional adjustment and establish very effective relationships with other people.

Key Trait: Personal Forcefulness

Assets	Shortcomings
Strong impact	Lack of tact
Dynamism	Insensitivity to feelings of
Tough-mindedness	others
Good organizing ability	Ruthlessness
Decisiveness	Strong ego
Supreme self-confidence	Intolerance
Production-mindedness (desire to get things done quickly)	Strong likes and dislikes
	Inflexibility
	Tendency to be too blunt and direct

Rationale

Because of the impact of his personality upon others, the forceful individual frequently manages to win election or promotion to positions of leadership. Such positions of course require decisive action and an ability to get the job done. If a person is to operate successfully as a leader, he has to learn to organize. To the leader, results are what count the most; and he is expected to obtain these results in the shortest possible period of time. The leader therefore becomes more concerned with the effectiveness of the group than he does with the problems of any one member of that group. Thus, he does not hesitate to make tough-minded decisions that may tread on the toes of the few, if such decisions are good for the many —the over-all organization. Remember, too, that it takes a great amount of confidence to make decisions at a high level. Decisions of this kind may have a pronounced, long-range effect on the entire organization. These are the decisions, moreover, that the timid, cautious individual finds it very difficult to make.

In his desire to get the job done quickly, however, the forceful individual sometimes gives too little thought to the people involved. Occasionally, such a person becomes so result-oriented that he does not care how he treats his people so long as he is able to accomplish his goals. This means of course that he is likely to be blunt, direct, and tactless. He may even be so insensitive to the feelings of others that he becomes ruthless. Because the experience of making decisions at high levels requires great self-confidence, the forceful person who has attained an important leadership position may become somewhat egotistical. If this occurs, he may come to regard his judgment as infallible, in which case of course he develops strong likes and dislikes, and tends to be inflexible and opinionated.

The above discussion pretty much depicts the "bull of the

woods" type of boss who was much more likely to be found in industry twenty or thirty years ago than he is today. Due in large part to pressure from the unions, such people find it necessary to modify their behavior if they are to maintain positions of leadership. The man promoted to foreman who throws his weight around without regard to the people who work for him runs head on into a series of union grievances. When such grievances become serious and time-consuming, the foreman's superiors call him on the carpet, telling him that he will have to modify his behavior or risk demotion to the ranks. The best of such foremen take stock of themselves and gradually come to the realization that they will have to learn to work with people amicably and adroitly if they are to survive. Happily, the vast majority of present-day managers have profited from hard knocks incurred on their way up. Obviously, too, management in general is much more enlightened today and recognizes the importance of the individual as a human being, regardless of union pressure.

It is easy to recognize the truly forceful applicant within the first five minutes of the interview because of the impact he has on the interviewer and because of his tendency to take the conversational ball and run with it. As soon as the interviewer realizes that he is dealing with a forceful person, he should immediately start probing for such possible short-comings as tactlessness, inflexibility, and a tendency to be egotistical and opinionated. When he finds evidence of such traits, he must decide how serious and deep-seated they are. In other words, is the candidate only somewhat egotistical or lacking in tact, or does he have these liabilities to such a serious degree that they would be likely to preclude the establishment of successful relationships with others?

Again, it must be remembered that many forceful people do not become leaders. And many forceful individuals may acquire very few of the assets or liabilities listed above.

Key Trait: Strong artistic interests

Assets	Shortcomings
Good intelligence	Impracticality
Creativity	Lack of mental toughness
Good cultural background	Oversensitivity
Social sensitivity	Questionable emotional adjustment
Breadth and perspective	Moodiness

Rationale

Since many forms of art are abstract, the artistically oriented person is normally equipped with relatively good intelligence. In other words, it takes a certain degree of intellect to appreciate and understand things in the abstract. Certainly modern music and modern painting represent art forms of such complexity that they are not easily understood or appreciated. And this holds true for many types of traditional music, painting, and ballet. The artistic individual often possesses an inquiring mind, and this sometimes leads him into numerous paths of creativity. In fact, his interpretation of various forms of art can be creative in itself. Appreciation of beauty in any form of art requires a relatively high degree of sensitivity. Such sensitivity, applied to social situations, finds its reflection in awareness of the reactions of others. A socially sensitive individual ordinarily acquires social judgment, judgment which enables him to sense how far he can press a point with an individual or a group of persons without incurring their displeasure. Consequently a socially sensitive person often develops a considerable amount of tact and adroitness in social situations. Because he is sensitive himself, moreover, he usually tries very hard not to hurt the feelings of others. It should be noted in passing, however, that some highly creative people become self-centered and egotistical. When this happens, they usually become less concerned about their approach to people. This is not because they lack the necessary social sensitivity but because they do not use the social intelligence they possess.

The study of art leads to an investigation of the history and development of the particular art form. This provides some insight into how people lived in the past in various countries throughout the world—their aspirations, their needs, and other things that were important to them. Thus, a study of art normally results in a better cultural background than might otherwise have been the case, and this develops the individual's breadth and perspective.

Many artistically inclined individuals become so completely immersed in their art that their lives take on an imbalance. They become wrapped up in their studies to such a degree that the more practical aspects of life take on less significance. Musicians, as a group, are notoriously inept when it comes to handling money matters. In fact, many of the more successful musicians find it necessary to engage managers to handle their personal funds as well as their business arrangements. The high degree of sensitivity developed by artistically inclined people often results in oversensitivity to criticism in their day-to-day relationships. Thus, they frequently interpret a remark as having deeper significance than was intended by the individual who made it. Lack of practical balance and oversensitivity are also occasionally reflected in some lack of emotional adjustment. Many artistic people have a tendency to be moody—to have their ups and downs. Of course all of us have such ups and downs, but these swings in mood are likely to be more protracted in the case of the person with strong artistic interests. In other words, the artistic person can suffer occasional periods of depression that may last for several days.

The interviewer obviously will not be able to identify the candidate with strong artistic interests in the first few minutes of the discussion. He may get no clues at all until he begins to discuss the candidate's extracurricular activities in school. At that point he may find that the candidate was exclusively involved in such activities as band, orchestra, glee club, and literary societies. When the interviewer subsequently gets ∴ to the candidate's present interests, he may find that the individual's hobbies are entirely concerned with the collection of musical records, symphonic concerts, the reading of poetry, ballet, and the theater. When the interviewer finally concludes that his subject does have strong artistic interests, he should begin probing for the possible existence of the above-mentioned traits.

A certain amount of interest in the arts, of course, represents a real asset. Who can say that such factors as breadth of perspective, social sensitivity, and cultural background do not represent a source of strength? As a matter of fact, many highly trained technical people have rather strong artistic interests. It is only when artistic interests become so strong that they seem to exclude other important areas of activity that the warning signals become evident. In such cases, the individual may possess a number of the shortcomings of this constellation as well as the assets.

Key Trait: Strong social drive
(Strong desire to help others—a do-gooder)

Assets	Shortcomings
Genuine love of people	Lack of mental toughness
Selflessness	Impracticality
Tendency to be unassuming	Not sufficiently suspicious of
Missionarylike zeal	others' motives
Enthusiasm	Tendency to take people at
Strong desire to encourage	face value
others' development	Tendency to see only the best
	in people
	Gullibility/naïveté
	Lack of critical thinking

Rationale

Applicants who reflect this trait constellation derive their greatest satisfaction from doing things for others. They are not primarily motivated by money, power, or prestige. For the most part, they tend to be selfless and unassuming. The YMCA director and the social worker, to cite members of two occupations that fit into this category, are certainly not motivated by the desire for financial gain. Their greatest satisfaction comes from helping other people to fight their battles. And they approach their work with as much or more enthusiasm than might have been the case were they primarily motivated by personal gain. The social worker will plunge into settlement house activity with the same kind of zeal shown by the salesman in his quest for new business.

Because of his strong desire to help others, the socially motivated individual is not always practical and tough-minded. Inclined to be overly sanguine, he is likely to believe that other people are guided by the same high principles that guide him. Since he is primarily concerned with helping others to better themselves, he tends to think only of their strengths, without giving proper consideration to their weaknesses. This is the type of a person, moreover, who is often considered a "soft touch." He willingly loans money without much concern as to whether or not it will be repaid. Helping another person in time of need is the primary consideration. Consequently, he tends to be naïve, easily taken in, and not very critical in his thinking.

A reasonable degree of social drive represents an asset in many types of jobs. For example, a woman does not become a great teacher unless she is strongly motivated to help the student learn—to stimulate his thinking and broaden his horizons. The effective supervisor in industry should also have a certain amount of social drive. He should be interested in bringing his subordinates along so that they can grow and develop. Again, as in the case of the other trait constellations, social drive presents problems only when it becomes inordinately strong. The individual whose social drive becomes so strong that it overshadows everything else frequently develops many of the shortcomings described above.

The interviewer will normally be unable to identify social drive in the early part of the discussion. In fact, he may not get his first clue until he approaches the end of the work-history discussion. Then, in response to the interviewer's questions concerning factors of job satisfaction, the applicant may say, "In order to give me satisfaction, a job must provide an opportunity to make some contribution to the welfare of mankind." Later on, in discussing his outside interests, the applicant may further reflect his social drive by the nature of his community activities. He may be entirely wrapped up in such affairs as boy scout work, YMCA work, hospital work, and community drives. The interviewer would then be prompted to probe for the *why* of such activities. If strong social drive seems to be indicated, he would of course probe for the possible existence of the shortcomings described above. Since it may not always be possible to identify social drive until the interview is almost over, the interviewer may have to rely upon the self-evaluation area as the primary means of obtaining documentary evidence of shortcomings related to this trait.

Precautions

Knowledge of possible trait relationships can provide the interviewer with a powerful tool in terms of his probing for clues to behavior. He must remember, however, that this knowledge only *suggests the possibility* of related traits, once the key trait has been identified. Moreover, only a fraction of the applicants will fall clearly into any one of the five trait constellations. And some applicants may reflect some of the strengths and shortcomings of two or three constellations. This knowledge must therefore be used cautiously and judiciously.

INTERPRETATION IN THE LIGHT OF THE APPLICANT'S STANDARDS

Before we leave the subject of general factors of interpretation, we must draw attention to the fact that what the applicant says about himself must be interpreted in the light of his own personal standards. It is not enough to know that the individual is telling the truth—important as that is. We must also determine whether his personal standards are realistic or not.

Subsequent chapters will make it abundantly clear that the interviewer's over-all evaluation of a candidate depends to a rather large degree on that individual's own self-evaluation, primarily because the applicant is encouraged to make a value judgment of his own abilities and personality traits throughout the interview discussion. At the end of the work history, for example, he is asked to relate the various abilities and personality traits that have become evident to him as a result of working on his various jobs. Later on, he is asked to compare his own personality with that of his parents, siblings, and spouse. Finally, at the end of the interview, the applicant is asked to summarize his major assets and shortcomings.

Since self-evaluation looms so important in this kind of an interview, the applicant's personal standards become genuinely significant. Throughout the interview, the interviewer must look for clues which may tell him that the applicant's standards are objective, unrealistically high, or perhaps unrealistically low.

If the applicant tells us that he is a hard worker and, if we have already determined that he is honest and objective, we can place a considerable amount of credence in that value judgment. But if we have determined that the person's personal standards are low—that he really does not demand a great deal of himself—then we are not very much impressed by his own view of his work habits.

Conversely, if the applicant tells us that he does not really work as hard as he should and, if we have already determined that his standards are unrealistically high in the sense that he expects too much of himself, then we do not necessarily take this statement at face value. In other words, we give him credit for working harder than he says that he does.

As material in subsequent chapters will point out, we rely upon many different techniques to provide us with clues to behavior. But the kind of self-evaluation that the applicant does throughout the interview nevertheless represents one of the more important techniques. Hence, when he does place a value on certain of his abilities or personality traits, we must view this not only in the light of whether or not we think he is telling the truth but also in the light of whether or not his standards are realistic.

TRAIT DESCRIPTION

If we are to rate a given applicant on a series of traits, our understanding of the meaning of these traits must be as clear as possible. Unfortunately, psychologists themselves find it difficult to agree specifically on the definition of many traits of personality, motivation, and character. Hence, it is expected that many people will quarrel with the definitions listed below. At the same time, these definitions do provide a functional description of the trait and should therefore be of assistance to the employment interviewer.

Emotional maturity: the ability to behave as an adult, to take the bitter with the sweet, to face up to failure without rationalizing or passing the buck, to acquire self-insight, to establish reasonable vocational goals, and to exercise self-control.

Personal forcefulness: aggressiveness in social situations; impact of one's personality upon other people—not to be confused with drive to get a job done.

Tough-mindedness: willingness to make difficult decisions involving people for the good of the organization, to stand up for what one thinks is right and not to shrink from confrontations with others when necessary.

Social sensitivity: awareness of the reactions of others; judgment in social situations.

Conscientiousness: willingness to put in additional time and effort on a given task in order to complete it in accordance with one's personal standards.

Self-discipline: ability to carry out the less pleasant tasks without undue procrastination.

Initiative: self-starter; willingness to try new methods, provide own motivation without undue prompting from superiors.

Analytical capacity: ability to break down a given problem into its component parts in a logical, systematic manner.

Ability to plan and organize: ability to lay out a given task in logical sequence, approaching first things first in a systematic manner, planning future steps in such a way as to accomplish the whole task efficiently and thoroughly.

Critical thinking: ability to dig down deeply in order to get to the bottom of problems, to probe beneath the surface in order to test the findings in terms of one's own experience, hence not to take things at face value.

Self-confidence: willingness to take action based upon a realistic assessment of one's own abilities

Emotional adjustment: ability to stand up under pressure, to take a reasonably cheerful outlook on life, to be at peace with one's self.

Team worker: willingness to do one's share of the work, ability to get along with other members of the team, willingness to subordinate one's ego to the extent that one does not try to become the "star" of the team or to claim too much credit for the joint accomplishment.

MINORITY CONSIDERATIONS

This book is primarily concerned with methodology—how to carry out a particular style of interviewing and how to interpret the information brought to light. Hence, a comprehensive or extensive discussion of the interviewing of minorities would detract from the major purpose of the book. In fact, a completely adequate treatment of the selection of minorities could conceivably involve an entire book in itself.

With the passage of the Equal Employment Opportunity legislation, however, employment interviewers must be guided by federal law that prohibits discrimination in hiring on the basis of race, religion, color, sex, age, marital status, disability, or national origin. And they have faced up to the fact that their work force does not include a high enough percentage of women, blacks, Spanish Americans, and other ethnic groups in higher-level positions. As a consequence, a relatively high proportion of applicants interviewed are now recruited from the so called minority populations. With this in mind, the second edition of this book now provides a treatment of some of the *major* considerations involved in the hiring of minorities—general factors in this chapter and specific factors in each of the chapters on work history, education, early home background, and present social adjustment.

Facing Up to Prejudice

Whether we realize it or not, most of us have certain built-in prejudices as a result of the way we were brought up. The interviewer, of course, is no exception. But there are some things that he or she can do to try to modify such prejudices.

In the first place, the interviewer can subject himself to self-analysis in an effort to face up to his prejudices. If this does not work, he can candidly ask some of his friends and business associates. And, once having determined what his prejudices are, he can keep these uppermost in mind so that they do not unduly bias his evaluation of people.

The Interviewer and Minorities

The question is often raised as to whether or not it is important to have the recruiting and selection of minority workers done by members of their respective ethnic groups. Many companies have found that recruiting is often more effectively accomplished when minorities are brought in for consideration by a member of their own group—one who is more familiar with the most productive sources. But the well-trained interviewer should be able to communicate with people—regardless of age, sex, race, or religion.

Women as a Minority Group

Because business and industry has long been considered a "man's world," women have had a difficult time gaining acceptance in the more technically demanding jobs as well as in managerial positions. But with more and more married women joining their single counterparts in the labor force and with governmental pressure being brought to bear as a result of Equal Employment Opportunity legislation, things are changing rapidly. But not rapidly enough!

As a group, women represent a still largely untapped bonanza in terms of qualified candidates for higher-level positions. Industry must therefore channel much more energy into their recruiting, preparation, and training for such positions.

Other Minorities

Although many minority and nonminority applicants obviously represent well-qualified candidates for important positions, there are other members of both groups who occasionally pose a problem to the interviewer.

With such individuals, the interviewer does have to make adjustments both in his approach and in his thinking when considering the applicant for employment. Largely because of lack of opportunity, some of these applicants have not had the benefit of a good education and hence may not do well on aptitude tests. And, because they have not been given a chance, they have sometimes had to settle for low-level jobs that have little relevance in terms of the job for which they may be now being considered. Yet experience has shown that many such applicants do have *potential* that has never been realized. Suggestions for identifying this potential will be found at the end of Chapters 8, 9, 10, and 11.

In the long run, interviewing the minority applicant is not all that different from interviewing applicants from the general population. The interviewer must try very hard to establish rapport. He will probably spend a little more time on small talk, will be quicker to give pats on the back, and will be especially careful to play down all unfavorable information. But once he achieves rapport, he can use all of the techniques recommended in previous chapters of this book.

Selection Standards and Minorities

There is nothing in the Equal Employment Opportunity legislation that precludes the selection of the best-qualified candidate from a pool of available applicants, provided such selection does not discriminate with respect to disability, sex, color, age, race, marital status, religion, and national origin. Hence, even though most companies are actively trying to hire as many minority applicants as possible, they need not and should not appreciably lower their selection standards.

CHAPTER EIGHT

Interpreting Work History

Having talked about general factors of interpretation in the previous chapter, we now look specifically at the work history, in terms of what this discussion may be able to tell us about the applicant's personality, motivation, and abilities. In addition to establishing the relevance of the candidate's previous work experience in terms of the job for which he is being considered, we should look specifically for clues to such traits as willingness to work hard, ability to get along with others, self-discipline, and emotional maturity.

In this chapter, suggestions for structuring the work history will be briefly discussed. This will be followed by an item-by-item discussion of the factors listed under work history on the Interview Guide.

STRUCTURING THE
WORK HISTORY

Much has already been said in Chapter 6 about structuring the work history. It seems appropriate at this point, however, to restate and elaborate upon some of the points previously mentioned. The reader will recall that the work-history discussion is launched with a comprehensive introductory question. This question should indicate to the applicant that he is expected to talk about his various jobs in chronological order, starting with the first job and working up to the present. The question should also include a request for information concerning duties, likes and dislikes, accomplishments, and earnings on each job. In talking about his various jobs, the applicant will normally provide spontaneous information concerning many of the factors listed under the work history on the Interview Guide. If he fails to provide such information—or if he does not discuss important factors in sufficient detail—the interviewer should prompt him to do so by adroitly worded follow-up questions and comments.

Remember, too, that we try to keep the work history pure, in the sense that we encourage the applicant to concentrate on his *jobs* without supplying much information about other interview areas. He starts with the jobs he may have had while going to high school; then he discusses the jobs he carried out at the time he was in college; and from there he discusses his postcollege jobs in chronological order. For each job, he is encouraged to supply information concerning duties, likes, achievements, dislikes, earnings, and reason for leaving. In the case of someone over thirty, the early jobs should be covered very quickly, confining the discussion to length of time employed on each job, number of hours worked per week, and reason for leaving provided such reasons are not obvious. In cases like these we are looking primarily for the work habits the individual established during adolescence. Once having established this information, we probe more exhaustively into the postschool experiences. On the other hand, we treat early jobs much more comprehensively in the case of an applicant still in his twenties. Such a person has had so little opportunity to accumulate work experience that we must do everything we can to probe for clues to behavior in every job situation with which he has been confronted.

Military service should be discussed whenever it occurs chronologically in the individual's work history and treated just like any other important job. Thus, in the case of a man who went into the Army after completing two years of college, we would discuss the jobs he had while in high school, and the jobs he carried out during his first two years of college. We would then launch into a thorough discussion of his Army experience. This would be followed by a discussion of the jobs he may have had during his last two years of college, and by a discussion of his postcollege jobs. Since the military experience normally represents a very important episode in the individual's life, it should be discussed in considerable detail. At the same time, we do not want to devote an inordinately large portion of the interview to it. Hence, the applicant should be encouraged to outline his various military assignments rather quickly. Provided with this overview, the interviewer then probes deeply for the applicant's reactions to the military experience as a whole. In other words, he should be asked about his over-all likes, dislikes, achievements, and relationships with superiors and associates. Such discussion may supply strong clues to adaptability, leadership, and ability to get along with people. It is also well to ask the applicant what he thinks he gained as a result of his military experience. Such a question may not only reflect the growth that took place in the individual but also provide leads for further probing later in the interview. For example, the applicant may say, "I really grew up while in the Army. Because I came from a pretty sheltered home situation, I was a real green, immature kid when I went into the service." The interviewer mentally catalogues this information, with the intention of reintroducing it at the conclusion of the discussion of early home background. He will subsequently be interested in learning about the factors that prevented the normal development of maturity during the individual's early life.

Achievements, development needs, factors of job satisfaction, and *type of job desired* are introduced at the end of the work-history discussion, after the applicant has talked about his most recent job experience and is therefore up to date. Suggestions for eliciting appropriate information concerning these job factors will be presented later in this chapter, together with suggestions for evaluating the total job accomplishment.

Attention now swings to a discussion of each of the factors listed under the work history on the Interview Guide. Each factor is treated in some detail, both in terms of how to get the information and how to interpret the resulting data.

DUTIES

As indicated previously, the applicant should not be permitted to devote too much of his time to a description of job duties, particularly in the case of the early jobs. When he gets to his more important experiences, however, he should be encouraged to talk in some detail about what he actually did on these jobs. Such discussion enables the interviewer to determine the relevancy of the candidate's previous experience in terms of the job for which he is being considered. With a mental picture of the job and man specifications before him, the interviewer continually compares what the subject has done in the past with what he will be expected to do in the future. For the most part, he does not expect the applicant to have performed duties that are exactly the same as those he will be responsible for in his new job. Rather, he evaluates the general nature of the candidate's experience, assuming that he should be able to carry out new duties that are generally similar to what he has done in the past. In hiring an engineer for the design of automatic-control systems for jet engines, it may not be absolutely necessary to find a man whose previous experience has been devoted to jet engines. If the candidate has successfully designed automatic-control systems for other highly technical power plants, such as those concerned with guided missiles or torpedoes, he should be able to assume his design responsibilities on jet-engine control systems without too much difficulty.

Information concerning the duties of the candidate's more important jobs also tells the interviewer about the degree of responsibility he has assumed. Such responsibility may have been highly technical or it may have involved the supervision of other people. In either case, the interviewer needs to know the degree of responsibility assumed—the exact nature of the technical duties or the number of persons supervised. To get this information, the interviewer may have to interrupt the applicant's story from time to time, encouraging him to be more specific. As the candidate goes from one job to another, the interviewer has an opportunity to note his progress in assuming responsibility. Such progress—or the lack of it—may provide clues to the individual's general ability. Where considerable progress has been made, the interviewer will probe for the *why*—those specific traits and abilities that have been responsible for the individual's success. Where lack of progress is evident, the interviewer will be equally interested in trying to find the underlying reasons. In the latter case, he will watch particularly for any attempt on the applicant's part to rationalize his failures, as a possible clue to immaturity.

In evaluating the degree of responsibility assumed in the course of military experience, the interviewer will be guided by the understanding that promotions frequently take place because the particular individual happened to be at the right place at the right time. In other military situations, the individual may have had little opportunity for promotion because he happened to find himself in a group where many of his associates had more experience and training in his particular specialty. At the same time, rapid promotion in the military establishment is normally based on ability and leadership qualifications. In such instances, the interviewer will naturally attempt to identify the particular factors responsible for the individual's success.

LIKES

Since attitudes and reactions to a particular job experience normally tell us much more about the person than a recitation of his job duties, a great deal of attention should be devoted to likes and dislikes. If the candidate omits this from his discussion, he should be reminded by such a follow-up question as, "What were some of the things you liked best on that job?" Moreover, the interviewer should not be satisfied with a single response. He should probe for additional likes.

Ideally, the most favorable situation develops when the applicant's likes on previous jobs correspond with important elements of the job for which he is being considered. If he has previously shown a liking for detail, for example, he should find little difficulty adjusting to the detail work on the job for which he is being evaluated. Or if he has shown a decided preference for jobs involving a considerable amount of contact with people, he should be able to adjust to the contact aspect of the new job with no great difficulty.

Likes on previous jobs can of course supply many clues to abilities, personality traits, and motivation. Someone who has shown a liking for responsibility—particularly where people are concerned—*may* have a certain degree of initiative and leadership ability. Someone who derives particular satisfaction from contacts with workers in the shop may possess a considerable amount of common touch. Since likes and abilities tend to be fairly highly correlated—in the sense that we tend to do best on those tasks we enjoy most—a liking for detail may indicate that the individual has a fair amount of aptitude for this type of work. In other words, he may be accurate, precise, and temperamentally suited for work of a confining nature.

But likes are equally valuable in providing clues to possible shortcomings. The man who liked a job because of its regular hours, frequent vacations, and lack of overtime work, may be the kind of a person who does not like to extend himself by putting in extra effort on a job. If this can be supported by subsequent clues pointing in the same direction, the interviewer will have come up with an important finding concerning the man's motivation. Or when a woman says that she enjoyed a job because she was able to deal with high-level people from the best families, the implication may be that she is prestige-oriented. Of course, such a clue in itself provides only the slightest evidence. The interviewer mentally catalogues it, however, and subsequently looks for additional specific clues that may confirm it. If such confirmation is eventually forthcoming, he will have identified an important shortcoming in terms of the individual's ability to get along with people. As indicated above, likes may provide clues to both assets and shortcomings. Someone who enjoyed a given job because he had a good deal of freedom may be saying that he is the kind of a person who, on the one hand, likes responsibility but, on the other hand, tends to be overly independent. In response to such a finding, then, the interviewer would do some two-step probing in an effort to find out what there was about having a completely free hand that gave the individual so much satisfaction.

THINGS FOUND
LESS SATISFYING

Having had a chance to discuss his likes in considerable detail, the candidate is normally quite willing to talk about his dislikes, particularly if good rapport has been established. At the same time, the interviewer should approach this subject adroitly by softening his follow-up question. Instead of asking about a person's dislikes, he should pose such a question as, "What were some of the things you found less satisfying on that job?" It is possible that an applicant may not have any actual job dislikes in a particular situation, but considered relatively there are always some aspects of a job that are less satisfying than others. In the event that the candidate is able to come up with very little in the way of things that were less appealing to him, the interviewer should stimulate the discussion by means of a laundry-list question. He can say, "What were some of the other things that were less appealing on that job—were they concerned with the earnings, the type of supervision you received, the amount of detail involved, or perhaps the lack of opportunity to use your own initiative?

If the interviewer has previously formed an initial hypothesis about certain possible shortcomings, he will include pertinent items in his laundry-list question. Thus, if he suspects insufficient attention to detail, he will be certain to mention this as a possible dislike. Or if he suspects laziness, he might include such an item as "and an overly demanding supervisor" in his laundry-list question as one of the possible job factors the individual may have found less satisfying. Remember, too, that probing for job dislikes often results in spontaneous information as to why the person eventually left the job. If we can get such information indirectly and spontaneously, we are more likely to get the real truth of the matter. The candidate may say, for example, "I just couldn't see eye to eye with my supervisor, and quite frankly that was why I left." In such a situation, the interviewer would naturally probe deeper by saying, "Some bosses are certainly very hard to get along with. What was your boss's particular problem?" Once he has obtained the full story, the interviewer would of course *play down* the resulting information, in that way reassuring the applicant.

Information concerning job dissatisfactions can provide a wide variety of clues to the individual's possible shortcomings. He may admit, for example, that the mathematical-calculations aspect of his job represented a factor of dissatisfaction, and he may further disclose the fact that he does not consider himself particularly qualified in this area. The interviewer would then have a strong clue to lack of mathematical aptitude. If test scores are available and if they show below-average numerical ability, the interview finding in this case would confirm the results of the test. Another applicant may volunteer the information that he disliked being left on his own so much of the time without much direction from above. This might provide a clue to lack of confidence and a tendency to be dependent upon others. In another job situation, the candidate may reveal that the assignment was not sufficiently well structured for him. This may indicate a clue to his inability to plan and organize, as well as a possible lack of initiative. Still another may complain about the fact that he was required to juggle too many balls in the air at one time. Such a comment might point to the possible lack of flexibility and adaptability. Lack of general mental ability might be another possible interpretation. In any event, the interviewer carefully catalogues such clues and looks subsequently for supporting data.

Discussion of job dislikes can also reveal clues to assets. In fact, the very willingness to talk about dislikes frequently provides clues to honesty, sincerity, and self-confidence. In supplying negative information, the individual in a sense says, "This is the way I am constituted; if you don't have a place for me here, I am confident of my ability to locate something somewhere else." When an applicant discusses negative information candidly and objectively, the interviewer soon comes to the conclusion that he is getting the complete story, and he gives the person credit for being honest and sincere.

CONDITIONED TO WORK?

A man who has become conditioned to hard work and long hours in the past can be expected to apply himself with like diligence in the future. Particularly when a person has found it necessary to extend himself by working sixty or seventy hours a week or by going to school at night while carrying on a full-time job during the day, he normally develops a greater capacity for constructive effort than might otherwise have been the case. In contrast, when he is subsequently confronted with an eight-hour day, he finds it quite possible to apply himself vigorously throughout the eight-hour period without feeling unduly weary. A boy brought up on a farm often gets up at five o'clock, milks the cows before school, and does the chores at night after having studied all day. Having become accustomed to long hours, he normally finds it very easy to work hard in the shop for a normal eight-hour period, provided he can adjust to the confinement of indoor work. A young woman who works after school and during summers while going to high school and college normally develops work habits that stand her in good stead later on. On the other hand, the college graduate who has never worked at all may be expected to find adjustment to his first postcollege job somewhat difficult. Of course, he should not be excluded from further consideration because of lack of any kind of work experience, but this should nevertheless be included in the over-all evaluation as a possibly unfavorable factor.

As the applicant talks about working conditions on his previous jobs, the interviewer should mentally compare such conditions with specifications of the job for which he is being evaluated. If the job requires working under pressure, for example, the interviewer will look specifically for any previous jobs carried out by the applicant where pressure was an important factor. In addition, he will try to get the subject's reaction to such pressure. If an individual found it hard to work under pressure and even includes this as a reason for leaving a particular job, his qualifications for the new job would be viewed with some question. Or, if the new job is fast-moving and requires quick changes of reference, the interviewer would look specifically for previous exposure of the applicant to situations of this kind. If he has enjoyed and been stimulated by such working conditions in the past, this would obviously represent a definite asset. On the other hand, expressed dissatisfaction with conditions of this kind would represent a negative factor.

In an earlier chapter of this book, we discussed the value of not tipping one's hand—getting the information from the applicant before giving information about the job. This is especially true with respect to working conditions. If the individual really wants the proposed assignment, he will hardly be inclined to express dissatisfaction about certain job factors that he knows exist in the position for which he is applying.

Working conditions also include the degree of supervision to which the individual has become accustomed. Here again, using the job specifications as a base, we try to determine the extent to which the type of supervision may be expected to represent an adjustment factor, in terms of the contrast between the degree of supervision to which the applicant has become accustomed and the supervision he would encounter on the proposed assignment. As we have already pointed out in another chapter, the person who has grown accustomed to relatively little supervision on past jobs—where he has ordered his own life, laid out his own work, and made many of his own decisions—will ordinarily chafe under close supervision in a subsequent job situation. Obviously, we do not exclude him from further consideration on this basis alone, but it nevertheless represents a negative factor. The type of supervision under which the person has worked in the past may provide clues to possible abilities and personality characteristics. If he has operated successfully without close supervision, for example, he may be the type of person who has a good bit of initiative and who has so much ability that his supervisors trust him to carry out day-to-day tasks without checking up on him very frequently. Moreover, the natural leader is normally one who likes to work without close supervision. He enjoys the degree of responsibility that such a situation permits. And he derives satisfaction from an opportunity to exercise his own initiative.

LEVEL OF EARNINGS

Since information about earnings may represent a somewhat delicate subject in the case of some applicants, it is well to approach this question with considerable adroitness. In the first place, the interviewer should get the candidate in the habit of talking about earnings by asking him to give this information on his early jobs. Since few people object to talking about the salary they made on jobs some years ago, they willingly supply these facts. If, moreover, they are encouraged to give salary information on each job, they provide salary figures on their most recent experience pretty much as a matter of course. On the other hand, if the interviewer waits for the most recent job experience before asking about earnings, the applicant may try to fence with him. A question such as, "What happened to your earnings on that job?" usually proves quite efficient, since the individual normally discusses both starting and termination pay.

Pattern of earnings over the years represents one important criterion of the individual's job progress to date. In cases where the applicant's earnings have gone up rather quickly, it can usually be assumed that he is a person of some ability and may also be able to sell himself. In cases like this, the interviewer will want to probe for the reasons why the individual has done so well, since such probing may provide clues to his major assets. On the other hand, earnings are not always a true reflection of ability. The person may have been in the right place at the right time, may have been given special treatment because his father was a partial owner of the company, or may have been successful in impressing his superiors on the basis of his persuasive personality rather than because of his real ability.

Just as a rapid rise in earnings normally points to the existence of assets, so does lack of salary progress frequently reflect a series of significant shortcomings. The man in his middle thirties who has shown relatively little salary progress in the last ten years is usually one who is lacking in either ability, effectiveness of personality, or motivation. In probing for the reasons, however, the interviewer may find that the applicant has been confronted with circumstances somewhat beyond his control. He may find that the individual has been working in a relatively low-paying industry such as the utilities industry and that he has been reluctant to give up the security of that particular job because of the serious illness of a member of his family. In probing for the real reasons, the interviewer should obviously avoid such a direct question as, "How do you account for your failure to earn more money over the years?" Rather, he should approach this situation more indirectly, bringing up the question under the discussion of job dislikes. If the applicant does not mention salary as a factor of dissatisfaction, the interviewer can say, "How do you feel about your salary? Are you relatively satisfied with what you are making or do you think that your job merits somewhat more?" The subsequent response may indicate a number of interesting clues to behavior, including lack of salary aspirations, bitterness over lack of salary progress, rationalization of the situation, or general recognition of shortcomings and willingness to accept his lot in life.

In evaluating salary progress, one should keep the level of the individual's basic abilities in mind. If the man is bright mentally and has good general abilities, lack of salary aspirations may point to inadequate motivation. In the case of the man who is somewhat limited intellectually but has nevertheless been moved along rapidly, subsequent frustration will almost certainly occur. Such a person has become accustomed to rapid promotion and hence expects this pattern to be maintained. The time will undoubtedly come, however, when his mental limitations will preclude further promotion, at which time he will probably become a most unhappy individual. On the other hand, a mentally limited individual who has learned to accept such limitations and not to expect too much has usually attained an admirable degree of emotional maturity.

In selecting an individual for a new job, consideration should be given to the relationship between the applicant's earnings on his last job and the starting salary on the job for which he is being considered. If he has already earned appreciably more than he can be expected to start at on the new job, serious dissatisfaction is likely to develop later on. At the time of the interview, he may profess a willingness to take the new job because of its greater opportunities. Once on that job, however, he will normally become relatively unhappy—at least until such time as his salary equals his previous earnings. On the other hand, the individual whose previous earnings have been substantially less than those of the job for which he is being considered represents a different kind of a problem. The interviewer naturally wonders why his earnings have failed to keep pace with his years of experience and probes for the underlying reasons.

REASONS FOR CHANGING JOBS

This is one of the most delicate aspects of the interview, since many applicants are sensitive about their reasons for having left certain jobs. Therefore, we try to get this information spontaneously and indirectly by probing for job dislikes. If this fails, however, we have to approach the situation more directly with a softened follow-up question such as, "How did you happen to leave that job?" In posing this question, the interviewer should of course give particular attention to his facial expressions and vocal intonations, in order to give the appearance of seeming as disarming and permissive as possible. Even so, some applicants may not give the real reason why they left a certain job. Hence the interviewer must be alert for any indication of rationalization, since this type of response usually means that the individual is trying to hide the real reason by attempting to explain away the situation. If the interviewer is not convinced that the person is telling the truth, he certainly should not challenge him at this point. To do so would be to risk loss of rapport and subsequent lack of spontaneous discussion throughout the remainder of the interview. Rather, he should wait until the interview is nearly concluded—when there is little or nothing to lose. If he is interested in the candidate's qualifications, he can reintroduce the subject by asking him more directly to elaborate upon his reasons for the job change in question.

Reasons for changing jobs frequently provide clues to a number of possible shortcomings, in the same way that job dislikes often point to such shortcomings. In his discussion of these reasons, for example, the applicant may so structure his remarks that general lack of ability to handle the job becomes apparent. He may even admit that he did not possess the specific aptitudes, such as mathematical ability or mechanical aptitude, that the job required. If those particular aptitudes are important in the job under consideration, the interviewer will have come up with some significant negative information.

When a candidate leaves a number of jobs to make a little more money on subsequent ones, he may represent the kind of person who has too strong an economic drive. Now strong desire to make money is a definite asset on some jobs—particularly those involving selling on a commission basis. The salesman who wants to make a lot of money is usually one who will work harder to get it. At the same time, when the economic drive becomes too strong, the individual often develops into something of an opportunist. In other words, he will immediately jump into any new situation that pays him a little more. Such a person seldom develops strong loyalties. The interviewer has a right to say to himself, "Since this person has a habit of leaving each job whenever he gets a chance to make a little more money, I wonder how long we would be able to keep him happy here?"

When an applicant leaves a series of jobs because of dissatisfaction with job duties or working conditions, he may be the type of a person who lacks perseverance and follow-through. Perhaps unable to take the bitter with the sweet, he "pulls up stakes" whenever he is confronted with anything really difficult or not to his liking. If such proves to be the case, a clear indication of immaturity will be apparent. When dissatisfaction appears to be chronic from job to job, the individual concerned may be poorly adjusted emotionally, in the sense that he may be somewhat bitter toward life and may take a negative attitude toward things in general.

If reactions to a series of jobs indicate friction with supervisors or coworkers, the interviewer should look specifically for indications of quick temper, inflexibility, intolerance, oversensitivity, and immaturity. When he suspects the possible existence of some of these traits, the interviewer should use such a question as, "How did you feel about your relationships with your superiors and associates on that job? Were you completely satisfied with these relationships or, in retrospect, do you think that they could have been improved to some extent?"

Discussion of reasons for leaving jobs may provide clues to assets as well as liabilities. In talking about a previous job from which he had been fired, for example, the applicant may assume some of the blame, indicating that he was "just off base" in that situation. Such candor often reflects objectivity, honesty, and maturity.

In leaving certain job situations, moreover, the individual may demonstrate such positive factors as initiative and desire for further growth and development. If he has been in a dead-end situation with little opportunity for promotion, he certainly cannot be blamed for leaving it. If he is a person of considerable ability and leaves a given job to obtain broader experience and responsibility, this is again something that one should expect in a competent individual.

In discussing job changes, it is often helpful to explore how such changes came about. Did the candidate take the initiative himself? Did the suggestion come from his superiors? Or was he recruited for a better job by another company? The latter, incidentally, may tell something about his general reputation in his field.

LEADERSHIP EXPERIENCE

Throughout the discussion of the work experience, the interviewer should carefully note the frequency with which the applicant has been promoted to supervisory responsibility, together with the person's reactions to such responsibility. If the individual has derived considerable satisfaction from this kind of experience, and if he has been asked frequently to take over the direction of others, he is quite probably a person of some leadership ability. Certainly, a number of his previous superiors have thought so. Moreover, one who has led successfully in any situation has acquired skills in handling people that nothing but experience of this sort will provide.

In evaluating the possible effectiveness of an individual as a supervisor, look specifically for demonstrated ability to plan and organize, ability to delegate important responsibilities to others, contagious enthusiasm, sense of fairness, and sensitivity to the feelings of others. It is equally important to find out whether the person has shown a tendency to dictate to others or whether he has been able to get other people to work for him because they like and respect him.

NUMBER OF PREVIOUS JOBS

In evaluating the applicant's work experience, the inter-viewer should note among other things the frequency of job changes. Since many students in school do not get very much in the way of vocational guidance, it sometimes takes them a little while to find the right type of job once they have graduated. Hence, frequency of job change is not particularly unusual during late adolescence or during the time the in-dividual is in his early twenties. But if this pattern extends through the late twenties and thereafter, it can be assumed that the individual may have some rather deep-seated prob-lems. If he fails to stay with any of his jobs at least three years, he may very well be the kind of a person who has not yet found himself and is still quite immature. Many "job jumpers" lack self-discipline, perseverance, and follow-through. Some of them are opportunists and still others are not very stable emotionally. At the very least, frequent job changes should alert the interviewer to the possible existence of serious shortcomings. In every case, however, he will want to probe specifically for the underlying reasons.

A certain number of job changes over a period of some years is of course to be expected. Many people have good reasons for leaving one job to go to another—to increase their earnings, enhance their opportunities for promotion, and broaden their experience. In some occupations, such as advertising, moreover, rather frequent job change is con-sidered something of a matter of course. An advertising agency may obtain a large account and hire as many as thirty or forty additional people to handle this additional business. At the end of the year, the agency may lose the account and be forced to terminate a considerable number of its em-ployees. Even so, such an organization can usually find a place for a new employee who has turned in an outstanding job performance.

ACHIEVEMENTS

Once the interviewer has discussed the applicant's complete job history—from the first position to the most recent assignment—he should try to help the individual summarize the *achievements,* in terms of abilities and personality traits, that have been brought to light as a result of his experience on his various jobs. We do this by formally introducing the technique of *self-evaluation* for the first time in the interview. In order to accomplish this, we utilize the question which appears on the Interview Guide: "What have you learned about your strengths as a result of working on all your various jobs? Have you found, for example, that you perhaps work a little harder than the average person, get along a little better with people, organize things better, give more attention to detail, just what?" It will be noted that the technique of self-evaluation is introduced by means of a laundry-list question. This is because most individuals will not have taken the time to analyze their strengths in terms of the abilities and personality traits we are seeking to identify. Hence, they need the assistance of the laundry-list question.

The interviewer should not be surprised if the applicant appears to have some difficulty coming up with a significant list of assets. Since this may be the first time he has ever been asked to develop such a list, he may find the going a bit difficult. The interviewer must therefore exercise considerable patience here and be prepared to "prime the pump" by suggesting an asset he may have observed during the applicant's discussion of his work history. He may say, for example: "Well, you seem to have worked hard and spent long hours on practically every job you have ever had and that certainly represents a very definite asset. What are some others?" (For further assistance with this self-evaluation technique, refer to Chapter 13, "Concluding the Interview.")

The interviewer should not leave this important subject until he has developed a significant list of genuine assets, even if he has to interject a number of these himself. Once the applicant has been encouraged to think critically about his own strengths, he frequently warms to the task and generates a considerable amount of very useful information here. He may reveal, for example, that he got along particularly well with people. And he may be able to document this by telling about the closeness of his relationships with certain individuals, pointing to correspondence and other contacts that he has had with those individuals since leaving the company, or by the fact that his friends surprised him with a dinner in his honor at the time he left. Or, he may list creative ability as one of his achievements. In probing more deeply for evidence of such ability, the interviewer may find that the applicant has several patents to his credit and has published a series of articles in the technical journals. When such evidence is presented, the interviewer will of course want to know whether these patents and articles came as a result of the individual's single-handed achievement or whether other people were also involved. Since the applicant is naturally interested in selling himself, his stated achievements cannot always be taken at face value. This is why he should be encouraged to supply documentary evidence.

It is extremely important that the interviewer help the applicant to develop a sizable list of assets, since this prepares him for a subsequent discussion of his shortcomings. In other words, one cannot expect a person to discuss his shortcomings at length if he is not certain that the interviewer is well-acquainted with his strengths. More important still, in successfully developing a list of the candidate's achievements, the interviewer will have planted the seed of self-evaluation at this relatively early stage of the interview. And, as a consequence, the applicant may spontaneously volunteer further self-evaluative material during his discussion of subsequent areas of the interview—education, early home background, and present social adjustment.

DEVELOPMENT NEEDS

Having had an opportunity to discuss his strengths at some length, the applicant normally finds it relatively easy to talk about some of the areas that need further development—his shortcomings. However, since this represents the first real confrontation in terms of asking him specifically about his shortcomings, appropriate rationale must be provided. In other words, in introducing this subject we draw upon certain helpful phrases, which have been developed in Chapter 13 under the heading of *Self-evaluation,* and interject these phrases at this point. The following question should prove extremely useful: "Did you get any clues to your development needs as a result of working on those jobs? You know, we all have some shortcomings and, the person who can recognize them, can do something about them. Was there a need to acquire more self-confidence, more tact, more self-discipline —to become firmer with people—just what?" Questions such as this and others appearing on the Interview Guide should be committed to memory verbatim, in that way helping the interviewer to develop more facility during the interview.

An inspection of the above question will reveal that the interviewer is trying to help the applicant acquire insight into his development needs. Again, having planted this seed relatively early in the interview, the interviewer will find it less difficult to get the applicant to summarize his shortcomings at various subsequent stages—particularly at the end of the interview under the area of self-evaluation. Actually, helping the candidate develop more insight should represent one of the interviewer's primary purposes. This approach not only helps the interviewer to get a clearer picture of the subject's shortcomings, but it also helps the applicant to crystallize his thinking about his own developmental needs. Clear recognition of shortcomings, together with a strong desire to do something about them, represents the first positive step in individual development.

However, just as the applicant may have had initial difficulty summarizing his strengths, so will he undoubtedly experience something of a problem in terms of identifying his shortcomings. This is why the introductory question here includes a laundry list of conceivable shortcomings. As the person listens to this list, he may immediately recognize a trait that does represent one of his own shortcomings and may volunteer this information quite candidly. As soon as this has been done, of course, the interviewer *plays down* the indicated shortcoming by pointing out that identification represents the first step in terms of doing something about it.

By the time the interviewer has helped the applicant discuss all his jobs, he will of course be aware of a number of the latter's shortcomings. Hence, he will not only be in the position of being able to judge the applicant's honesty and candor here but should normally get further documentation of clues to behavior he has observed earlier. If one of the applicant's indicated shortcomings surprises him, he should ask for further elaboration and documentation.

If the laundry list of conceivable shortcomings does not prove sufficiently productive, the interviewer should become a bit more direct, introducing the double-edged question at this point. For example, if he has noted a tendency to be too soft and yet the applicant makes no mention of this, the interviewer can say: "What about firmness with people? Do you think you have as much of this as you would like to have or is this something you could improve a little bit?" Again, in warming to the discussion of development needs, the applicant may candidly admit that he lost his temper too frequently, was inclined to procrastinate in carrying out less-pleasant duties, or was so retiring that he did not always stand up for what he felt was right. Such information supplies clues to lack of motivation, self-discipline, aggressiveness, and maturity. The individual who cannot get himself to carry out the unpleasant as well as the pleasant aspects of a job is frequently one who cannot take the bitter with the sweet. Such a person generally suffers from some degree of immaturity. The individual who lets things slide may in fact be a bit too easygoing and hence lacking in conscientiousness as well as willingness to work hard.

The extent to which a person is able to talk about likes, achievements, dislikes, and development needs—without undue prompting—may provide strong clues to analytical ability. There are persons who would honestly like to provide clear-cut information about their reactions to a job situation but find themselves so unable to analyze such reactions that they do not come up with very much. This is usually an indication of lack of mental depth. Other individuals can talk about all their favorable aspects but seem able to offer little or nothing that they found less satisfying. If this pattern continues from job to job, the interviewer must conclude that the individual is either withholding an important part of the story or remarkably uncritical in his thinking. The person who likes everything is frequently found to be näive and uncritical. At any rate, it is the interviewer's task to decide whether an individual's seeming inability to discuss development needs represents lack of analytical ability or sheer unwillingness to divulge this type of information.

FACTORS OF JOB SATISFACTION

At this point, we have not only discussed the applicant's jobs but have tried to plant the seed of self-evaluation by asking him to summarize strengths and development needs of which he has become aware as a result of working on these various jobs. Hence, we can now give our attention to a very fruitful area—factors of job satisfaction. It is well to introduce this subject with another laundry-list question: "What does a job have to have to give you satisfaction? Some people look for money, some look for security, some want to manage, some want to create, some like to work with details while others do not—what's important to you?" Again, the applicant's response to such a depth question may provide clues to his analytical ability and his intellectual depth. One individual may say, "Oh, I just want a job where I can be happy and make an honest living." Another person may reflect a great deal more discernment and intellectual depth by such a remark as: "In looking for a new job, I have given this subject a great deal of thought. I am looking primarily for an opportunity to grow and develop—to find the type of job that will provide the greatest challenge and do the most to bring out the best that is in me. Money is of course important, but I consider that secondary. Security probably ranks at the bottom of my list, since I feel that I can always make a living somewhere." A response such as this tells the interviewer a good bit about the individual's drives and aspirations, as well as about the quality of his thinking. The lack of emphasis on security, moreover, may provide a clue to self-confidence.

If a candidate "blocks" at this point, give him a chance to organize his thinking by making use of the *calculated pause.* If he still seems to have a problem, repeat part of your laundry-list question or select one of the items and ask him rather directly how he feels about it. The interviewer may say, "Well, how do you feel about security, for example? Is this important to you or perhaps not so much so?"

Actually, discussion of job-satisfaction factors presents the interviewer with an excellent opportunity to obtain further confirmation of clues that have come to his attention earlier in the work discussion. For example, if he has noted some dislike for detail, he can include the phrase, "Some like detail while others do not," in his laundry-list question. If the applicant seizes upon this with the statement, "Well, for one thing, I certainly do not want to be involved with much detail; I prefer to delegate this to others," the interviewer is presented with additional confirmation of his original hypothesis. If the interviewer has a suspicion that the candidate may be lazy, he can include in his laundry-list question the phrase, "Some people want regular hours while others do not mind spending extra time on a job—time that may interfere with family life." Again, the applicant might say, "I believe that seven or eight hours a day on a job is enough for anybody. My family certainly comes first and I don't intend to let my job interfere." Such a statement may indicate that an individual is unwilling to make present sacrifices for future gains, and this also may provide an additional clue to lack of motivation.

In presenting the applicant with a laundry-list question, it is always important to include at least four or five items. The interviewer should then note items that the candidate talks about first, since those items may be the most important to him and hence may tell more about him as a person.

Factors of job satisfaction represent a very fruitful area for discussion; hence, at least four or five minutes should be devoted to this subject. The interviewer should then mentally compare the applicant's expressed desires with the specifications of the position in question. If the individual is looking for a job that provides a great deal of mental challenge, for example, it would be a mistake to assign him to a job situation that made few mental demands. Or, if he seems to be greatly interested in money, this factor should be considered in terms of the salary opportunities in the position for which he is being considered. Of course, many young people just out of school may not be able to come up with very much in the way of job-satisfaction factors. This obviously should not be held against them, since they have not been exposed to enough job situations to enable them to form any real conclusions as to the factors that give them greatest satisfaction.

TYPE OF JOB DESIRED

The work-history discussions should be concluded with a question concerning the kind of job for which the candidate is looking. In the case of older people with some years of specific experience in a given area, this question may be unnecessary, since they may be applying for a definite type of work. This may also be true in the case of persons who were referred to the company as a result of a newspaper advertisement. On the other hand, many younger people have no specific job situation in mind. In fact, many such individuals are looking for some kind of guidance in this respect. If they do mention the kind of a job they think they would like to have, it is well to say, "What is there about that type of job that you think might interest you?" The ensuing discussion may reveal that the individual has some good and valid reasons for his choice and, in the case of a younger person, this would provide a definite clue to emotional maturity.

When a candidate says he really does not know what he wants, however, the interviewer should attempt to narrow the field for him to some extent. In the case of a recently graduated engineer, for example, he could say, "Well, do you think you might prefer basic research, development work, production, or technical service work?" The interviewer would then try to get the individual's reaction to these fields of work and compare these reactions with what he has already learned about the person as a result of the previous discussion. The individual frequently does a little self-evaluation at this point. He may say, for example: "Well, I certainly know that I don't want research or development work. I learned in school that I am no whiz on a purely technical assignment." If, on the basis of available test results and previous work-history discussion, the interviewer concurs with the candidate, he may then explore the individual's possible interest in production or technical service. Or, he may decide to postpone this particular discussion until the end of the interview—until he has learned more about the individual and thus has a better basis for helping him with his placement decision.

As the work-history discussion draws to a close, the interviewer mentally reflects on the candidate's total job accomplishment. Has the individual made normal progress in terms of salary? Has he acquired a solid background of experience in his specialty? Has he shown an ability to assume gradually increased responsibility? If the answer to any of these important questions is negative, the interviewer may begin to have a real reservation concerning the candidate's overall qualifications. In some cases, in fact, the situation may be so clear-cut that the interviewer can decide then and there not to hire the applicant. In such a situation, he would talk very briefly about the individual's educational background and then terminate the discussion. Not only is it unfair to waste the applicant's time but the interviewer also has to be economical with his own time.

WORK HISTORY AND MINORITIES

As pointed out earlier, many members of so-called minority groups need no special consideration with regard to interpretation of work history. Their impressive vocational achievement speaks for itself.

But what about those minority men and women who, because of circumstances largely beyond their control, have not been given the opportunity to demonstrate their abilities? Certainly many such persons have *potential* to do far better than their employment record may indicate. And it is the interviewer's job to ferret out such potential.

In many cases such applicants will not have had the usual avenues of employment open to them. As a consequence, they have often had to settle for whatever jobs they could get. Many of their jobs, therefore, may have been routine and undemanding in nature. This should not be held against them. At the same time, we are always looking for that individual who has been able to rise above this situation to demonstrate a somewhat better vocational achievement.

Pay particular attention to how each job was obtained as a possible indication of an applicant's initiative. Note also any increased responsibility within a job, even though the job may have been rather routine. For example, was the applicant promoted to lower levels of supervision, such as lead man, straw boss, or chief clerk? Probe also for any indication of hard work, such as inordinately long hours or physically demanding job duties. Finally, even though many of the jobs may have been routine, has there been any significant progress from job to job in terms of more responsibility and higher pay?

Since many of the jobs available to some minority applicants are temporary in nature, a record of rather frequent job changes is not unusual. Here, reasons for changing jobs should be investigated carefully in order to determine the basic motivation. Certainly, we cannot expect an individual to stay with a low-level, uninteresting job for any great length of time if he can substantially better himself by moving to a new job situation. In each of these job changes, therefore, try to determine whether or not the new job really did represent a measurable improvement over the previous one or whether the person moves from job to job because he finds it difficult to stay put.

For all applicants, the discussion of *achievement* and *development needs* at the end of the work history can be difficult. Hence, the interviewer must exercise more patience in exploring these two areas. He must do more "pump priming" in the sense that he will have to lubricate the discussion by introducing strengths and shortcomings he has already noticed. Once the applicant has acquired a thorough understanding of what he is expected to do, however, he can often come up with some surprisingly valuable information about himself.

In discussing *factors of job satisfaction,* give special attention to the person who seems to have a genuine desire to make something better of himself, even though he may not yet have been given much of an opportunity. If he still aspires to a better situation and has not given up hope, this is a very good sign—particularly in contrast to the individual who has become cynical and pessimistic. At the same time, aspirations should not be out of reach in terms of what seems to be his basic abilities. As pointed out in an earlier chapter, a decided gap between basic abilities and aspirations represents a rather strong clue to immaturity.

In reflecting upon the individual's entire work history, try to determine whether the person was consistently overqualified for many of the job situations in which he found himself, in the sense that he could easily have handled more responsibility if he had been given the opportunity. If it can be determined that the applicant has been consistently over-qualified for the jobs he has held, there is a good chance that, with special training, he may be able to handle the position for which he is being considered, even though his work experience may not be relevant to the job in question.

CHAPTER NINE

Interpreting Education

Applicants for most higher-level jobs will usually be college graduates, and many will have gone to graduate school. These years represent a large segment of the individual's life, during which time he has had ample opportunity to display a considerable number of assets or shortcomings, as the case may be. Interpretation of the educational history, then, is not only concerned with whether or not the individual has acquired sufficient training to carry out the job in question; it is also concerned with the evaluation of abilities, personality traits, and motivation.

In the case of younger applicants, in particular, the educational experience may represent the most important period of the individual's life and, as such, may provide the greatest source of clues to behavior. Although education does not represent quite such a dominant factor in the case of older applicants, it is nevertheless exceedingly important. The traits that an individual develops while in school often remain with him throughout his life. Moreover, the discussion of educational history frequently provides additional confirming evidence of traits that had been tentatively identified during the discussion of work experience. Thus, the applicant who tends to be lazy on the job can be better understood if it can also be determined that he did not apply himself in school. In other words, he has never been conditioned to hard work and hence has never developed strong motivation.

In this chapter, we shall discuss the items appearing under education and training in chronological order as they are listed on the Interview Guide. Each item will be discussed not only in terms of its contribution to the individual's educational attainment, but also in terms of possible reflection of clues to abilities, personality, and motivation.

STRUCTURING THE DISCUSSION OF EDUCATION

Having completed the discussion of work history, the interviewer uses a comprehensive introductory question to launch the subject of education. In so doing, he tries to make the transition from the first interview area to the second in such a way that the discussion appears to be a *continuing conversation,* rather than a segmented one. Thus, the interviewer may preface his comprehensive introductory question by saying, "That gives me a very good picture of your work experience; now tell me something about your education and training." In the comprehensive introductory question the interviewer should point out that he would like to have the applicant talk about such factors as subject preferences, grades, and extracurricular activities. He should also indicate that he would like to have the individual start with a discussion of his high school experience and go on from there to college.

Chronology is just as important here as it is in work history. The interviewer should get the full story of the candidate's high school experience before permitting him to talk very much about college. If the candidate jumps ahead by beginning to talk about college before he has given a complete picture of his activities in high school, the interviewer should control the situation by making a positive comment and redirecting him to the high school area. He might say, for example, "Being able to play on the college football team must have given you a great deal of satisfaction. By the way, were there any other extracurricular activities in high school?" In getting the high school story first, the interviewer can trace the candidate's progress through school. He may note, for example, that the individual did quite well with his high school studies but experienced more difficulty as the subject matter became more difficult in college. Or he may observe that the candidate was a "big frog in a little puddle," while in high school but, up against sterner competition in college, was not able to compete successfully. Findings such as these represent probable indications of some limitations and help the interviewer to establish the level of the candidate's vocational ceiling.

In response to an adroitly worded comprehensive introductory question, the candidate will normally discuss much of his school experiences spontaneously. If he leaves out important items or does not discuss certain topics in sufficient detail, the interviewer will use appropriate follow-up questions in an effort to get the complete story. He will also use such questions to probe more deeply for the underlying implication of certain of the applicant's remarks. After the individual completes his discussion of the high school experience, the interviewer may wish to repeat part of his comprehensive introductory question by saying, "Suppose you tell me a little about college now—your subject preferences, grades, extracurricular activities, and the like."

BEST AND POOREST SUBJECTS

If the candidate forgets to include subject preferences in his discussion, the interviewer should approach this by asking about his subject interests, particularly since interests tend to correlate with abilities. He can say very simply, "What were some of the subjects you enjoyed most in high school?" Preference for such highly verbal subjects as English, history, and languages normally reflects a certain amount of *verbal ability,* particularly when grades in such subjects have been relatively high. If verbal ability represents one of the job requirements, the interviewer will have identified strong clues to an important asset. Another applicant may reflect strong scientific interests through his preferences for chemistry, biology, and physics. When such preferences are combined with interest and ability in mathematics, considerable aptitude for work of a technical nature would normally be indicated.

In discussing subject preferences in college, it is well to ask the individual whether he most enjoyed the more practical subjects or the more highly theoretical courses. In the case of an engineer, for example, the interviewer might say, "Did you enjoy the more practical courses such as unit operations and your laboratory work, or did you derive more satisfaction from the more highly theoretical courses such as thermodynamics?" Lack of interest and ability in the more theoretical courses may sometimes indicate certain mental limitations—inability to deal with things in the abstract. This interpretation of course becomes all the more valid if test results reflect mediocre mental equipment. Other things being equal, the more practically oriented engineers usually derive greatest satisfaction from assignments in production, applications engineering, or technical service. The more theoretically inclined technical people usually get more satisfaction from research and development.

Subject dislikes, introduced by such a question as, "What were some of the subjects you found less satisfying?" can provide important clues to shortcomings. When an applicant dislikes a subject, it may mean that he either has little aptitude for that subject or failed to study hard enough to awaken an interest in it. When a person does poorly in a subject that represents an important factor in the specifications of the job for which he is being considered, an important shortcoming will have been identified. And this is particularly true when poor performance in school is supported by low aptitude-test scores. Some knowledge of course content in various fields is also helpful to the interviewer. If a given individual has relatively poor mathematical ability, the interviewer can understand the candidate's difficulty with physical chemistry, since this course has a rather high mathematical content.

It is not enough to know that an applicant liked or disliked a certain subject. The interviewer should be interested in finding out *why*. He does this by using the second step of the two-step probing question, "What was there about physics that seemed to trouble you?" In response the applicant might say, "Oh, I was completely over my head in that subject. Even though I studied hard, I never could quite seem to understand the theoretical aspects." Or in response to a question as to why he did not like quantitative chemistry, an applicant might say, "That subject requires a good memory, and memory has never been one of my attributes." As indicated in an earlier chapter, probing for the *why* of subject preferences often provides clues to analytical ability and intellectual depth. Some people may be unable to give other than superficial reasons whereas others can provide detailed, analytical statements. In any case, the information that flows from this particular discussion should be carefully checked with the requirements of the job specifications.

GRADES

If the candidate does not specifically mention his grades, the interviewer may say, "What about grades? Were they average, above average, or perhaps a little below average?" Note that such a question makes it relatively easier for the individual to admit that his grades were below average. Where grades are indicated as above average, an attempt should be made to determine the applicant's actual ranking in the class. Was it upper half, upper third, upper quarter, or upper tenth? When he provides a ranking, such as ninth in his class, he should be asked about the number in the class. It is conceivable that the entire class may have had no more than eleven or twelve students. On the other hand, a standing of ninth in a class of four hundred would represent a real achievement.

School achievement as reflected in grades may provide clues to *ability* and *motivation*. They also may reflect the academic standards of the school. In any case, the interviewer should make a real effort to identify the major factors responsible for grade level, whether such level is high or low.

If test scores are available, the interviewer's interpretation of grade level is greatly facilitated. A high score on a mental test means, among other things, that the individual has the ability to learn rapidly, absorbing new information quickly. Hence, he is expected to get good grades in school. When an individual with a high mental-test score indicates that he made poor grades in school, the interviewer should be alerted to the possibility that he did not apply himself. Further probing may indicate lack of perseverance, procrastination, or disorganized study habits. Moreover, many gifted people find it possible to get along in school without "cracking a book." Such people not only fail to make the best use of their abilities but may develop habits of superficiality, never learning to dig down to the bottom of things. If this habit persists through life, the individual is seldom able to realize his full potential.

In the case of an applicant with a mediocre mental-test score and top grades in school, the interviewer is faced with at least three interpretive possibilities. First, there is the possibility that the person may not be telling the truth. Secondly, the academic standards of the school may have been relatively low. Or in the third place, the individual may have studied so hard that he obtained high grades despite his somewhat limited mentality. If the latter proves to be the case, the individual is almost certainly hard-working, persevering, and highly motivated to succeed.

High grades in a school of established high academic standards normally provide clues to both intellect and motivation. This is particularly true, of course, where the applicant has selected a difficult major course of study. In the best schools, a student has to have a reasonable degree of mental ability and has to study reasonably hard in order to achieve a good academic record.

COLLEGE BOARDS

The majority of people today under the age of twenty-five or twenty-six will have taken SAT's (Scholastic Aptitude Tests) during their senior year of high school, and most of these people will have been told their specific scores on these tests. Scores on these tests give us a good "fix" on the applicant's mental ability, verbal ability, and quantitative or numerical ability. High school seniors take two specific tests prepared by Educational Testing Service in Princeton, New

Jersey—one test on verbal ability and another test on quantitative or numerical ability. 800 represents a perfect score on each of these two tests. The table below represents the distribution of scores on each of the two tests made by the high school senior population.

Test Score	*Interpretation*
700–800	Excellent
575–700	Above average
425–575	Average
300–425	Below average
Below 300	Poor

However, the above distribution includes a great many people who never made it to college. Hence, the distribution for college graduates—the population we are dealing with here as candidates for high-level jobs—is appreciably higher than that shown above.

In fact, today the colleges with the highest academic standards look for a combined score on these two tests of 1300 to 1350. This means that a boy might be taken into a good engineering school with a verbal score of 575 and a numerical score of 725, since the engineering course content places greater demand on mathematical aptitude. Or, a girl with a score of 750 on verbal ability might be accepted into a top school of journalism even though her math score was no more than 550.

Even the less-prestigious schools look for a minimum combined score on the SAT's of at least 1000. Hence, a score of less than 500 on either the verbal or the math test reflects a relatively low aptitude for a person who has graduated from college. And, of course, the higher the score, the better the aptitude.

As noted above, most young people will have been told their College Board scores and will remember them because of their importance in getting into the college of their choice. Yet, some of them may be reluctant to disclose their scores, particularly if they are not especially good. As a result, they may simply say they have forgotten the scores.

In approaching this question, the interviewer *assumes consent* with such a direct question as, "What were your College Board scores?" Note that he does not say, "Do you remember your College Board scores?" or "Did you take the College Board Examinations?" The applicant is much more likely to respond to a direct, definitive question here since the interviewer does not make it easy for him to "get off the hook." If he professes not to remember his scores, the interviewer can say, "Well, were they in the 500's, 600's, or 700's?" Or he may say, "Did you do better on the verbal or the mathematical test?"

It has been the author's experience that most younger people will respond to the question on College Board scores, particularly if good rapport has been established and maintained. The resulting information—providing you feel that you can believe the individual—can be unusually helpful, particularly if it is consistent with clues to intelligence and aptitudes which have come to light previously. Of course, some applicants may not remember their SAT scores correctly or may even lie about them. Hence, if the reported scores do not seem consistent with other clues to aptitudes, they should be disregarded.

The tests are normally taken in the junior year of high school for practice and taken again in the senior year. The latter represents the official score and is often appreciably better than the score achieved during the junior year. Hence, the interviewer must make certain that the scores the person provides resulted from tests taken during the senior year.

Since these tests are taken during the high school experience, the subject of College Boards should be introduced during the discussion of high school, immediately after getting the individual's high school grades and class standing.

EXTRACURRICULAR ACTIVITIES

The degree to which the individual has participated in extra-curricular affairs may provide many important clues to personality traits. If little or no participation has taken place, the individual may have a tendency to be shy, self-conscious, inhibited, and introverted. In fact, he may freely admit that he tended to be "backward" and retiring at that stage of his life. Of course, such a person may have changed materially over the years, but the chances are very good that certain vestiges of these shortcomings may remain with him today. On the other hand, a person may say that he did not participate in student activities because he did not care very much for the type of classmates with whom he was associated. Such a remark should prompt the interviewer to get further elaboration as a possible indication of snobbishness, intolerance, or a "sour grapes" attitude. The latter in particular may indicate some lack of emotional adjustment. Obviously, still other people fail to participate in student activities because of lack of motivation. They are content with the social relationships they develop on the outside. Finally, there is the "bookworm" or "grind." This type of person devotes all his energy to getting top grades. As a result, he often graduates with honors but fails to achieve the social development acquired by the average college graduate. People who fall into this category are often the first to admit later in life how much they failed to get out of college. Since many jobs require a fair amount of social facility, such people often find themselves inadequately equipped to deal with others.

Those who do participate in extracurricular activities, however, often develop appreciably on the social side during their four years of school. In dealing with others of their own age, they frequently become more sociable, develop more tact, become more aggressive, and acquire traits of leadership.

A girl elected president of her sorority, for example, is confronted with responsibilities that are entirely new to her. She is naturally anxious to show up well in the eyes of other members of the group and therefore takes particular pains to do the best jobs she can. In the course of shouldering these responsibilities, she often matures perceptibly, acquiring new poise, learning how to handle the more difficult people, and developing the kind of infectious enthusiasm that sparks an organization.

Participation in athletics—contact sports in particular—often fosters the development of competitive spirit, cooperation, and ability to serve as an effective member of a team. One who has a tendency to "hog the show" is frequently batted down rather quickly by his teammates.

It is often helpful to ask an applicant how old he was when he went to college. If he happened to be appreciably younger than his classmates, he may have experienced severe adjustment problems. Such a person often has difficulty gaining acceptance on the part of his older associates. They frequently have a tendency to "write him off," taking the view that he is not old enough to appreciate their thinking or to engage in their activities. Inability to compete successfully with one's contemporaries in college—either academically or socially—can have a marked effect on the individual's behavior. It is at least conceivable that he may develop a feeling of inferiority that will remain with him throughout his life. If such turns out to be the case, he may have a tendency to underestimate his real abilities and may lack the confidence necessary to achieve up to his potential.

HOW MUCH EFFORT?

The subject of amount of effort expended should be introduced after the discussion of extracurricular activities, so that the individual will be not quite so likely to relate effort to grades. In other words, we first talk about all the academic factors such as subject preferences, grades, and College Boards before we discuss extracurricular activities. Only after the latter have been thoroughly explored do we bring up the question of effort. This should be introduced with the question that appears on the Interview Guide: "How conscientious a student were you? Did you work about as hard as the average person, a little harder, or perhaps not quite so hard?" If the individual seems to have difficulty with this question, help him to become more definitive: "Well, how many hours a day did you study on the average and what time did you normally get to bed at night?"

Information developed in this area can provide excellent clues to both intellectual level and motivation. If a candidate obtained good grades in a school with high academic standards without working unduly hard, it can be assumed that he possesses good mental ability. On the other hand, if he obtained no better-than-average grades in the school with questionable academic standards despite unusual effort, there would seem to be some question about the level of his mental ability. The latter individual, however, can be given credit for strong motivation. It is not unusual for such a person to say, "I really had to work for everything I got. I certainly burned a lot of midnight oil. In fact, I used to be envious of my roommate who was always able to get things twice as easily as I could."

When interpreting grades in terms of the amount of effort expended, it is also necessary to factor in the amount of time spent on extracurricular activities as well as time spent on part-time jobs. A person with average grades in a good school who has devoted a great deal of time to student activities or to financing his own education of course deserves credit for his over-all accomplishments. Such a person often develops social skills and work habits that stand him in good stead later in life. Moreover, the person who crowds in a great many activities, does a considerable amount of part-time work, and also manages to make good grades is usually one who has learned to organize his time effectively. Normally, he works on a specific schedule and does a considerable amount of planning.

SPECIAL ACHIEVEMENTS

The interviewer should be alert to the possibility that a given individual may have attained achievements beyond those of most of his classmates, and such achievements may provide additional clues to mental ability, specific aptitudes, and leadership strength. Some individuals are basically modest and may not reveal this type of information unless they are specifically asked to do so. Hence, when a liberal arts student indicates that he made top grades in college, the interviewer should ask him if he made Phi Beta Kappa. A top technical student should similarly be asked if he achieved any academic honors, such as Tau Beta Pi or Sigma Xi. Persons achieving such honors are normally those who possess both high mental ability and strong motivation.

If asked about special achievements in high school, an applicant may say that he won the mathematics prize, the physics prize, or the oratorical contest, thus revealing the possible existence of special aptitudes. Likewise, it is well to ask an athlete if he was ever elected captain of a team. Again, responsibility of this kind fosters the development of leadership traits. In the case of persons elected to the student government or to the presidency of the student body, the interviewer has a right to assume that the individual was popular with his contemporaries and probably possessed some degree of leadership ability. Of course, school politics are responsible for the fact that some people are elected to class offices, but the person involved usually displays some traits that set him apart from the crowd. At the very least, he is ordinarily one who is liked by others, who has a genuine interest in people, and who has developed an ability to get along amicably with others.

TRAINING BEYOND THE UNDERGRADUATE LEVEL

Where the application blank indicates graduate training, the interviewer explores this area immediately after getting the complete description of the college experience. Even in the case of those who do not have graduate training it is well to ask, "Did you ever give any thought to going to graduate school?" A question such as this frequently provides clues to the strength of the individual's theoretical drive. A man may say, for example, "I had enough of studying in college; I'm not the academic type, you know. As soon as I finished college I wanted to do something practical where I could earn some money."

Except for the fact that he usually does not ask about extracurricular activities, the interviewer explores graduate training in much the same way that he carried out the college discussion, concentrating on subject preferences, grades, amount of effort involved, and any special achievements. In some graduate schools, grades are either satisfactory or unsatisfactory, but other schools give letter grades, insisting that courses counted for graduate credit must be at a B level or better. In such a case, it is interesting to learn whether the graduate student obtained mostly B's and a few A's or made practically a straight A record.

Special attention should be devoted to the individual's thesis or dissertation. Even though the applicant's field may not be very familiar to the interviewer, the latter can still ask the individual about the problems he encountered and how he went about solving such problems. Evidences of creative ability may be revealed here, particularly in cases where the candidate solved most of his own problems rather than relying upon his sponsor. It is also well to ask about the extent to which the research findings may be expected to make a contribution to the field. In some cases, individuals publish articles in technical journals even before they are awarded their degree. In evaluating graduate training, again consider the academic standards of the school. A Ph.D. from some schools means a great deal more than it does from others.

Consideration of postgraduate training should not be confined to formal courses taken with a view to getting a master's or doctoral degree. Many people take special courses of one kind or another, including extension work, correspondence courses, and company-sponsored courses. Moreover, many such courses are taken at night, after putting in a full day on the job. Such attempts to improve oneself frequently provide clues to perseverance, aspiration, and energy level. In going to school at night an individual often extends his capacity for constructive effort. Many courses taken in the evening also equip the individual to turn in a better performance on his job.

After-hours courses may also reflect an individual's attempt to broaden his horizons. Sensing a lack of cultural background, he may take courses in history, art appreciation, or government. In a sense then, the selection of evening courses may tell as much about a person as the kind of courses he selected as electives in college.

HOW WAS EDUCATION FINANCED?

The interviewer will have acquired much of this information as a result of having discussed the applicant's early jobs under work history. But it is well to reconsider such information mentally while discussing the applicant's educational background. As indicated above, awareness of the fact that the individual worked his way through school may cast a different light on the kind of grades he received or on the extent of his participation in extracurricular activities. The individual who has to work his way through school by carrying out part-time jobs frequently develops greater maturity and motivation than the person who did not have to earn any of his college expenses. When an individual helps to finance his own education, he usually appreciates it all the more and tries to get the most out of it. In the course of this experience, he frequently develops sound work habits, perseverance, and resourcefulness. On the other hand, someone whose parents pay for his entire education may become accustomed to having things too easy. In fact, he may suffer a rude shock when he does finally get out into the world and finds it necessary to earn his own living. Certainly, his adjustment to industry will be more difficult than that of the person who has already learned to earn his own way.

Scholarships are awarded to certain individuals as a means of financing part of the educational expense. In this case, it is important to know whether the scholarship was awarded on the basis of previous academic achievement or on the basis of economic need. The latter of course represents less of a factor in the individual's favor than the former.

Many people will say that if they had it to do over again they would borrow money rather than work so hard while going to college. They seem to feel that they missed a great deal by not being able to participate in extracurricular activities, for example. All things considered, the greatest over-all development probably comes to the student who tries to maintain some kind of balance with respect to academic work, extracurricular activities, and part-time jobs. Too much concentration on any one of the three at the expense of the others usually has some retarding effect on the over-all growth of the individual.

As the interviewer concludes the discussion of education, he mentally evaluates the entire experience in terms of the extent to which it has equipped the person to handle the job under consideration. In making this evaluation, he of course includes formal courses in high school and college, training acquired while in military service, special company-sponsored courses, extension work, and correspondence courses. He then asks himself whether or not the applicant has the specialized training that the job requires, whether he has developed the necessary skills, and, equally important, whether or not he has developed the kind of thinking demanded in the job for which he is applying. Many job descriptions indicate simply that the incumbent should be a college graduate. This usually implies a certain degree of cultural background, the ability to think logically and to reason from cause to effect, and the ability to get along successfully with other people on the college level.

In evaluating the factors mentioned above, the interviewer naturally takes into consideration all major achievements such as grades, participation in sports, membership in clubs, offices held, and any special effort involved in financing education. He also thinks in terms of how much the individual benefited from the educational experience. Did he look for the easiest way out by selecting the easiest possible major course of study and by taking snap courses as electives? Or did he choose a reasonably difficult major course of study and take electives designed to broaden his cultural background? Is there any indication that the individual became so interested in his subjects that he did additional reading that was not required? Did he do any really significant research work in connection with his graduate studies? Answers to questions such as these help to cast the educational experience in its true perspective.

Obviously, too, the interviewer will evaluate the educational history in terms of resulting clues to abilities, personality traits, and motivation. And he will be particularly interested in those clues which supply further confirming evidence to support interpretive hypotheses he established at the time he was discussing the applicant's work experience. It is to be expected, in addition, that the interviewer will have picked up some clues to behavior that are new, in the sense that he did not become aware of them during the earlier discussion. For the most part, these new clues will have added to his understanding of the candidate. At the same time, some of the newer clues again provide only tentative hypotheses. For example, he may have noted that the individual's extracurricular activities in school were confined to such artistic pursuits as glee club, band, orchestra, literary club, and dramatics. Suspecting that the individual may possibly fall into the artistic trait constellation, the interviewer will look for further confirming evidence in subsequent areas of the interview and will probe specifically for the possible existence of such traits as oversensitivity, impracticality, lack of tough-mindedness, and the like.

Finally, the interviewer must take the long view with respect to traits that the candidate developed while in school. If the individual is an older person, it is probable that he has grown and developed considerably since his school days. For example, he may have been quite immature as a student, but may have caught up with his chronological age group in this respect long since. The fact that the individual did not apply himself while in high school and college need not mean that he does not work hard today. Experience has nevertheless shown that a person is seldom able to "change his spots" entirely as he grows older. In other words, if his performance in school reflected serious, deep-seated shortcomings, there is a good chance that vestiges of these shortcomings still remain with him as part of his make-up today.

EDUCATION AND MINORITIES

The interviewer must be reminded again that many members of minority groups need no special consideration as far as interpretation of education is concerned. Many such men and women will have done well in schools with high academic standards, will have made favorable scores on their College Board Examinations, and will have made good scores on aptitude tests.

Some minority members, on the other hand, will have attended schools with poor academic standards and will not have done well on aptitude tests. This means that the individual probably did not have the advantage of a high-quality education. Again, this may explain in part why he did not do well on the aptitude tests that may have been administered to him or why he did not obtain better scores on the College Board Examinations—in the event that he took the SAT's during his senior year of high school.

Even though the academic standards of the school leave something to be desired, a person who gets good grades in such a school nevertheless deserves special credit. If he ranked high in class without expending an inordinate amount of effort, the chances are good that he has reasonably good mental capacity. As in our discussion of work history, we are searching here for the individual who is able to compete successfully with his peers and hence establish a better record than that achieved by many of his classmates. Remember that in our attempt to select the best-qualified applicants from both minority and nonminority groups alike, we are searching for those who are a cut above the average in every respect.

The College Board Examinations represent a special problem to some minorities, particularly since high scores on these tests are often required for admission to the better colleges and universities. Yet, as explained earlier, it is not fair to expect such individuals to do as well on these tests as some others if they have not had a good-quality education—particularly since the tests have been standardized on people from a different culture.

Even though we might not expect high scores on these tests, we are nevertheless impressed with the individual whose scores are higher relative to his group. Because many of the colleges realize that the SAT's do not represent a completely fair and accurate measurement of the ability to learn for a minority population, they have decided to take some individuals with lower College Board scores and, once those individuals are admitted, to make every conceivable effort to enable them to succeed. The fact that many such people with lower Board scores have done well in some of the better colleges represents proof in itself that the SAT scores do not necessarily accurately predict success in college.

It is important to note the kind of effort the individual expended on his studies, not only as a possible clue to mental ability but also as a clue to his general motivation. Good grades without unusual effort normally reflect good basic abilities, and of course we are always impressed with the person who consistently gave his best and made every effort to do what was expected of him. Moreover, the ability to put first things first—in the sense that he was able to concentrate on his studies in the face of the ever-present temptation to oversocialize—represents a strong clue to maturity.

Since we are always looking for people who get along well with others, it is well to give a fair amount of attention to extracurricular activities. People with a history of doing things with others are more likely to have developed important social skills as well as a sense of teamwork.

It is sometimes more difficult for minority applicants to get a college education. For example, it can be harder for them to come up with the necessary funds. Hence, special credit must be given to those who have achieved higher learn-ing, since they have often accomplished this in the face of appreciable difficulty. In so doing, they have often acquired great determination and a strong drive for achievement.

If, in reviewing the entire educational experience of such a candidate, the interviewer comes up with the finding that his mental ability is reasonably good in spite of lower apti-tude scores, lower College Board scores, and poorer-quality schools attended, he will have obtained an important finding indeed. Mental capacity is the single most important ingre-dient in that intangible quality we refer to as *potential*. And, if it can be determined that a candidate has potential, he is worthy of employment. This kind of person can profit from special training and learn to do a job well even though he does not meet the traditional educational criteria for selection.

CHAPTER TEN

Interpreting
Early Home Background

Although early home background represents an extremely important interview area, this aspect of the applicant's life is highly personal and hence must be handled with unusual adroitness and sensitivity. *Consequently, the inexperienced, untrained interviewer should not attempt to explore this area, unless of course he has had considerable formal training in clinical psychology.* The development of highly personal information requires skill that normally comes only as a result of extended practice under the supervision of a competent, highly experienced trainer. When the approach to personal information is awkward, the interviewer frequently loses rapport with the candidate and thus is unable to get spontaneous responses during the remainder of the discussion.

The experienced interviewer, on the other hand, will often

find the applicant's early home background an exceedingly fruitful area for investigation. By the time he gets to this part of the discussion, he will already know a great deal about the applicant, as a result of having spent approximately an hour with him talking about his work history and education. Having acquired a rather clear picture of many of the candidate's assets and liabilities, the interviewer should regard the exploration of early home background as a real intellectual challenge. For it is in this area that we frequently learn *why* the individual developed into the kind of person he is today. Knowledge of cause-and-effect relationships provides us with a great deal more understanding of the individual and, in addition, helps us to appraise the amount of personality growth that has taken place since the early years.

Influences brought to bear upon the individual during childhood have a great deal to do with the development of his character, motivation, interests, and personality traits. Therefore, the more we can learn about the individual's early environment the better we should be able to understand the forces that helped to determine his make-up. Early environment of course includes relationships with parents and siblings, the strictness of the upbringing, and the economic level of the home.

Throughout the discussion of this portion of the individual's life, the interviewer will look particularly for the *effects* of environmental influences on the individual's development, giving special attention to any unusual advantages or disadvantages he may have had. It is important to realize, however, that the effect of early influences cannot always be predicted, and hence no assumptions should be made unless they can be confirmed by documentary evidence. It cannot be assumed, for example, that a given individual developed selfishness because he was an only child. Many parents are aware of the problems faced by an only child and thus do everything possible to ensure his normal development. Nor can it be assumed that a person necessarily developed emotional maladjustment just because he came from a broken-home situation. Many adolescents, after losing the male parent, take part-time jobs to help support themselves and even contribute to the support of the rest of the family. In so doing, they often develop a sense of responsibility and resourcefulness they might not have achieved otherwise. In every case then, the interviewer must probe for the real effect of environmental influences during the early formative years.

STRUCTURING THE DISCUSSION OF EARLY HOME BACKGROUND

In bridging the gap between education and early home background, the interviewer can use such a casual statement as, "Let's talk a little bit now about your early life." He then follows directly with his comprehensive introductory question. Because early home background represents an area that the candidate has seldom been called upon to discuss in other interviews, the comprehensive introductory question should include a statement concerning the reasons for desiring this information. The applicant can be told, for example, that a knowledge of some early influences helps the interviewer to understand him better and facilitates proper placement. The remainder of the comprehensive introductory question of course includes a request for information concerning some of the items appearing under early home background on the Interview Guide—items such as the parents' occupations, the personalities of father and mother, number in the family, and the strictness of the upbringing. Normally, the skilled interviewer will have developed very good rapport with the candidate by the time he has arrived at this stage of the interview. He should therefore encounter little difficulty in getting the appropriate information. In order to ensure proper response, however, he should give particular attention to facial expressions and vocal intonations in the course of "selling" the comprehensive introductory question. He should also *assume consent,* giving the impression that this is the kind of information he discusses with all applicants and that there is nothing new or unusual about his request.

In response to an adroitly worded comprehensive introductory question, most applicants talk willingly and spontaneously about their early experiences. In so doing, they include appropriate information about many of the items appearing on the Interview Guide. In such cases, the interviewer simply has to ask about items that the candidate fails to include in his discussion. When, after listening to the comprehensive introductory question, the candidate seems to hestitate, the interviewer should start the discussion by asking for the father's occupation. He follows this with questions concerning the father's personality make-up, the mother's personality, number in the family, and strictness of upbringing. Questions about the effects of early influences should come toward the end of the early-home-background discussion. By that time, the interviewer will have noted a number of the effects and he will be able to prompt the applicant's discussion.

PARENTS' OCCUPATIONS
(Socioeconomic level)

In one sense, discussion of the occupations of the applicant's parents sets the stage for exploration of the early home background experiences, for this factor alone plays an important part in establishing the socioeconomic level of the family. Note that, due primarily to inflationary pressures and a desire for individual self-expression, more and more married women are entering the labor market. Their earnings often substantially raise the socioeconomic level of the home. But if the parents held low-level, unskilled jobs, it can be assumed that there probably was not very much money in the home and that the candidate did not have the advantage of many cultural influences during his early years. If the parents made their living in lower-level jobs, moreover, they probably had relatively little education and hence may not have been much of a factor in stimulating the candidate's intellectual development. There is the further probability here that the friends the applicant's parents entertained in the home were also persons of less education and cultural attainment. The fact that the candidate may show some rough edges and lack of tact and social sensitivity today may stem directly from lack of exposure to cultural influences as a child.

Where there is relatively little money in the home, however, children are more likely to take part-time jobs, such as baby-sitting and grocery-store work, in order to contribute to the family income. Such experience of course brings them into contact with other adults in a customer-salesman or a supervisor-employee relationship. In getting a glimpse of life through the eyes of adults other than their parents, they sometimes mature more rapidly and broaden their horizons to some extent. In carrying out early part-time jobs, moreover, boys and girls often develop a willingness to work hard, a sense of responsibility, initiative, and resourcefulness.

Children raised in higher-level socioeconomic circumstances often have the advantage of many fine cultural and financial influences. Where the parents are professional people or well-paid executives, children may have access to a sizable library right in the home. They may therefore cultivate the important habit of reading at an early stage in life—reading which obviously stimulates intellectual development. Furthermore, successful parents tend to entertain friends of equal accomplishment in the home. In getting to know other higher-level people on a social basis in the home, children frequently develop more poise and confidence than might otherwise have been the case.

If the applicant has been raised in high-level socioeconomic circumstances, however, there is always the possibility that he may have had things a bit too easy for his own good during the formative years. Because there was no economic pressure in the home, he may never have been motivated to take part-time jobs. Perhaps he may even have spent all his time with his family during the summer months while going to high school and college, without contributing to the financing of his education. When a person has too many things handed to him on a silver platter, he frequently matures less rapidly, becomes overly dependent upon others, and fails to develop good work habits. Such individuals often fail to take full advantage of their educational opportunities in school and subsequently find adjustment to their first postcollege job somewhat difficult.

TEMPERAMENT OF PARENTS

When the applicant omits a description of his father as a result of the comprehensive introductory question, the interviewer should remind him by saying, "What was your father like in personality?" If the man seems to have difficulty coming up with a series of traits, the interviewer can stimulate the discussion with a laundry-list question, "How else would you describe your father? Was he aggressive or unaggressive, calm or quick-tempered, extroverted or introverted, hardworking or inclined to take it a bit easy?" As we shall subsequently see, it is important to get a list of at least five or six of the father's traits. Once this has been accomplished, the interviewer asks about the mother's traits in a similar manner, again making certain to get at least five or six descriptive characteristics. If the indivdual seems to have difficulty describing his mother, the interviewer can say "Well, in what ways did your mother differ in personality from your dad?"

As soon as the individual has described his parents by listing a number of the traits of each, he should be asked to compare his own personality with that of his parents. The interviewer may say, "In retrospect, which of your parents do you think you are most like in personality?" If the individual answers, "Oh, I have a mixture of both of their characteristics," the interviewer should ask him to be more specific by saying, "Well, in what respects do you take after your father?" After the ensuing response, he should follow up by saying, "Now, in what ways do you resemble your mother as far as personality is concerned?"

Asking the candidate to compare his own personality with that of his parents frequently results in highly significant self-evaluation. After having described his father as "forceful, hard-working, opinionated, and inflexible," for example, the applicant may later say that he is like his dad. In response to the interviewer's subsequent question he may say, "Well, I guess I have a lot of his stubbornness; once I get something in my head, it's pretty hard for anyone else to dislodge it." A finding such as this may provide confirming evidence to clues obtained while discussing the applicant's work history and education. The interviewer may already have noted signs of inflexibility and stubbornness in the way the individual reacted to various job situations and in some of his relationships with his teachers. In another situation, a candidate may say that he is like his mother, in the sense that he derives so much satisfaction from helping people that they sometimes take advantage of him. Again, the interviewer may already have noted this tendency in the course of probing for the individual's effectiveness as a supervisor. With this additional evidence, moreover, he begins to suspect that the applicant may possess some of the shortcomings frequently found in the person with a high social drive—shortcomings such as tendency to lack tough-mindedness, practicality, objectivity, and criticalness of thinking. Hence, in subsequent sections of the interview he probes specifically for the possible existence of these traits.

Stimulation of self-evaluation is only one of the important reasons for wanting to know as much as possible about the applicant's parents. Among other things, we would like to know something about the *effects* the parents may have had on the growing child. For this reason, the interviewer should be alert to any possible clues to the *relationship* the individual enjoyed with his parents. Does he seem to have been quite close to them and to have real affection for them? Or does he now seem to be ashamed of their lack of education and cultural background? The latter reaction would certainly tell something about the individual's standard of values as well as providing a clue to possible immaturity.

Where the parents have been extremely successful vocationally, a special effort should be made to try to determine what effect this may have had on the candidate. Does the individual owe some of this current drive to the fact that he was stimulated by his parents' success and is anxious to match the latter's achievement? Or in growing up in the shadow of a successful parent, did he find the competition so difficult that his basic self-confidence was undermined? Many successful parents tend to expect a great deal of their children. As a result, they sometimes become unduly critical, to the point that nothing the boy or girl ever does seems quite to satisfy them. Over a period of years, an influence of this kind may partially destroy an adolescent's feeling of self-worth. He eventually gets the feeling that he just does not "measure up" and will never be able to match his parents' achievement. An experience such as this can leave a serious scar on an adolescent. In fact, he may never be able to acquire the amount of self-confidence he needs.

It is interesting to note that some adolescents acquire certain strong assets in large part because their parents lacked these qualities. A boy or girl whose father drank to excess, for example, sometimes becomes a teetotaler. With the example of their father constantly before them, they resolve never to follow in the latter's footsteps.

If in the course of the discussion it becomes apparent that the individual was not brought up by his own parents, the interviewer should of course probe for the relationships that existed between him and the individuals who were responsible for his early direction. This is particularly true in the case of a stepparent. Such a person may have no real love for a youngster not directly related and may tend to reject him, especially if the stepparent has children of his or her own. Rejection at any time represents a serious problem and may leave deep-seated scars on the individual's emotional development. Psychological research has shown that, in order to develop a normal, secure personality, a growing child needs love and affection in almost the same way that he requires food and shelter.

NUMBER OF BROTHERS
AND SISTERS

This information will of course be available from the application blank. If the applicant has indicated no brothers or sisters, the interviewer will already have determined beforehand to probe for possible effects of having been raised as an only child. It is well known that parents sometimes tend to spoil an only child. Such a child is often given too much and permitted too often to occupy the center of the stage. As a consequence, he sometimes develops habits of selfishness and willfulness. Upon occasion, too, he becomes self-centered and egotistical. A child brought up in a large family, on the other hand, frequently learns to share and share alike. And he has the added experience of learning to get along with other people in a group relationship. As a consequence, he is likely to become more cooperative and better adjusted emotionally.

The youngest child in a family sometimes experiences some of the problems faced by the only child. Realizing that she is unlikely to have any more children, a mother frequently continues to think of her youngest child as the "baby." She gives him correspondingly more attention and sometimes tends to overprotect him. He may thus become excessively dependent and may not mature as rapidly as otherwise might have been the case.

The oldest child in the family, on the other hand, is sometimes expected to take some of the responsibility for bringing up his younger brothers and sisters. And he is likely to be the first one of the family to get a part-time job and thus contribute to the family's income. Given relatively greater responsibility, then, he often develops faster in an emotional sense, acquiring more maturity, dependability, and resourcefulness.

The interviewer must also be on the alert for indications of early sibling rivalry. Unfortunately some parents do tend, perhaps unwittingly, to favor one child over another. And they may even hold up this one child as an example to the rest. In such situations, one or more of the children may feel that he is rejected—that he actually does not have the love of his parents. As indicated above, this can lead to serious emotional problems. Some parents, though perhaps well-meaning, tend to set up sibling rivalry by constantly asking a chid why he cannot get as good grades in school as his older brother. Now it may very well be that the younger child does not have the mental equipment possessed by the older boy. In this case, try as he may, he never finds it possible to match the latter's academic achievement. Since he is constantly being made aware of this painful situation by his parents, he sometimes develops deep-seated feelings of inferiority that remain with him throughout life.

Just as he often gets significant self-evaluation by asking a candidate to compare his own personality with that of his parents, so can the interviewer get similar data by asking the candidate to compare his personality with that of his brothers. He may say, "Were you and your brother pretty much alike in personality at the time you were growing up or not so much so?" To such a question the response may be quite revealing, "Oh, no! He was the bright one in the family. He always did a lot of reading, always got top grades in school, and took a very conscientious attitude toward other things." By implication, the candidate is saying that he has some awareness of his own mental limitations. He is also implying that he himself is perhaps not too scholarly and, in addition, may not be particularly conscientious. At the very least the interviewer is supplied with clues that he certainly will want to follow up during subsequent areas of the discussion.

HOW STRICTLY RAISED?
(Parental guidance)

If this information does not develop spontaneously, the interviewer may use such an open-end question as, "In thinking back about your early childhood, would you say that you were raised fairly strictly or perhaps not quite so much so?" In responding to such a question, the individual usually talks primarily about the degree of parental guidance and discipline he received. He may indicate, for example, that he was expected to be in at a given time every evening throughout the adolescent period. And he may talk at some length about the regularity of his weekly attendance at church and Sunday school. If the discussion does not appear to be meaningful, the interviewer may probe a bit more deeply by saying, "Who was the real disciplinarian in your home; was it your father or mother?" A question of this kind may stimulate some highly significant information. Among possible responses, the candidate might say, "My father was the one who made us toe the mark. He was a very strict man and had quite a temper. In fact, I guess we were all a little afraid of him. Mother was more sympathetic and used to try to intercede for us, but Dad usually had his way. Actually, we were raised very strictly—much more so than most of the kids in the neighborhood."

When discipline in the home is unduly strict, the child's emotional development may be considerably retarded. In such a home, parents tend to be overprotective. In such a rigid and sheltered environment, too many of the child's decisions are made for him. He is told when he can come and go, where he shall go to school, and in some cases what major course of study he must pursue. Because he has so little chance to try his own wings in an environment such as this, the child sometimes becomes insecure, finding little opportunity to develop resourcefulness, and little opportunity to learn by his own mistakes. Consequently, he may fail to develop a normal degree of maturity.

The child who remains "tied to his mother's apron strings" until he leaves home to go to college usually faces a similarly difficult adjustment problem. He is the type of person who gets homesick and who has difficulty establishing successful relationships with the other students. And because he is unable to make an appropriate emotional adjustment, he finds it difficult to focus his energies on his studies. Many a bright boy has flunked out of college in his freshman year because he was not emotionally prepared for the experience.

Other young people held under tight wraps at home take undue advantage of their new-found freedom in college. Presented with an opportunity to do what they please for the first time in their lives, they sometimes try to taste too many new experiences at once. Thus, they often do more drinking than they should, devote too much time to social parties, and consequently neglect their studies. Emotionally unprepared for the college experience, youths like this often fail to make the grade. Unfortunately, they frequently have to experience such a rude awakening as flunking out of school before they settle down and find themselves.

A strict upbringing may also result in rebellion. Adolescents with strong minds of their own often rebel against undue restraint. As soon as such youngsters get old enough, they openly challenge the discipline of their parents and begin making too many of their own decisions. As a consequence, they sometimes become extremely independent and subsequently have difficulty submitting to authority of any kind— whether it be the authority of the teacher in school, the superior officer in the military service, or the supervisor on a job.

Obviously, insufficient parental discipline is just as harmful to an adolescent's development as too much direction. This occurs more frequently in homes where the male parent spends a great deal of time away, devotes himself almost exclusively to his business, or is not in the family picture at all. At any rate, when parental control becomes lax, the adolescent has a strong temptation to take advantage of the situation. At the very least, he may become too self-assured as a result of having a chance to make too many of his own decisions and may have subsequent difficulty in relating to authority. Or, he may choose the most exciting and daring of his associates for his steady companion, begin running in gangs, and eventually get into trouble.

Normal development of the individual seems most likely to take place where parents begin to subject a child in his early teens to *psychological weaning*. They control the youngster just tightly enough so that he learns the meaning of right and wrong, becomes accustomed to judicious discipline, and acquires respect for his elders. At the same time, they encourage him to learn the hard way by giving him an opportunity to make some of his own decisions. And they try to inculcate the thought that they know the child will do nothing really wrong because they have trust in him. While steadfastly avoiding overprotection, they nevertheless spend as much time as possible with their child, invite his confidences, and try to help him work out his own problems. They give him constant encouragement to do his best at school and make certain to attend an athletic event or performance of any kind in which he participates. In short, they try to support him rather than to overprotect him. Upbringing of this kind usually results in the development of a normal, secure personality. At the same time, the individual acquires moral standards that stay with him throughout the rest of his life.

AGE OF FINANCIAL INDEPENDENCE

The interviewer will undoubtedly have already acquired this information as a result of his discussion of the candidate's earliest jobs. At the same time, he should factor these findings into his over-all evaluation of the individual's early life experiences. It will be found, for example, that some adolescents have earned enough money to pay for their own clothes and provide their own spending money since the age of twelve or thirteen. As pointed out previously, such individuals usually develop good work habits, become more responsible, mature more rapidly, and learn to look at life from an adult point of view.

Other young people not only fail to contribute to their educational expenses but continue to accept financial help even after they have graduated from college and occasionally after they have married. Needless to say, individuals of this type find it more difficult to develop sound work habits and a mature outlook. It has often been noted, too, that individuals from wealthy families who have an independent income all their lives often feel less need to give their complete attention and energy to the jobs they undertake.

EFFECTS OF EARLY HOME INFLUENCES

Having discussed the parents' occupations, their temperament, number of brothers and sisters, and strictness of upbringing, the interviewer is now in a position mentally to summarize his conclusions by considering the over-all effect of the early home influences. As a means of clarifying his findings in this area, he solicits the candidate's assistance by such a question as, "In thinking through your early home experiences, what effect do you think these influences may have had on your early growth and development?" The applicant's reply may not only supply information to substantiate some of the clues that have already occurred to the interviewer but may also help the individual himself to acquire a little more insight. Perhaps for the first time in his life, he has systematically reviewed some of the important things that happened to him as a youngster. In attempting to summarize the effects of these influences, he may develop a better understanding of himself in terms of how he happened to develop into the person he is today. And once an individual has acquired better self-insight and understanding, he has taken a positive step in the direction of further growth and development.

Some people—particularly those with poor powers of analysis—find it difficult to summarize the effects of their early home influences. The interviewer then attempts to stimulate the discussion by pointing out some of the positive factors he has observed. If he has noted, for example, that the applicant was brought up in such a way that he learned the difference between right and wrong, attended Sunday school and church fairly regularly, and acquired respect for his elders, he could say, "Well, you seem to have developed very fine moral and ethical standards as a child. What other effects do you think the early influences may have had on your development?" Or, if he has observed that the person worked unusually hard and spent long hours on his early jobs, he could say, "Certainly, you seem to have developed good work habits during the early years."

After helping the individual to interpret the positive effects of the early influences, the interviewer may then probe for possible negative information. If the individual seems to have been overprotected by a dominant mother, for example, the interviewer might say, "Do you think that you matured as rapidly as the average boy during the early years or perhaps a little less so?" In the event the applicant admits that he matured less rapidly, the interviewer may ask him what particular effects he thinks this may have had on his early development. The individual might conceivably reply, "Oh, I suppose that was one reason why I was always so shy and bashful in school. In fact, I guess I really never quite eliminated those tendencies. Even today, I find it difficult to talk to strangers and get nervous when I am called upon to present an idea to a group of my superiors."

Having already become aware of many of the applicant's characteristics by the time he has reached the end of the early-home-background discussion, the interviewer may probe specifically for the underlying reasons for such behavioral development. If, for example, he has already concluded that the individual is quite introverted, he might say at this point, "Is it possible that you spent a good bit of time by yourself as a youngster?" To this the candidate might conceivably reply, "Yes, I did. There were no other children of my age in the immediate neighborhood, so I consequently spent a lot of time reading or working alone in the basement with my radio equipment. That's how I became a ham radio operator, you know."

Remember, time spent discussing the effects of the early home influences may prove very fruitful. Among other things, this discussion may throw considerable light on the individual's basic motivation. If the interviewer can get a true picture of these influences—and this is not always possible—he may learn a great deal about the individual's drives. And, as indicated previously, he may be able to obtain a much better understanding of the personality make-up of the candidate. No matter how skilled the interviewer, however, there will always be cases where he is unable to obtain much significant information from the discussion of the person's early home background. In such instances, he simply relies upon other interview areas to supply him with the data he needs to get a clear picture of the individual's over-all qualifications. In our search for relevant information, we cover as many areas as possible in the time allowed. If one area proves relatively unproductive, we try all the harder to dig out the required information in other areas. Actually, the interviewer should not feel discouraged if he is unable to obtain significant information in every case from the discussion of the individual's early home background. We might point out here that, even in the case of very young children, studies have revealed that the subjects possessed traits that were not readily explainable in terms of environmental influences.

Interpretation of early-home-background data should be

tempered by the knowledge that most people are capable of considerable growth and development. The human organism, being as flexible as it is, can take a great deal. Hence, there are those who are capable of overcoming serious disadvantages suffered during childhood. Consequently the interviewer should be careful not to make inferences of a sweeping nature based on his interpretation of the candidate's early environment.

EARLY HOME BACKGROUND AND MINORITIES

It has been argued that because some minority members are the products of difficult early life experiences, this area of the interview should be eliminated because it is unfair to the individuals concerned. This argument fails to take into consideration the fact that our emphasis here is not on circumstances of the life situation but rather on the *effect* such circumstances may have had on the individual's growth and development. For example, many products of "broken homes" develop into mature, well-adjusted adults. And many girls and boys who grew up in the inner city develop into strong, resourceful adults with a good set of values because the *effect* of a father's or mother's influence has been so positive.

The fact that the *early home background* is the area of the interview most likely to provide clues to the individual's value system amply justifies exploration of this area in applicants for higher-level positions. While there may be less justification for concern about the value system of lower-level employees, this looms as a most critical factor in the relationships and decision-making of men and women who may eventually help to determine the course of a given company. An organization makes a large investment in employing people for higher-level positions and hence is entitled to know as much as possible about the ethical standards of such employees.

In exploring the early home background of some minority members, we will certainly encounter people who have had difficult early home experiences. In some cases, there may have been considerable privation; in other cases there may have been limited educational opportunity. But no matter how difficult the situation, it must be remembered that this was all outside his control.

But look particularly for any special positive influence of one or perhaps both parents. Even though the parents may not have had very much to give their children in the way of worldly goods, they may have been able to give them things that are more important—love, a sense of security, and a good set of moral and ethical values. Make a special note, too, of the father's or mother's occupational history. If either or both of them have stayed with one company for a period of years, they are probably stable people and some of this may have rubbed off on the children.

Again, it may be more difficult to develop information concerning temperament of parents as a possible basis for self-evaluation. For the person who has not been trained to think analytically may have a problem providing a list of traits of each of his parents. In that case, the use of the laundry-list question on the Interview Guide will help a great deal. But this question may have to be repeated from time to time until a sufficiently detailed account of the traits of the father and mother has been obtained.

Keep in mind that we are not as much concerned with the early home background per se as we are with the *effects of that background on the development of the individual*. It has often been observed that some people have the capacity to rise above a difficult early existence in such a way that they seem to develop greater strength of character, resilience, and resourcefulness. In sharp contrast, other people from a similar background seem never to be able to escape the effects of that early conditioning.

An important evidence of an individual's rate of growth and development will be found in the extent to which he is a different person today than he was as an adolescent. If appreciable positive changes have taken place during that time, the person can be said to have taken on a considerable amount and may be still developing at a very good rate today. On the other hand, if he still reflects the immaturity, hot temper, and lack of responsibility that characterized his behavior as a youth, relatively little real development would seem to have taken place and hence the prognosis here is not very favorable.

In any event, the greatest attention in this area must be concentrated on the *effects* of the early influences rather than on the early home situation itself.

CHAPTER ELEVEN

Interpreting Present Social Adjustment

Having talked with the applicant about his childhood and adolescent experiences, the interviewer brings him up to the present with a discussion of his current social situation. As in the case of all the other interview areas, this discussion can also provide many clues to the individual's emotional adjustment, motivation, personality traits, and abilities. In particular, the resulting information often brings into focus such factors as sociability, intellectual breadth, and marital adjustment. Obviously, discussion in this area is usually less significant in the case of young men and women just out of college than with persons somewhat older. In talking with young people about their extracurricular activities in college, the interviewer will already have learned a great deal about their social adjustment.

In the discussion of social activities, the interviewer has an excellent opportunity to determine the amount of personal growth that has taken place since the early years. Does the candidate still show evidences of the shortcomings he developed earlier in life? Or does he seem to have grown up emotionally to the point where he has largely overcome the effects of any early disadvantages?

STRUCTURING THE DISCUSSION OF PRESENT SOCIAL ADJUSTMENT

The interviewer leads the applicant into this area by means of a simple question concerning present interests and hobbies, rather than by using the more comprehensive approach. Most people find it easy to talk about their off-the-job activities and hence have no difficulty initiating the flow of conversation. A comprehensive introductory question here, moreover, might alert the individual unduly to some of the more delicate areas the interviewer wishes to explore. It is therefore more adroit to start with a discussion of present interests and subsequently use tactfully worded follow-up questions to get information concerning the remaining items that are listed under present social adjustment on the Interview Guide.

PRESENT INTERESTS AND HOBBIES

Since interests often provide many clues to behavior, they should be discussed in considerable detail, particularly with respect to the kind of satisfaction the individual derives from them. In every case, then, be sure to include such possible activities as sports, participation in community affairs, reading, and interest in the arts.

Sports

The individual who continues to participate in such sports as golf, tennis, handball, and softball is frequently one who tries to keep in good shape physically. This obviously represents an asset, since a healthy person may have fewer absences from work and may be able to devote more energy to the job. Participation in sports, as in the case of many other types of interests, may provide strong clues to energy level. When a person is able to carry out a considerable amount of activity in the evening after having put in a full day on the job, his energy level may be appreciably above average.

Participation in Community Affairs

Note whether the applicant seems to prefer the more solitary pursuits such as hiking, chess, reading, and stamp collecting, or whether he is more group-oriented. The person who spends a great deal of time by himself or with one or two companions may tend toward introversion and may lack facility in establishing easy relationships with others. The person who devotes a considerable amount of his time to group activities in the community, on the other hand, may be more outgoing and extroverted. He also may be the type of person who takes his community responsibilities seriously, thus reflecting attributes of the solid citizen. Give special attention also to any indications of leadership in community affairs. In general, one who invites social exposure in connection with community activities acquires additional skills in getting along with others.

At the same time, the interviewer should be on the alert for the person with a strong social drive. When an individual devotes himself almost exclusively to such activities as fund drives, hospital work, YMCA work, and helping out with the boy scouts, he may be sincerely motivated by a strong desire to help other people. If this turns out to be the case, the interviewer will be alerted to the possibility that the man or woman may possess some of the assets and shortcomings frequently found in persons fitting the description of the social-drive trait constellation. He would then probe specifically for the possible existence of these characteristics in the next area of self-evaluation.

Reading

This subject may be introduced by such an open-end question as, "What about reading? Do you have any opportunity at all to read or do your other activities leave little time for this?" In evaluating reading habits, look for indications of intellectual depth and breadth. Does the individual confine his reading to westerns and mystery stories? Or does he range far afield, reading practically everything and anything he can get his hands on? Specifically, too, does he show any evidence of trying to keep abreast of developments in his field? Finally, do the individual's reading habits reflect unusual intellectual curiosity? The latter may represent an important clue, since persons with a high degree of intellectual curiosity are more likely to be creative in their thinking.

Interest in the Arts

Preference for good music, painting, ballet, and the theater may reflect breadth as well as a good cultural background. In discussing artistic interests, however, the interviewer should try to learn whether such interests are superficial or deep-seated. Does the applicant with musical interests collect records and, if so, what kind of records? Is he interested in operatic and symphonic music or do his tastes run toward popular and semiclassical works?

Although, as indicated in the previous chapter, individuals with strong artistic interests frequently possess such assets as good intelligence, breadth and perspective, and social sensitivity, they may also have a tendency to be overly sensitive, soft, moody, and a bit impractical. When the interviewer notes that the candidate's interests are strongly artistic to the exclusion of practically everything else, he will resolve to probe specifically in the next interview area of self-evaluation for the possible existence of shortcomings associated with the artistic trait constellation. Of course, he will be equally interested in determining whether the person also possesses the assets normally associated with this constellation.

MARITAL STATUS

Since it is now illegal in many states to ask an applicant if he or she is married, this information will often not be available from the application blank. Nor can the interviewer ask this question of the applicant directly. In many cases, however, the candidate will volunteer this information during the course of the discussion, in which case it is perfectly legitimate to discuss items found on the Interview Guide under Present Social Adjustment. In the event that the marital situation does not come up voluntarily, the interviewer will skip to Financial Stability on the Interview Guide.

SPOUSE'S INTERESTS AND PERSONALITY

When the interviewer proceeds immediately to a discussion of the spouse's interests, after getting the complete story on the applicant's off-the-job activities, the candidate normally talks very freely about his spouse. Once on this topic, moreover, he seldom confines his discussion to the spouse's interests alone. In fact, his discourse frequently provides a considerable amount of spontaneous information concerning the marital relationship. A man may say, for example, "Oh, her interests are primarily concerned with her home and children. Actually, she is a wonderful mother and helpmate. Without her support over the years, I certainly would not be where I am today." Comments such as these—provided they can be taken at face value—obviously reflect an excellent marital adjustment. And, if a person is happy at home, he is more likely to be able to give his full energies to his job.

With the intent of stimulating further discussion about the spouse and perhaps to set the stage for a little self-evaluation as well, the interviewer may say, "Are you and your husband quite alike in personality or perhaps somewhat different?" The response may not only provide further clues to the marital adjustment but may also add to the accumulated knowledge of the applicant's behavior. She may say, for example, "Actually, we are not at all alike as far as personality is concerned. He has a great deal more patience, is a wonderful manager of family funds, and has an excellent sense of organization." By implication, the individual may be saying that she is somewhat deficient in these traits. In many cases, of course, the applicant's implied admissions here may provide evidence that tends to support clues to such shortcomings picked up during the discussion of the work history, education, and early home background. If, on the other hand, the applicant's response comes as some surprise to the interviewer, he will want to investigate the situation further by bringing up these traits as possible shortcomings under the discussion of self-evaluation.

When the approach to marital adjustment is handled adroitly and indirectly, the applicant frequently discusses his marital problems quite candidly. He may indicate, for example, that his wife comes from a wealthy family and has never learned how to handle money. Or a woman may make remarks which by implication are critical of the way her husband handles the children. Rarely, of course, will an individual discuss an impending separation. But the interviewer may nevertheless be able to determine that all is not well in the home situation. Certainly, he has a better chance of getting such information if he relies upon indirection than if he uses the direct approach.

SPOUSE'S ATTITUDE TOWARD RELOCATION

When employment on a new job would mean moving from one location to another, the interviewer should ask about the spouse's possible reaction to such a step, provided, of course, that the applicant has already *volunteered* that he is married. Studies of employee turnover, by the way, have indicated that a relatively large percentage of employees who leave their jobs do so because their spouses are unhappy with the community. Hence, it is well to ask, "How do you think your wife (or husband) would feel about moving to this community?" The response, incidentally, may not only reveal the spouse's attitude toward relocation but may also give a clue as to who makes the decisions in the family. It may become apparent from the individual's remarks, for example, that most of the major family decisions are left up to the wife. In that case, the interviewer may get additional clues to the candidate's lack of aggressiveness and self-confidence. Or, the man may say, "I never discuss decisions involving my work with my wife; it is her job to keep the home and mine to support the family." A response of this kind may raise some question as to how good the marital relationship really is. Furthermore, it may suggest clues to over-aggressiveness and inflexibility. The ideal situation exists, of course, when the man and his wife consider major problems together, talk these problems out on an objective basis, and arrive at joint decisions.

Because of the importance of the spouse's attitude, many companies suggest that the prospective employee defer the decision until his wife or her husband has had an opportunity to visit the community and help investigate such factors as housing, schools, and the community in general.

ATTITUDE TOWARD DEPENDENTS

As the applicant talks about his family, particular attention should be paid to the remarks he makes about his children. Does he seem to be particularly close to his children? Does he seem to spend as much time as possible with them? Has he made any plans for financing their college education? Answers to questions such as these tell a great deal about the person's sense of responsibility, family loyalty, stability, and long-range planning. Family loyalty of course represents an important aspect of character. And a loyal family member is likely to prove to be a loyal employee.

FINANCIAL STABILITY
(Housing, insurance, etc.)

Although the application blank may provide some information of a financial nature, it is nevertheless advisable to discuss this important matter with a prospective employee. Since the subject of finances is a highly personal one, the interviewer should use a tactfully worded question such as, "Has there been any opportunity to acquire a little financial reserve, or has this been rather difficult in the light of your family responsibilities?" If good rapport has been established, the individual will often talk quite freely about his financial situation, revealing such factors as the equity he has in his house, the insurance he carries on himself and his family, and the manner in which he has invested his surplus funds.

Information of this sort often provides further clues to his sense of responsibility, maturity, self-discipline, business sense, and long-range planning.

It is particularly important to try to determine whether the applicant usually lives within his income. If he seems to be careless about money matters and to have a tendency to overextend himself financially by purchasing expensive automobiles and major appliances on credit, he may be the kind of a person who is not particularly practical, conscientious, or mature. A person who incurs sizable debts—for reasons other than financing his home and medical expenses—should be looked upon with considerable reservation.

Obviously, younger people with growing families cannot be expected to have accumulated much in the way of a financial reserve. But older individuals who have made a good salary over a considerable number of years should normally have something to show for this in the form of savings, investments, or a sizable equity in their home. When a person has done his best to provide for his family's security in the event of his death, this again reflects stability, responsibility, and family loyalty.

HEALTH STATUS
(Physical vigor and stamina)

Even though most companies today require a medical examination before placing a new person on the payroll, the interviewer should nevertheless discuss the applicant's health, as a function of his possible effectiveness on the job. A question such as, "What about health? Have you had a physical checkup lately?" should start the conversational ball rolling on this topic.

In discussing the candidate's health, note particularly any prolonged sicknesses or major operations. Of course, many persons completely overcome the effects of such illnesses, but in some cases the person's energy level is seriously impaired. When prolonged illnesses occur during childhood and adolescence, moreover, it is well to find out whether this caused the person to miss several grades in school. When a child falls behind in school, he may find upon his return to class that he is the oldest one in the group. Unfortunately, other children are not reluctant to bring this continually to his attention, referring to him as a "dumbbell" and the like. As a result, the person may develop feelings of inferiority that may persist for years.

An applicant's reaction to an obvious physical disability should be evaluated very carefully. If he seems reluctant to discuss the handicap or appears to be oversensitive or to indulge in self-pity, the chances are that he has not been able to adjust to the situation adequately. Such a person may be expected to find it difficult to establish good relationships with coworkers. On the other hand, if the individual is able to talk about his handicap openly and objectively, there is an equally good chance that he has achieved very good adjustment indeed. Moreover, a person who succeeds in making an appropriate adjustment to a physical handicap may be able in large part to compensate for the disability by developing a particularly effective personality or by being unusually faithful on the job. Perhaps because it is not easy for such a person to get a new job, he is often more appreciative of the opportunity to work. Accordingly, he usually shows up on the job every day and works to the best of his ability.

If the applicant appears to be nervous and high-strung, it may be well to ask if he ever has any problems with sleeping or digestion. It is well known, of course, that insomnia, many types of ulcer conditions, and allergies frequently stem from mental worry. Thus, if a person does suffer from any of these ailments, there is at least the possibility that they may be of psychosomatic origin. The person who takes things too seriously and worries excessively is usually one who is not particularly well-adjusted emotionally. He may be able to function successfully at a given vocational level, but when his responsibilities are increased and he is placed in a situation involving greater pressure, he may not be able to stand up under the added load.

Interviewers obviously should make no attempt to diagnose medical problems but, when they do develop relevant health information, they should pass this along to the company doctor for his interpretation.

ENERGY LEVEL

High energy level, vigor, and stamina obviously represent extremely important assets. In fact, few people attain genuinely high vocational achievement unless they possess these important qualities in some abundance. Given a reasonable degree of intellect, educational training, and personality effectiveness, the degree of energy and stamina a person possesses may account in large part for his ability to win promotions over his associates.

By the time the interviewer has reached this stage of the discussion, he will of course have acquired numerous clues to the individual's energy level and stamina. For example, the individual may have been able to work long hours over a protracted period of time without showing any serious defects. Or he may have secured his college education by going to night school over a period of six or seven years while carrying on a full-time job during the day.

If the interviewer is not certain of the applicant's amount of energy at this stage of the interview, he may ask him specifically about this by saying, "How would you describe your energy level—as average, somewhat above average, or perhaps a little less than average?" Most younger people like to think that they have an above-average energy level. Hence, if they admit that they have no more than an average degree of this important quality, they may have even less than that amount. Other clues to lack of energy may be reflected in the applicant's tendency to take the easy way out, to procrastinate, to be unwilling to make present sacrifices for future gains, and by a phlegmatic general manner.

PRESENT SOCIAL ADJUSTMENT AND MINORITIES

Since it is illegal in some states to ask about marital status, most of the discussion in this area will center around interests, finances, health, and energy. As indicated earlier in this chapter, however, if the applicant *volunteers* information about his spouse—as a large percentage of applicants will—it is then permissible to ask about the spouse's interests, the extent to which the personality traits are the same or different, and possible reaction to relocation.

Members of this group cannot always be expected to have developed truly broad interests. At the same time, when we encounter an individual who has broadened his horizons, we are truly impressed.

We cannot always expect to find many people with a high degree of financial stability among the minorities. Some of them have simply not been given the opportunity to work in the types of jobs that pay relatively high salaries. Hence, when you find a person who is buying his home and has purchased a reasonable amount of insurance, this represents a decided mark in his favor as well as providing clues to maturity, resourcefulness, thrift, and a sense of responsibility.

As in the case of our development of all the other interview areas, we are looking here again for the person who has "been able to do a little more with what he had to work with." This sets him up as a person apart and one in whom we are particularly interested.

CHAPTER TWELVE

Mental Ability, Motivation, and Maturity above All Else

The interviewer is required to search for so many traits and abilities that it seems justified here—at the risk of some redundancy—to point out that three factors take precedence over all others. These factors may be referred to as the 3 M's —mental ability, motivation, and maturity, the level of importance being perhaps in that order.

If an applicant is bright mentally, highly motivated to succeed, and mature emotionally, he undoubtedly represents a good candidate for some kind of a job in any given organization. The specific job for which he is qualified, of course, depends upon such secondary factors as relevance of his work experience, educational background, specific aptitudes, and temperament.

In this chapter, then, we shall point out the reasons why mental ability, motivation, and maturity loom so importantly in our evaluation of any candidate. And we shall review the major clues which help to identify these three factors, bringing together material from a number of the previous chapters.

Just as mental ability, motivation, and maturity represent the three most important factors to be identified in selecting an employee for industry, so do they also represent the three most important requisites to be considered in selecting students for college. This will be discussed in some detail at the end of this chapter.

MENTAL ABILITY

As implied above, mental ability probably represents the single most important factor to be considered in any evaluation of a candidate for a higher-level position. Despite this seemingly obvious fact, many highly placed managers in industry have been observed evaluating candidates for important positions without making any real effort to determine the individual's intellectual level or to give appropriate weighting to that important factor. The reason for this omission may lie in the fact that most managers have not been trained in interviewing techniques and therefore do not know how to judge a candidate's mental capacity.

Yet, mental ability represents the *power* factor, in the sense that it means the individual's ability to acquire new information, to generate new ideas, and to solve complex problems. And when we think of *potential* for ever-increasing responsibilities, we must again give major consideration to the level of the individual's mental capacity.

Keep in mind, too, that there are some jobs which cannot competently be performed by a person who is not really bright—such jobs as demanding research positions, engineering design, and high-level management.

It is equally important to identify the intellectual factor in candidates for less intellectually demanding jobs—jobs that have a fair amount of routine detail, such as laboratory control work, some types of engineering testing, and door-to-door sales. Most really bright people, placed in a job that is routine and not at all intellectually challenging, become quickly "fed up" and leave. Obviously, therefore, it is necessary to staff such jobs with persons whose intelligence is no better than average or perhaps even slightly below average.

Although aptitude tests represent the best means of establishing the individual's intelligence, most companies are still not equipped to give these tests, and many organizations shy away from them because they are afraid of being accused of unfair employment practices. In many cases, such fears are of course groundless, but they nevertheless represent some deterrent as far as the use of aptitude tests is concerned. Consequently, it becomes all the more important *to be able to identify mental ability without giving additional tests.* Actually, an applicant's mental ability can be quite accurately assessed by means of a comprehensive interview, *provided the interviewer is well-trained and has developed a broad frame of reference, in the sense that he has evaluated many hundreds of people and can thus compare a given applicant's qualifications against those of many others he has seen for that same type of job.* Although clues to mental ability have been brought to light in several of the preceding chapters, it will perhaps best serve our purposes if these clues are pulled together and presented again here.

High School and College Grades in Relation to Effort Required to Make Such Grades

Although grades *per se* are not a reliable indication of mental ability, they become significantly more reliable when considered in the light of the amount of effort the individual expended in order to get these grades, particularly if the academic standard of the school attended is factored into this equation. Thus, if a person attained relatively high grades in a school of acknowledged high academic standards without having to expend a great deal of effort, it can be assumed that he is a reasonably bright individual. In sharp contrast, if a person was not able to obtain better-than-average grades in a school of questionable academic standards, despite a great amount of effort and long hours of study, he is quite probably somewhat limited intellectually. (Refer to Chapter 9 for a more complete discussion of this subject.)

College Board Scores

Most individuals twenty-five or younger will have taken SAT's (Scholastic Aptitude Test) during their senior year of high school, will have been informed of their scores, and will undoubtedly remember them still. Actually, Scholastic Aptitude Tests are made up of two separate tests—*verbal* and *quantitative,* or numerical. 800 represents a perfect score on each of these tests. In our attempts to identify a given individual's mental ability, we must consider the *combined score* resulting from both of these tests. Thus, if a person obtained a score of 575 on the verbal test and 625 on the numerical test, the combined score of 1200.

Most colleges today look for a certain minimum combined score on the SAT's to qualify for college entrance. And the level of this minimum required score tells us a good bit about a given college's academic standards. Many of our most prestigious colleges and universities require a minimum combined score of at least 1300, although some other colleges require no more than a combined minimum score of 1000.

Since most mental ability tests are made up of verbal and numerical items, the combined score on an individual's SAT's represents quite a good indication of his intellectual level.

The table below represents a distribution of the combined scores on the two SAT's for the high school senior population.

Combined Test Score	Interpretation
1400–1600	Excellent
1150–1400	Above average
850–1150	Average
600– 850	Below average
Below 600	Poor

As pointed out in Chapter 9, however, the above distribution includes many people who did not make it to college. Therefore, the distribution on the college population is much higher. In fact, a combined score of 1000 represents a rather marginal score for a college graduate. Scores ranging higher than this, of course, reflect higher mental ability—the higher the combined score, the brighter the individual.

Graduate Record Examination Scores

A person applying for graduate study leading to a master's or a Ph.D. degree in most of the better colleges and universities will be required to take the Graduate Record Examination. A perfect score on this examination is 800 but, since the test is appreciably more difficult than the Scholastic Aptitude Test, relatively few people make scores in the 700's on this test. A minimum score of at least 500 represents a requirement for entrance at most of the better schools. Scores ranging above 500, of course, reflect higher-level mental ability—the higher the score, the brighter the individual.

In talking with persons who have done graduate work—or have even applied for graduate study—it is often helpful to ask them about their score on the Graduate Record Examination. Practically everyone who has taken this examination will remember his score because it is pivotal in gaining admittance to the university of his choice.

Quality of Response to Depth Questions

Although the interviewer should be alert to the quality of the applicant's responses throughout the discussion, he should give particular attention to certain items appearing on the Interview Guide. These are items i, j, and k (achievements, development needs, and factors of job satisfaction) under Work History and item f (effects of the early home influences) under Early Home Background. The interviewer should be equally alert in examining the quality of the applicant's responses to the Self-Evaluation section at the end of the interview.

The areas identified above—perhaps more than any of the others—require a great amount of concentration, analysis, and in-depth thinking on the part of the applicant. Hence, his responses in these areas should be carefully evaluated in terms of the extent to which they reveal analytical power, perception, self-insight, and intellectual breadth and depth. Obviously, analytical power, perceptiveness, and perspective are directly related to a favorable degree of mental ability.

Achievements Reflecting Mental Ability

High academic achievement such as election to Phi Beta Kappa (liberal arts student) or Tau Beta Pi (engineering student) normally reflects high-level mental ability. Of course, there is the occasional student who attains these high honors by dint of inordinate effort rather than because he is particularly bright, but such persons are few and far between. Hence, it can usually be assumed that a person who has attained either of these two scholastic honors has very good mental capacity.

Because certain academic courses require a rather high degree of abstract thinking, persons who like and do well in such courses as philosophy, logic, thermodynamics, and differential equations are usually relatively bright. It is equally true that demonstrated ability to handle intellectually demanding jobs represents a further clue to good intelligence. As noted earlier in this chapter, such jobs include important research positions, engineering design, and high-level management.

MOTIVATION

As important as intellect is, it cannot do the job alone. Unless a person is motivated to utilize what he has, his over-all achievement may not be particularly great and will most certainly be less than that of which he is capable. Moreover, many people with average intelligence coupled with high motivation attain a greater success than some other more intellectually gifted people who fail to make maximum use of what they possess. This is another way of saying that many people find it possible to compensate for something less than a brilliant mind by means of unusually strong motivation. As a matter of fact, high-level vocational achievement in certain areas may stem more from strong motivation than from any other single factor.

In view of the relationship of motivation to achievement, therefore, no evaluation of a candidate's qualifications is complete unless the degree of his motivation has been identified and its relationship to his over-all achievement spelled out. In fact, motivation ranks almost as important as intellect as far as the candidate's qualifications are concerned.

As we did in the case of mental ability above, therefore, we have pulled together clues to motivation from various parts of the interview in order that we may treat this important factor here as an entity.

High Energy Level

There is a direct relationship between the amount of energy a person possesses and the achievement he is likely to attain. One needs only to look around him in almost any business situation to understand the truth of this statement. The people at the top—those in important management jobs—will almost invariably be equipped with a great amount of energy. In fact, a highly placed person who does not have great energy will certainly represent a rather rare exception.

Energy appears to be largely inherited, with environment playing a secondary role. Thus, if a person is born without a great deal of energy, there is not very much he can do about it. On the other hand, if he is equipped from the beginning with a high degree of energy, he possesses an extraordinarily important asset, particularly if he learns to harness and focus that energy.

Since energy is so important to the prediction of success on a job, it seems surprising that there has been so little research effort expended in the direction of attempting to develop a valid and reliable measurement. If we could obtain as good an objective measurement of energy as we have of mental ability through intelligence tests, we would have a tremendously valuable tool for predicting behavior.

A well-trained interviewer—one with a broad frame of reference—can do quite an accurate job in assessing the candidate's energy level. He normally picks up clues to this important factor in all the interview areas. By means of adroit questioning, he can usually tell whether the applicant was able to handle certain enervating jobs without undue difficulty or whether they actually seemed to have drained him of his energy and stamina at that time.

The interviewer is equally alert to the degree of energy required during the applicant's educational experience. If a

student was able to take a heavy academic load and still participate in many extracurricular activities or carry on an outside job, the evidence speaks for itself. Such an individual
must have a high degree of energy.

It is furthermore helpful to note the kind of activities a
person is able to carry out after completing a hard day on the
job. Some people have enough energy left to participate in
all types of physically demanding sports or to "moonlight"
on another job. Other people appear to become completely
"bushed" at the end of a normal work day.

Finally, the interviewer can discuss the subject of energy
quite directly, providing he has developed sufficient rapport.
Such a discussion often results in additional important
evidence.

Vocational and Educational Achievement in Terms of Mental Level

In an applicant whose mental ability has been assessed by
the interviewer as not much better than average, there must
be some other factor responsible for unusual vocational or
educational achievement. That factor is almost invariably
strong motivation. Many people have attained rather unusual
success in industry on the basis of strong motivation as the
primary factor. In fact, *in cases where other qualifications are
reasonably good,* strong motivation is often the single most
important factor in vocational success.

Some people make such maximum utilization of their
rather modest abilities that they manage to do very well in
high school and college. Such people are often referred to as
"overachievers"—people who have attained a higher level of
achievement in school and on the job than might have been
expected of them in the light of their level of intelligence.
Many of these people manage to do so well on their way up

that they develop the philosophy that they can achieve anything at all providing they are willing to work hard enough. Unfortunately, that philosophy only works well until the individual is confronted with a task that is highly demanding intellectually. At that point, he often discovers that hard work alone is not enough.

Conditioned to Work

People who have developed successful work-habit patterns have become accustomed to working hard and expect to extend this type of behavior throughout the rest of their lives. In interviewing such a person, it is easy to tell the extent to which he has become conditioned to work by probing for likes and dislikes on his various jobs, by noting the amount of overtime hours he regularly puts in on many of his assignments, and by making observations about the kind of things which give him satisfaction.

Strong Drive for Achievement

A person with strong motivation is normally one who "sets his sights high." In the words of Emerson, he has a strong drive to "become." Motivated by a drive to "make something of himself," he is usually willing to pay whatever price may be required as far as hard work is concerned.

Clues to high aspirations are most often brought to light during the discussion of *factors of job satisfaction* at the close of the discussion of work history. There it is frequently fruitful to ask a candidate what level of job he expects to attain at the end of five years and then at the end of ten years.

MATURITY

Some bright, highly motivated people fail because they lack *emotional maturity*. As discussed in previous chapters, the development of this important trait stems largely from environmental factors—the major influences which have been brought to bear on the individual from the time of his birth until the time of his appearance at your employment office. Just as in the case of mental ability and motivation, however, the individual has little actual control over the extent to which he matures emotionally. He is not able to select his parents; he has nothing to do with the early environment in which he was raised; for the most part, he has no choice of his teachers; and even his playmates during the early years have to be chosen on the basis of the immediate neighborhood in which he lives.

Although most immature people have had very little to do with this lack of development, they nevertheless possess a shortcoming which very frequently stands in the way of success. This becomes immediately apparent when we go back to our earlier definition of emotional maturity: the ability to take the bitter with the sweet without rationalizing, the ability to acquire self-insight, the ability to exercise good judgment, the ability to establish reasonable vocational goals, and the ability to exercise self-control.

If one lacks judgment, he often makes the wrong choice when confronted with important alternatives at critical stages of his life. He may take the wrong kind of job, may leave a job for the wrong reasons, may select the wrong college major, or may do a poor job in planning his personal and financial affairs.

When a person lacks self-insight, he does not know who he is or where he is going. This often means that the factors he tends to emphasize in his life may not be appropriately related to success or achievement. He may not even realize the fact that he tends to rationalize his failures because he does not face up to his own shortcomings and hence is inclined to blame others for his difficulties. Furthermore, the immature person is often self-centered, expects too much from others, and is too open in his criticism when things do not suit him.

Again, clues to emotional maturity should be brought to light in all the interview areas and have therefore been discussed in previous chapters. However, the factor of emotional maturity is so important that a certain amount of repetition seems justified and we are therefore summarizing some of these clues below.

Emotional Foundation in the Home

We now know that love and a sense of security are as important to a child's emotional development as are food and drink to his physical growth. The love and attention of both parents, reasonable freedom from economic privation, and the right amount of parental guidance loom importantly in the individual's early development. Clues to early emotional development of course appear most frequently in a discussion of the individual's early home background as he talks about the temperament of his parents, the extent to which he was raised strictly, and the effects of the early home influences.

Relationships with People

As noted above, lack of self-control represents a shortcoming that frequently mars a person's relationships with people. An astute interviewer, moreover, may be able to determine that the primary reason for an inordinate amount of job jumping stems from the fact that the individual has not been able to get along with either supervisors or co-workers on any of his jobs. Although it happens rather infrequently, sometimes a student will resign from his fraternity because he cannot "fit in" with his fraternity brothers. On the other hand, frequent election to offices or team leadership usually mean that the individual gets along with others quite well.

Good Judgment

Lack of good judgment in leaving a given job, in selecting a major field of study, or in handling finances usually represent a sign of immaturity. Judgment is also a pivotal factor in deciding the type of job the individual desires, in terms of the extent to which that job realistically draws upon his ability and personality assets. Reasons for undertaking graduate study provide further clues to judgment, particularly in the sense that those reasons are consistent with his goals and "make sense" in terms of his previous educational background and work experience.

Demonstrated Ability to Put First Things First

The mature individual has enough self-discipline so that he is able to make himself do the things that have to be done but may not be particularly pleasant. Such a person resists the temptation to do too much socializing in college, making certain that he gets his homework done first. The ability to resist the temptation to buy a new car every other year in favor of saving for a down payment on a home also shows indications of maturity.

Reasonable Vocational Goals

When, in the discussion of factors of job satisfaction, it becomes apparent that a person with very modest abilities aspires to a position which is way beyond his reach, it becomes clear that he has not recognized his limitations and learned to live with them.

In assessing the degree of a candidate's emotional maturity, he must be compared with his chronological age group. Since maturity is a dynamic rather than a static factor, one normally develops more of this trait as he grows older. Hence, we do not expect a nineteen-year-old to be as mature as a twenty-five-year-old, despite the fact that some nineteen-year-olds are far more mature at that age than some other young men and women of twenty-five.

It can be noted in passing that there are at least two other forms of maturity—intellectual maturity and social maturity. Sometimes a person brought up in a home where the father is a professional man develops more breadth and perspective than others of his age. Social maturity, on the other hand, implies an ability to handle one's self well in social situations, particularly with one's peers. Thus, the extremely shy person who finds it difficult to relate to other people of his own age is said to be socially immature.

IMPLICATIONS FOR SELECTION OF COLLEGE STUDENTS

Many colleges still do a relatively poor job of selection, as reflected in the attrition at the end of the first semester or at the end of the first year. In these times of rising costs when many institutions are struggling to remain solvent, inefficient selection creates an unnecessary demand for more classroom space, more laboratory facilities, and more dormitory space and puts an additional burden on the teaching staff. Moreover, students who fail to make the grade often lose confidence and never try again. This is something of a tragedy since many of those students are capable of doing college work but simply *were not ready at the time they applied for admission.*

Now, if we think of the college-admission situation in terms of the 3 M's discussed in this chapter, we find that the colleges have no problem dealing with the factor of mental ability. This is because most applicants today take the College Boards, an examination which clearly determines whether or not a boy or girl is bright enough to do college work. But some institutions are modifying their ideas of fixed-minimum-score requirements, now realizing that certain individuals are capable of *compensating* for something less than a brilliant mind. As a matter of fact, even the prestigious colleges are discovering that a student does not need a combined score of 1300 or better on the SAT's in order to handle the academic work competently. Accordingly, they are experimenting, taking in some applicants with lower scores, providing they have *something else* in abundance, usually athletic prowess, demonstrated leadership in extracurricular affairs, or perhaps unusual talent in music.

However, the colleges would be well-advised to look for that *something else* in the direction of unusually strong motivation and emotional maturity beyond the student's chronological years. Most students fail because they are not sufficiently motivated to study or are so immature that they cannot adjust to the college situation.

It seems quite clear that much of the attrition that takes place during the first year of college could be largely eliminated if the colleges would staff their admission offices with trained interviewers. These interviewers should not be so young, incidentally, that they have not yet had an opportunity to do a great deal of interviewing and hence to have acquired a broad frame of reference. The latter is important in enabling the interviewer to compare one applicant with many others that he has interviewed over the years.

Once the colleges were staffed with trained interviewers, they would be in a position to consider the all-important factors of motivation and emotional maturity, in addition to their current concentration on mental capacity. At that point, it would be perfectly logical to take some young people with lower SAT's, provided these individuals possessed strong motivation and a high degree of emotional maturity.

CHAPTER THIRTEEN

Concluding the Interview

With the completion of the discussion of the applicant's present social adjustment, the interviewer will have accumulated the information he needs to make his decision concerning the candidate's over-all qualifications. If he has been interpreting the various clues to abilities, personality, and motivation as they have occurred throughout the discussion—as indeed he should have been doing—he will have formed his over-all judgment of the candidate at this point. Hence, he is ready to conclude the interview. If he is a relatively inexperienced, untrained interviewer, he can do this directly in accordance with suggestions found later in this chapter. Or, if he is highly skilled and well-trained, he may employ the self-evaluation technique prior to terminating the discussion.

This chapter includes a discussion of the self-evaluation technique together with suggestions for terminating the interview—suggestions pertaining both to applicants who are to be rejected as well as to those considered qualified.

THE SELF-EVALUATION TECHNIQUE

As indicated above, *this technique should not be attempted by the inexperienced, untrained interviewer.* The technique demands the utmost in terms of adroitness on the part of the interviewer. And it can be used successfully only when the interviewer has already developed a rather clear-cut mental picture of the candidate's assets and shortcomings.

In the hands of a skilled person, the self-evaluation technique provides two major advantages. It permits the interviewer to obtain additional confirming evidence of assets and shortcomings that have come to light in the previous discussion, and equally important, it enables the candidate to acquire greater self-insight. It is entirely conceivable that the latter may never have given any comprehensive, systematic thought to his own strengths and weaknesses. A discussion of this kind with him then often clarifies his thinking about those traits and abilities he already possesses in some abundance as well as the characteristics that need some improvement, in terms of his further development.

Structuring the Discussion of Self-evaluation

Much of the success of this technique depends upon the wording of the comprehensive introductory question. The interviewer should ask the individual to summarize his qualifications. He should then point out that everyone possesses a number of important assets and, on the other hand, since no one is perfect, everyone also has some areas in which he might with advantage improve himself.

The individual should first be asked to discuss what he thinks of as his principal assets. Most individuals find it rather easy to discuss this pleasant subject. Moreover, they will subsequently find it much easier and will be much more willing to discuss their shortcomings if they are certain that the interviewer has a full appreciation of their strengths.

Helping the Candidate Discuss His Assets

In concluding the comprehensive introductory question, the interviewer should ask the individual to start with a discussion of his assets, pointing out that he should do this objectively without any feeling that he is bragging. Immediately after each asset has been presented, moreover, the interviewer should *lubricate the situation* by giving the candidate a verbal pat on the back. If the individual indicates that he is a hard worker, for example, and if the interviewer has already seen abundant evidence of this trait, he might say, "I'm sure you are a very hard worker, and that's a wonderful asset to have!" On the other hand, if the interviewer has a question about the individual's motivation, he will simply nod his head, ask the applicant to indicate some of his other assets, and resolve to reintroduce the subject of hard work later on when talking about the individual's shortcomings.

Some candidates may find it difficult to list their real assets. In this case, the interviewer should stimulate the discussion by pointing out one or two strengths he has already observed. Thus, he might say, "Well, I have observed that you seem to get along unusually well with people, and this of course is a tremendous asset in any job situation." After "priming the pump" with one or two such observations, the interviewer should pass the conversational ball back to the candidate, asking him to tell about some of his other strong points. If he seems to be unable to come up with any additional assets on his own, make use of the *calculated pause*, in this way giving him an opportunity to organize his thoughts. If, after ten or twelve seconds, he is still unable to come up with anything, the interviewer should "take him off the hook" by introducing another asset which he has observed during the interview. In some cases, a considerable amount of "pump priming" may be necessary before the candidate begins to talk about some of his own strengths, but the interviewer should "wait him out," using as much patience as he can muster.

The interviewer should draw out a list of at least eight or ten assets and should spend at least five minutes in so doing. Otherwise, the applicant may be quite reluctant subsequently to discuss his shortcomings. Remember, a person usually feels confident about discussing his shortcomings only if he feels that the interviewer has a full appreciation of all the major assets.

It is true of course that the applicant's own listing of his assets may have to be taken with a grain of salt, particularly if he has shown any previous tendency to overplay his hand or to withhold important information. Remember, too, that the individual is trying to get a job and is therefore anxious to sell himself.

Helping the Applicant Discuss His Shortcomings

After the individual has had a full opportunity to discuss his strengths, the interviewer should reintroduce the subject of shortcomings, pointing out that everyone possesses certain traits that could stand a little improvement. He should then try to "sell" the applicant by indicating that, if the individual can be helped to recognize some of the areas in which he is a little less strong, he can consciously work on those areas and develop himself faster than might otherwise be the case.

In discussing the applicant's developmental needs, always use the word "shortcomings" rather than "weaknesses," "faults," or "liabilities." The latter three words carry the connotation that the trait may be so serious that he can do very little about it. The word "shortcomings," on the other hand, implies that the trait is just a little short of what it might desirably be and that hence the person may be able to improve upon it or eliminate it. In talking about shortcomings, moreover, refer frequently to the phrase "ways in which you can improve yourself." Thus, instead of saying, "What are some other shortcomings?" it is better to say, "What are some other ways in which you might improve yourself?"

Immediately after each shortcoming has been presented, the interviewer should "play it down," in much the same way that he plays down any other unfavorable information throughout the interview. When the individual admits, for example, that he needs to develop more self-confidence, the interviewer might say, "Well, confidence is a trait that a lot of people need to develop further. I'm sure you can improve yourself in this respect over the next few years." When a person admits a particularly serious shortcoming, such as laziness, the interviewer should play this down by complimenting the individual for having recognized it and for facing up to it. Thus, he may say, "You deserve credit for being able to recognize this. And, because you have recognized it, you probably have already taken certain steps toward eliminating it."

When the applicant finds it difficult or seems reluctant to present any of his shortcomings, the interviewer may stimulate the discussion by the use of *double-edged questions.* If the interviewer has already noted that the applicant is quite lacking in self-discipline, for example, he may say, "What about self-discipline? Do you think you have as much of this as you would like to have, or does this represent an area in which you could improve to some extent?" Such a question makes it easy for a person to admit his shortcomings. Again, if the interviewer has noticed a general tendency to be lazy, he might say, "What about work habits? Do you think that you usually work as hard as you should, or is this something that you could improve a little bit?"

For the most part, indicated shortcomings can be taken pretty much at face value. Seldom will one draw attention to shortcomings that do not really exist. At the same time, there is the occasional individual—one who is exceedingly insecure and tends to underestimate his abilities—who will bring up something as a shortcoming that is not a deficiency.

The interviewer's role in the self-evaluation discussion is a pivotal one. If he tries to stimulate the discussion by introducing assets or shortcomings that are not part of the applicant's make-up, the latter quickly loses respect for him. On the other hand, if the interviewer is able to introduce traits that go to the very heart of the individual's personality and motivational pattern, the latter gains appreciable respect for him.

The Value of the Self-evaluation Technique

As noted above, this technique can be of considerable value to both the applicant and the interviewer. The applicant gains by getting a clearer picture of his strengths and developmental needs, thus acquiring greater insight. And the interviewer gains because he is frequently able to get more documentary evidence concerning the candidate's over-all qualifications.

When the interviewer is able to get the applicant to agree with him on the presence or absence of certain traits, this obviously provides strong support for the original diagnosis. When, for example, he has seen several clues to insecurity throughout the interview, he waits expectantly for some indication of this in the candidate's self-evaluation. If lack of self-confidence is spontaneously admitted, or admitted as a result of probing with a double-edged question, the interviewer has of course developed further confirmation of his original hypothesis. And since the person is aware of this developmental need, he may be able to do something about improving himself in this respect.

Occasionally the applicant will mention a trait that may not have consciously crystallized in the interviewer's mind but for which he sees abundant evidence as soon as it is verbalized. In other words, he may have been only vaguely aware of the trait but, when the applicant mentions it specifically, he can immediately think of a number of clues that actually pointed in that direction. If the applicant had not mentioned this trait, the interviewer might not have factored it into his over-all decision.

When the candidate mentions an asset or shortcoming for which the interviewer has seen no support, it is well to ask the individual to elaborate. His subsequent remarks may convince the interviewer that the applicant actually possesses the trait in question, thus bringing to light valuable information that might otherwise have been missed. To illustrate this point, let us assume that the individual mentions creative ability as an asset. If the interviewer has seen little or no evidence of imagination, he might say, "What are some of the things you have done in the past that helped you reach this conclusion?" In the ensuing discussion, the candidate may point to a series of patents and technical publications that had not previously come up in the conversation. After getting this additional information, the interviewer may be quite convinced that the individual really is creative. In this instance, the self-evaluation technique operated as insurance against leaving out something that was really important. In trying to justify creative ability as an asset, on the the other hand, the individual's supporting reasons may be altogether superficial. In that case, of course, the interviewer would simply nod his head and ask for additional strong points, still not convinced that the person is imaginative.

TERMINATING THE INTERVIEW

As noted in Chapter 8, it is occasionally permissible to terminate an interview before all the suggested background areas have been discussed. This is only done in cases where a predominance of negative information results from the early discussion. If after a discussion of the work history and education, for example, it becomes clearly evident that the candidate is not at all suited for the job in question, the interview may be terminated at that point. However, the interviewer should guard against snap judgments, making certain that his decision not to carry the interview any further is based upon adequate factual evidence rather than upon an emotional reaction to the individual concerned. There are occasions, too, when the interviewer's impression of a candidate may change materially after the first half-hour of discussion, swinging from a rather negative impression to an entirely positive one. Hence, the accumulation of negative findings must be substantial in the case of an early interview termination.

In a well-designed selection program, applicants scheduled for the evaluation interview will already have been screened by preliminary interviews, application forms, aptitude tests, and reference checkups. For the most part, such applicants will represent likely prospects and will merit the complete interview. And the more likely a prospect the candidate seems to be, the more the interviewer needs to know about him, in terms of his possible shortcomings as well as his assets. Thus, early termination of an interview in which the findings are positive is never justified.

Since the vast majority of applicants will get the full interview, termination will normally take place at the end of the discussion of present social adjustment. Or, if the discussion is being carried out by a well-trained, experienced interviewer, the conversation will be concluded with the completion of the individual's self-evaluation. Termination, in the sense that we are using it here, involves more than the wind-up of the information-gathering aspects of the interview. It also includes the information-giving aspects. As noted below, every applicant should be given some information about the company and, in particular, about the job for which he is being considered.

Terminating the Unqualified Applicant

Even in the case where the applicant is to be rejected, a certain amount of information-giving should take place at the end of the interview. Directed toward the objective of public relations, this should be kept general. In other words, the applicant should be told about general factors, such as company organization, company policy, products manufactured, and the like—rather than about specific factors such as wages, hours of work, and employee benefits. The latter are important only in the case of an applicant who is to be offered a position. Five minutes will ordinarily prove sufficient to tell the unqualified applicant about the company. However, courteous and informative answers should always be given to any questions he raises.

An attempt should always be made to terminate the interview on a positive tone. Such a statement as the following will often accomplish this objective, "Well, you certainly have a long list of impressive assets—assets that will stand you in good stead throughout your working life. And, at the same time, you seem to have some insight into the areas to which you should give your attention in terms of further development. I will discuss your qualifications with other interested persons within the company and will let you know the outcome within a day or two. Thank you very much for coming in; I certainly enjoyed talking with you."

Once the interviewer has decided to terminate the discussion, this should be done with dispatch. Otherwise, the conversation will deteriorate into meaningless chitchat. Hence, after the interviewer has made a statement such as the one noted in the paragraph above, he should rise from his chair, shake the applicant's hand, and escort him to the door.

Rejection of an applicant is always a difficult task at best and, as such, must be handled with care and finesse. First and foremost, the applicant must be rejected in such a way that his feelings are not unduly hurt and his self-confidence is not undermined. In the second place, the company's public relations are at stake. In other words, rejected applicants should be permitted to "save face," so that they do not bear ill will toward the company. Because this task requires so much skill and finesse, many companies prefer to inform applicants of an unfavorable employment decision by letter. Actually, the latter means is almost uniformly used in the case of applicants for high-level jobs. A carefully worded letter not only represents an expression of courtesy but carries the implication of more thorough consideration. At the same time, the letter should be sent within a day or two after the interview, thus freeing the unsuccessful candidate to concentrate on other job possibilities.

Whether the applicant is informed of the unfavorable decision by letter or at the end of the interview, the reason for the rejection should be phrased in terms of the job demands rather than in terms of the individual's personal qualifications. The candidate should be given credit for his real assets but, at the same time, should be told that, in the interviewer's opinion, the job will not make the best use of his abilities. Instead of deprecating the individual's personal qualifications, this approach simply implies that he will probably be able to find better use for his unique qualifications in some other job with another company.

Another way to help a person "save face" involves a comparison with other candidates for the job in question, on the basis of his experience and education. He can be told, for example, "Although you possess many fine assets, there are one or two other candidates being considered for this job whose specific experience and training are somewhat more appropriate." Note that this statement makes no mention of personal characteristics such as ability to get along with people, willingness to work hard, or leadership traits. In general, it is far easier for an individual to face up to the fact that his experience or training does not quite fit the job than it is for him to admit that he does not qualify because of personal characteristics.

The more aggressive applicant may occasionally press the interviewer for further reasons as to why the job may not make best use of his abilities. In such a case, the temptation to inform the individual about specific test or interview findings should be resisted at all costs. The "feedback" of specific information of this kind represents a difficult task. Because it requires specific experience and training, it can lead to a discussion that may easily get out of hand. Hence, it is much better to keep the discussion general, elaborating on previous remarks. The interviewer might say, "As a member of the personnel department here I have a rather thorough knowledge of job requirements and, in my opinion, our current job openings are not likely to make the best use of your abilities. In fact, I have seen one or two other candidates whose experience and training are a little more appropriate."

Once in a while an individual will ask for vocational guidance. He may say, "If your jobs will not make best use of my abilities, what kind of a job do you think I should look for elsewhere?" In answer to such a question, the interviewer should refer the individual to a professional vocational guidance counselor. Guidance requires a great deal more academic preparation than does interviewing. Moreover, an interviewer is normally familiar only with the requirements of the jobs in his company. To do an adequate guidance job, the counselor must have knowledge of job requirements in a great many different fields. Hence, an applicant who expresses a desire for vocational guidance should be referred to a competent psychologist specializing in this field.

Terminating the Interview of the Qualified Applicant

Although the interviewer ordinarily has the authority to reject unqualified applicants, he does not always have final responsibility for placing qualified candidates on the payroll. The latter responsibility usually rests with the head of the department to which the applicant is being referred. Even when the interviewer's decision is entirely favorable, he should not communicate this to the applicant. Rather, he should express his real interest in the individual's qualifications and tell him that he feels sure that the department head would like to talk with him further.

The information-giving aspect of the interview takes on even greater importance when the interviewer's decision is favorable. In these situations, he does everything possible to sell the candidate on the job. And he is in a unique position to do this. With the full knowledge of the applicant's abilities and qualifications in mind, he can specifically point out the extent to which these qualifications apply to the job. Where the decision is favorable, moreover, the interviewer should talk in terms of job specifics—earnings, employee benefits, and subsequent opportunities for promotion. In addition, he will also talk about company policies, products, and the organization's position in the industry. At the same time, he will be careful not to oversell the job, knowing that this might lead to eventual disappointment and poor morale.

CHAPTER FOURTEEN

Completing
the Interview Rating Form

This chapter provides instructions for recording interview findings on the Interview Rating Form found in the back of the book. To help the interviewer summarize his thinking, moreover, the chapter also includes a cross-reference section, showing how possible clues from each of the major interview areas can be used to form judgments of the candidate's rating on traits of personality, motivation, and character appearing on the back of the Interview Rating Form.

The write-up of the case represents an important, integral part of the interviewing process. Experience has shown that, as the interviewer records his results, his thinking crystallizes with respect to the applicant's qualifications. By the time the applicant leaves the room, the interviewer will normally have made up his mind as to whether the man or woman is qualified for the job in question. But the write-up of the case represents an extension of his decision-making. As he records the findings, he becomes more definitive in his value judgments and hence is normally able to assign a more precise rating to the candidate's qualifications. The case write-up forces the interviewer to weigh all the relevant factors, and as a consequence he is usually in a much better position to decide whether the applicant's qualifications merit a slightly above-average rating, a well-above-average rating, or perhaps an excellent rating.

Because the recording of interview findings represents such an essential aspect of the entire process, the Interview Rating Form should be completed immediately after the candidate leaves the room. With all the essential facts still fresh in his mind, the interviewer usually finds it possible to complete the form within forty-five minutes. If he postpones this task, twice the amount of time may be required, and he may be unable subsequently to recall all the salient information.

In writing up the Interview Rating Form, use the space provided under each interview area for recording major findings pertinent to that area. Since the space is obviously limited, the interviewer will have to decide which findings in each area contribute most to understanding the applicant's behavior and to his over-all qualifications for the job in question.

The recording of interview results should not be confined to facts alone, since many of these facts will already have appeared on the application blank. Rather, the interviewer should try to indicate his interpretation of these facts, in terms of the extent to which they may provide clues to the individual's personality, motivation, or character.

Writing Up Work History
Data should be recorded chronologically, in much the same way as it is obtained during the interview. Thus, there

should be a brief treatment of early jobs, followed by a discussion of post-college jobs in chronological order. Because of space limitations, early jobs may be treated as a group rather than discussed singly.

The discussion should be primarily *interpretive*, drawing upon factual information to highlight clues to personality, motivation, and character. Obviously, it is impossible to draw off meaningful interpretations from every single fact presented, but clues to behavior should nevertheless be sprinkled frequently throughout the discussion of work history.

At the end of the work history discussion, the interviewer should be sure to indicate what he thinks of the applicant's work experience and how relevant he believes it is in terms of the job for which he is being considered. The following represents an example of how work experience should be recorded on the Interview Rating Form:

> Early jobs (lifeguard, pressing apples, part-time farming) provided an introduction to work but did not seem to extend him to any great degree or to do a great deal for his development.
>
> Worked two summers (fork-lift operator, testing carburetors) but did not find either job very interesting.
>
> Enlisted in the Navy in 1963 just prior to taking exams that would have graduated him from college—apparently in a fit of anger because the college failed to extend a loan. This obviously reflected poor judgment, immaturity, quick temper, and impulsiveness. Did radar and missile electronics maintenance in the Navy and thus acquired relevant experience with electrical hardware. Elected to stay on two more years after four-year enlistment "because I could earn $75 more a month and go overseas." This seems to reflect some lack of initiative in the sense that he took the path of least resistance. Did not have any significant leadership experience. Says he "does not like to offend people" and admits to a lack of confidence and mental toughness.

Now earning $11,500 at Crocker Electronics, doing testing work in the Manufacturing Section. Has enjoyed his work over the past year but now wants something "more professional" such as design or field engineering.

Although he does have some good electrical hardware experience, job history is not impressive for a man of thirty-one, reflecting some lack of drive as well as some failure to make maximum utilization of his abilities.

After completing his write-up of the work-history area, the interviewer should assign a rating to this area by placing a check mark on the horizontal line that extends across the top of this area. Note that the horizontal line represents a continuum, in the sense that the check mark can be placed at any point on the line—directly over any of the descriptive adjectives or, for example, between "average" and "above average." The rating should be made in terms of the job that appears in the upper right-hand corner of the form—the job for which the applicant is being considered. In cases where most of the interpretive comments are favorable, an "above average" rating would normally be expected. If the majority of comments are unfavorable, a "below average" rating would normally be indicated. Where favorable and unfavorable comments are about equally weighted in terms of their importance, an "average" rating would usually be made.

Writing Up Education and Training

As in the case of the treatment of the work history, educational data should also be recorded in chronological order. This means that initially there should be a discussion of high school followed by a treatment of the college experience. Any graduate experience should of course be recorded last.

Again, the recorded information should be largely interpretive, with a liberal use of factual data for documentation.

Thus, actual grades and class standings should be noted here. Be sure to record extracurricular activities as well as the extent to which the individual seems to have applied himself.

Here, as in the previous area, be sure to indicate names of schools, employers, and the like. This report should be sufficiently complete so that the reader does not have to refer to the application blank for additional information. An example of the manner in which the educational information should be recorded appears below:

> Did very well at Moravian High School, ranking eighth in a class of seventy. Apparently made this achievement without any unusual effort. Played basketball one year and made letter in track but otherwise not active in extracurricular affairs.
>
> Majored in electrical engineering at the University of Rhode Island and did well during the first three years, maintaining better than a "B" average (3.5 out of 4.0 during the first year), but, because she did not take her examinations in her fourth year, was given three "E's" and one D. This brought her overall average down to 2.4. Was a member of a college sorority but held no offices. Nor did she follow up on the athletic activities she had begun during her secondary schoolwork.
>
> Had the good sense to return to the University of Rhode Island after getting out of the Navy and apparently worked somewhat harder. During this last year, she made one A, three B's, three C's, and one D. Enjoyed and did well in most of her electrical engineering courses but had trouble with some of the more abstract and theoretical subjects like thermodynamics.
>
> Now working on a master's degree in electrical engineering at Northeastern but is only attending school one night a week.
>
> Seems well-trained academically. Educational record reflects a good but not outstanding intellect. Probably would

have done better still if she had applied herself more diligently.

Once the interpretive comments have been recorded in this area, the interviewer should assign his rating on the line at the top, in accordance with suggestions discussed above in connection with the rating of work history.

Writing Up Early Home Background

Because of the space limitations here, much of the recorded information should be concerned with the *effects* of the early influences on the individual's initial growth and development. Thus, if too much is said about the parents and siblings, there will not be enough room to record how the early influences may have affected the applicant's behavior. The following represents an illustration of the manner in which early home background data should be recorded:

> Father, a very successful sales manager of a national company, is apparently an extremely dominant, inflexible, opinionated, and hard-driving man. Mother died when applicant was six years old, and the father remarried soon thereafter. However, applicant apparently got along well with stepmother whom he describes as a "saint."
>
> But father was so dominant and made so many of the son's decisions that applicant probably did not develop as normally as might otherwise have been the case. To this day, he has some lack of self-confidence and is not as aggressive or tough-minded as might be desirable. Too, he tends to be moody when things do not go well.
>
> On the positive side, though, he does seem to have acquired his father's penchant for hard work and to have developed high moral and ethical standards.

After recording the appropriate interpretive comments in

this area, the interviewer should again assign a rating by placing a check mark on the horizontal line at the top.

Writing Up Present Social Adjustment

Interpretive comments in this area should be concerned primarily with value judgments as to the man's or woman's interests, financial stability, and health. Illustration of such comments appears below:

> Interests fairly broad and somewhat intellectual—reads five or six books a month, like to make her own clothes, has student license as a pilot, and enjoys listening to classical music.
>
> Seems responsible financially—has saved $1,850 and is still paying off college loans.
>
> Health apparently good, although she is quite overweight.
>
> Energy level is admittedly no better than average and, in truth, may be somewhat less than average.
>
> Seems something of a "loner" and not altogether happy, raising a question concerning her emotional adjustment.

Again, after recording the appropriate information in this area, the interviewer should assign a rating to the area by placing a check mark at the appropriate point on the horizontal line at the top.

Rating Personality, Character, and Motivation

Each of the fourteen traits listed under this area is preceded by a set of parentheses. This permits the interviewer to assign a rating to each trait. As in the case of ratings made in all the other interview areas, value judgments should be formulated in terms of the demands of the job for which a person is being considered. Using a five-point scale, the interviewer places a + in the parentheses if he believes that the applicant has a high degree of the trait in question, an A+ if he thinks that the individual has an above-average amount of the trait, an A in the parentheses if he believes the applicant has an "average" or adequate amount of the trait, an A— if he thinks that the applicant has a below-average degree of the trait, and a — if he thinks the individual is seriously lacking in that characteristic. If the interviewer is unable to make up his mind about a given trait or, if the particular trait has no relevance in terms of the job under consideration, he leaves the parentheses blank.

In devising a form such as the Interview Rating Form, it is of course impossible to include all the traits of personality, motivation, and character that should be considered in evaluating applicant characteristics for a wide range of jobs. The fourteen characteristics listed on this particular form simply represent some of the traits which experience has shown to be most relevant in assessing applicants for high-level jobs in general. Other characteristics deemed of particular importance in a given case can be listed as representing either a strength or a weakness on Section VI of the Interview Rating Form, summary of assets and of liabilities.

In rating an applicant on traits of personality, motivation, and character, the interviewer is called upon to summarize his thinking, in terms of the variety of clues to these traits that have come to light as a result of his discussion of the man's work history, education and training, early home background, present social adjustment, and self-evaluation. To take a specific example, his rating of the applicant as a "hard worker" will be based upon such considerations as the extent to which he seems to have applied himself on his various jobs, the amount of effort he gave to his studies in school, the extent to which he may have developed sound work habits as an adolescent, and his capacity for constructive effort as reflected in his outside interests or in his demonstrated ability to carry a heavy academic load in night school while working on a full-time job during the day.

The material presented below is designed to aid the interviewer in thinking through the various kinds of information that might be used to support a rating on each of the fourteen traits listed on the back of the Interview Guide. It is of course impossible to produce an exhaustive list of items that could conceivably merit consideration in rating an applicant for a given job on each of these traits. Hence, the questions appearing below under each trait are designed simply to stimulate the interviewer's thinking, in terms of the kind of positive and negative information that would ordinarily be factored into the rating of that trait. Items preceded by a minus sign represent examples of unfavorable findings with respect to a given trait; those preceded by a plus sign represent examples of favorable or positive findings.

MATURITY

— Any tendency to rationalize his failures?

+ Has he learned to accept his limitations and live with them?

— Chronic dissatisfaction with job duties and working conditions, reflecting an inability to take the bitter with the sweet?

+ Well-formulated vocational goals?

— Though in his late twenties, still living at home with parents?

+ Responsible attitude toward his family?

— Overly protected and sheltered as a child?

— Effort in school confined only to those studies which he liked?

+ Good financial stability?

EMOTIONAL ADJUSTMENT

+ Has he shown an ability to maintain composure in the face of frustration?

+ Has he been able to maintain his emotional balance and

mental health in the face of trying personal circumstances, such as a cronically ill wife?

— Have there been problems with supervisors, teachers, parents, or the marital partner which reflected a decided tendency to "fly off the handle"?

+ Is he able to deal with the shortcomings of subordinates calmly and patiently?

— Is he admittedly moody and inclined to experience more than the normal degree of ups and downs?

— Is he inclined to sulk in the face of criticism?

— Do current marital difficulties seem to stem in part from his tendency to be sarcastic or hotheaded?

+ Is there considerable evidence that he does not allow his emotions to color his judgment?

TEAMWORKER

+ Does he seem to have operated successfully as a member of a team, in connection with sports activities in school, community activities in the neighborhood, or group activities on the job?

— Is he strongly motivated to be the "star" of the team, taking more than his share of credit for accomplishments?

+ Does he seem to place the accomplishments of the group ahead of his personal feelings and ambitions?

— Did he have difficulty getting along with his associates while in the Army or Navy?

+ Does he have the degree of tact and social sensitivity necessary for the establishment and maintenance of good interpersonal relations with other members of a team?

— Does he show any pronounced tendency to be inflexible, intolerant, or opinionated?

TACT

+ Does the manner in which he has phrased his remarks during the interview reflect tact and consideration for the interviewer?

— Has he talked disparagingly about minority groups without any real knowledge as to whether or not the interviewer himself may be a member of such groups?

— Has he made a number of remarks during the interview that have been unduly blunt and direct?

+ In discussing his relationships with subordinates, does he seem to have reflected genuine consideration for their feelings?

+ Is he sensitive to the reactions of others to the extent that he is able to structure his approach without antagonizing them?

+ Does he show any evidence of being a good listener?

ADAPTABILITY

+ Did he adjust easily to Army or Navy life?

+ Has he shown a liking for jobs involving contact with many types of people and diverse situations?

+ Has he shown an ability to handle a number of job assignments simultaneously?

+ Has he demonstrated the ability to move from one job to a completely different kind of job without undue difficulty?

— Was he unable to do well in certain subjects "because of the teacher"?

— Was he raised in a provincial home atmosphere where there was relatively limited exposure to diverse situations and different types of people?

— Does his approach to a job reflect such a tendency to be a perfectionist that he has to do everything "just so"?

TOUGH-MINDEDNESS

— Does he have a strong dislike for disciplining subordinates?

+ Is he willing to take a stand for what he thinks is right?

+ Has he demonstrated an ability to make decisions involving people that, of necessity, work to the disadvantage of the few but have to be made for the good of the many?

— Is he insufficiently demanding of subordinates, in the sense that he is reluctant to ask them to work overtime or to "push" them to some extent when there is a job to be done within a certain deadline?

— Is he a product of a soft, sheltered, early life where there was little opportunity to become conditioned to the seamier side of existence?

— Does he give the impression of being too sympathetic or overly concerned about the feelings of others?

+ Is he willing to delegate responsibilities even though inadequate performance on the tasks delegated may reflect directly upon him?

SELF-DISCIPLINE

— Has he shown a tendency to procrastinate unduly in carrying out the less-pleasant jobs assigned him?

+ In connection with his academic career, has he shown a willingness to apply himself diligently to those courses which he disliked?

— Did he fail to take full advantage of academic opportunities because he was not able to make himself "dig deeply enough" really to understand the subject?

+ Does he assume his share of civic responsibility, even though community activities in general do not appeal to him?

— Has he been so conditioned by a soft, easy life that there has been relatively little need to cope with difficult problems or situations?

+ Has he demonstrated a willingness to give first attention to those important aspects of a job which are perhaps of less interest to him?

INITIATIVE

+ Has he demonstrated an ability to operate successfully without close supervision?

— Does he show a dislike for situations that have not been structured for him?

+ Does he reach out for ever-increasing responsibility?

+ Is there any evidence to indicate that he is a self-starter, in the sense that he does not have to wait to be told what to do?

— Does he seem to have fallen into a job rut, in the sense that he has been unwilling to extricate himself from a dead-end situation?

+ Has he demonstrated a willingness to depart from the *status quo* in order to accomplish a given task in a new and perhaps more efficient manner?

FOLLOW-THROUGH

+ Did he show perseverance in college by completing his undergraduate work despite a lack of good scholastic aptitude?

— Has he changed jobs too frequently?

+ Once he starts a job, does he continue with it until it has been completed, resisting any tendency to become distracted?

+ Has he completed an appreciable portion of his college education by going to school at night?

— Does he find it inordinately difficult to complete tasks on his own, such as correspondence courses where he does not have the stimulation of group effort?

— Is there evidence to support the view that he starts more things than he can finish?

SELF-CONFIDENCE

— Was confidence undermined by overly demanding parents who tended to be perfectionists?

+ Does he reflect a realistic appraisal of his abilities and a willingness to take action?

— During the early years was he unable to compete successfully with those of his own age in athletics or in academic affairs?

+ Does his general manner reflect poise and presence?
− Did he suffer in comparison with a brighter brother or sister?
− Did he grow up in the shadow of a very successful father?
+ Does he have sufficient confidence in his assets so that he is willing to discuss his shortcomings objectively?
− Has he been reluctant to take on additional job responsibility because of fear of failure?
− Did he limit his extracurricular activities in school because of a fear of lack of acceptance on the part of his classmates?

PERSONAL FORCEFULNESS

+ Does his personality have considerable impact?
+ Has he done a considerable amount of participation in contact sports where aggressiveness represented an important requisite?
− Has he shown a tendency to let others take advantage of him because of lack of self-assertiveness?
+ Has he operated successfully in sales, expediting, or production supervision—types of jobs conducive to the development of personal forcefulness?
+ Is his history replete with evidences of leadership in school, on the job, or in connection with activities in the community?
− Does he tend to be introverted in the sense that he shies away from group activity?

CONSCIENTIOUSNESS

+ Did he show conscientiousness in school by doing more than was actually required by the teachers, in order to satisfy his own standards?
− Does his record on the job reflect a tendency to let things slide?
+ Is he inclined upon occasion to work evenings and week-

ends, even though this is not actually required by his supervisor?

— Does he tend to be a clock-watcher?

+ Does he have high personal standards of workmanship?

HARD WORKER

+ Has his history been such that he has become conditioned to hard work and long hours?

+ Did he get good grades in school despite limited mental ability?

+ Did he earn a relatively high percentage of his college expenses?

— Does his general manner seem phlegmatic, reflecting a possible below-average energy level?

— Has he shown a strong dislike of overtime work?

+ Has he had any experiences that may have extended his capacity for constructive effort, such as going to school at night while carrying on a full-time job during the day?

— Does he seem always to look for the easy way out?

+ Does he seem to be in excellent health, reflecting a considerable amount of vigor and stamina?

HONESTY AND SINCERITY

+ Was his early home environment such that he developed good moral and ethical standards?

+ Has he "come clean" during the interview discussion, in the sense that he has shown a willingness to talk about the unfavorable aspects of his background as well as the favorable aspects?

— Is there any evidence to support the view that he is exclusively oriented in the direction of personal gain, to the point that he does not develop strong loyalties to any organization or perhaps even to his own family?

+ Is he willing to give credit where credit is due?

— Does he seem to derive satisfaction from the discussion

of situations where he has been able to get the better of the other fellow or to "pull a fast one"?
— Does he have any appreciable tendency to exaggerate his own accomplishments?
— Does his story seem to be inconsistent in terms of other selection findings, such as information developed from the application form, the preliminary interview, the aptitude tests, or the reference checkups?

After completing the ratings on the fourteen traits of personality, motivation, and character, assign an over-all rating to this area by placing a check mark at the appropriate point on the horizontal line at the top. In making this rating, the interviewer will of course be guided by the preponderance of pluses or minuses, as the case may be. At the same time, he should not add the pluses and minuses algebraically, since certain traits obviously merit a greater weighting than others. For example, a minus rating on "honesty and sincerity" would undoubtedly be sufficient to outweigh plus ratings on all the other traits. Moreover, certain traits such as maturity, emotional adjustment, and willingness to work hard are more important to job success than traits such as tact, tough-mindedness, or personal forcefulness. In assigning an over-all rating on this area, the interviewer must also be guided by the demands of the job for which the candidate is being considered. The trait of personal forcefulness, for example, would be given more weight in the case of a man being considered for production supervision than in the case of an applicant being evaluated for a job as office manager.

Writing Up the Summary of Assets and Shortcomings

Items listed under assets and shortcomings in this section of the Interview Rating Form should be concerned with the most important findings, in terms of the applicant's over-all qualifications. And these items, for the most part, should in themselves represent a summation of a number of individual factors. For example, the interviewer would list as an asset an item such as "effective sales personality," rather than trying to list all the factors of which the so-called "sales personality" is composed—factors like aggressiveness, sense of humor, poise, presence, social sensitivity, and persuasiveness.

The summary of assets and shortcomings should include major findings from all the selection steps, with special emphasis of course on aptitude tests and interview results. Thus, in addition to principal interview findings, this section should include any available test results such as mental ability, verbal ability, numerical ability, mechanical comprehension, or clerical aptitude. The interviewer should also combine test and interview findings in such a way that he summarizes the *quality* of the applicant's thinking. Items concerned with quality of thinking would of course be expressed in such terms as: analytical ability, ability to plan and organize, criticalness of thinking, and intellectual breadth and depth.

In writing up the summary of assets and shortcomings, the interviewer should select items of particular importance in terms of the job for which the candidate is being considered. Thus, in addition to listing appropriate items of ability, personality, motivation, and character, he should always note the relevance of the candidate's work history and educational preparation.

Writing the Over-all Summary

In the space found at the bottom of the reverse side of the Interview Rating Form, the interviewer writes a brief summary of the candidate's qualifications for the job in question. This takes the form of three paragraphs—the first paragraph devoted to a summation of the applicant's principal assets, a second paragraph which describes his most serious short-comings, and a third paragraph in which the interviewer seeks to resolve the major assets and shortcomings in such a way that he shows whether the assets outweigh his short-comings or vice versa. And, in this third and final paragraph, he shows how he arrives at his over-all rating. The three para-graphs of the over-all summary will of course draw upon the summary of assets and the summary of shortcomings which appear above. Hence, there will be some obvious redundancy but every effort should be made to word the summary in such a way that the individual seems to "come to life" as a unique person. An example of an appropriately worded over-all summary appears below.

Harland Smith deserves credit for doing as well as he has in the light of the unfavorable influences brought to bear upon him in early life. In spite of this, he seems to have developed good traits of moral character as well as a high degree of perseverance. That he eventually made it through college represents something of a monument to the latter trait. Harland has a relatively good intellect, possesses a good mathematical aptitude, and is quite well-trained academically. He has also acquired some good, relevant electrical hardware experience.

Unfortunately, however, Harland has never learned to make full utilization of his abilities, primarily because he is not strongly motivated. He seems to ask relatively little out of life, and hence it does not take a great deal to satisfy him. This means of course that his personal standards are not as high as might be desired. Harland does not express himself well and does not have a great amount of analytical power. Because he is still very inhibited and insecure, he does not have much in the way of leadership strength. Finally, he is not particularly well-adjusted emotionally.

In summary, Harland does not represent an especially good employment risk. He is probably capable of doing quite an adequate job in product-support organization as a field service engineer but, even there, he does not rank above some of the other men currently available for employment. Certainly, Harland is not at all qualified for design work. Nor does he seem to have a great deal of long-range potential for moving up to higher-level responsibilities in our organization.

Making the Over-all Rating

By placing a check mark on the line at the bottom of the reverse side of the Interview Rating Form, the interviewer makes the final selection decision. In so doing, he weighs the evidence that has been accumulated from all the selection steps. Thus, he not only considers the ratings he has made in each of the six major interview areas on the Interview Rating Form but also bears in mind all pertinent information that has been derived from the preliminary interview, the application blank, the aptitude tests, and the reference checkups.

In making his final rating, the interviewer will of course be guided by the extent to which the applicant's assets outweigh his liabilities, or vice versa. Remember, no applicant is expected to possess all the qualifications listed in the man specifications for a given job. The interviewer's task is to weigh the strength of the applicant's assets against the severity of his shortcomings. The interviewer asks himself how much the candidate's shortcomings are likely to handicap him in the job for which he is being considered. And, at the same time, he estimates the extent to which the individual's assets should help him to turn in a successful job performance.

The interviewer must remember, too, that assets of considerable strength may compensate for certain shortcomings.

For example, in some cases strong motivation, relevant work experience, and good intellectual qualifications may compensate for below-average educational preparation. In such instances, an "above average" over-all rating might be justified, despite the "below average" rating on education and training.

As pointed out earlier in this chapter, however, certain liabilities may be so damaging to the candidate's cause that they disqualify the individual regardless of the number of favorable ratings in other categories. An applicant decidedly lacking in honesty and sincerity, for example, or one exceedingly immature would undoubtedly merit a low over-all rating despite the number of high ratings he may have been given in other important areas.

In assigning a final, over-all rating, the interviewer thinks in broad terms. Does the person have the appropriate skills to handle the job? Is he willing to work hard and apply these skills? Has he demonstrated ability to get along with people? Is he basically a person of good character? In addition to these broad considerations, the interviewer may have to factor into his decision some important specific items, such as evidence of serious health limitations.

Over-all ratings are of course made in terms of the job demands. In other words, an over-all rating of "average" means that the candidate should be able to turn in an average job performance, not much better and not much worse. Applicants rated "above average" should be able to turn in a good performance, while those rated "excellent" should, in the interviewer's opinion, be able to do a top-notch job.

The over-all rating of "excellent" is normally reserved for applicants who have a great many assets and whose shortcomings are not at all serious. People rated "above average" are well-qualified individuals whose shortcomings, while a little more serious than the excellently rated person, are not serious enough to handicap them unduly. Candidates rated "average" are those whose assets and liabilities are about equally weighted. However, none of their shortcomings should be serious enough to keep them from turning in an adequate or average job performance.

Ideally, only those individuals with excellent or above-average ratings should be hired. In a tight labor market, however, it may be necessary to employ a number of applicants with only "average" qualifications. Candidates rated "below average" or "poor" should not be hired under any circumstances, both in terms of the good of the organization and in terms of the long-range benefits to the individuals themselves.

In making the final decision, the interviewer should be guided by one further consideration—the applicant's potential for further growth and development. Thus, although the candidate's qualifications for a given job may be only "average" at the present time, he may be a person of such potential that he could one day become a most productive employee. The age of the individual of course represents an important factor in this connection.

FURTHER USES OF THE COMPLETED INTERVIEW RATING FORM

In the case of those individuals who are employed, the completed Interview Rating Form becomes an important part of the employee's permanent file. And since the individual's shortcomings have been carefully recorded, this information can become the basis for his further development. Apprised of the new employee's developmental needs, his supervisor can take immediate steps to help him from the day he reports to the job.

The completed Interview Rating Form also can provide

the basis for follow-up studies designed to improve the selection procedures. The over-all interviewer rating can be subsequently compared with performance on the job. Such follow-up information helps the interviewer to identify his own interviewing weaknesses and makes it possible for him to make an effort to eliminate these weaknesses in his future discussions with other applicants. Moreover, follow-up studies of this kind enable the employment manager to evaluate his interviewing staff, in terms of both additional training needs and possible reassignment to other employment functions.

Interview Guide

INTERVIEW GUIDE

Name _____ Date _____ Interviewer _____

1. WORK HISTORY

a. Duties?

b. Likes?

c. Things found less satisfying?

d. Conditioned to work?

e. Level of earnings?

f. Reasons for changing jobs?

g. Any leadership experience?

h. Number of previous jobs?

i. Achievements?

j. Development needs?

k. Factors of job satisfaction?

l. Type of job desired?

2. EDUCATION AND TRAINING

a. Best – poorest subjects?

b. Grades?

c. College Boards?

d. Extracurricular activities?

e. How much effort?

f. Special achievements?

g. Training beyond the under-
    graduate level?

h. How was education financed?

(continued)

3. EARLY HOME BACKGROUND

a. Father's and mother's occupations?

b. Temperament of parents?

c. Number of brothers and sisters?

d. How strictly raised?

e. Earliest age partially or
wholly financially independent?

f. Effects of early home influences?

4. PRESENT SOCIAL ADJUSTMENT

a. Present interests and hobbies?

b. Spouse's interests and personality?

c. Spouse's attitude toward relocating?

d. Attitude toward dependents?

e. Financial stability?

f. Health status?

g. Energy level?

5. PERSONALITY, MOTIVATION, AND CHARACTER
   (+, A+, A, A−, −)

( ) a. Maturity ( ) f. Tough-mindedness ( ) k. Personal forcefulness

( ) b. Emotional adjustment ( ) g. Self-discipline

( ) h. Initiative ( ) l. Conscientiousness

( ) c. Team worker ( ) i. Follow-through ( ) m. Hard worker

( ) d. Tact ( ) j. Self-confidence ( ) n. Honesty and sincerity

( ) e. Adaptability

INTERVIEW GUIDE

Name_____Date_____Interviewer_____

1. WORK HISTORY

a. Duties?

b. Likes?

c. Things found less satisfying?

d. Conditioned to work?

e. Level of earnings?

f. Reasons for changing jobs?

g. Any leadership experience?

h. Number of previous jobs?

i. Achievements? "What did you learn about your strengths as a result of working on those jobs? Did you find, for example, that you worked harder than the average person, got along better with people, organized things better, gave more attention to detail—just what?"

j. Development needs? "Did you get any clues to your development needs as a result of working on those jobs? You know, we all have some shortcomings and, the person who can recognize them, can do something about them. Was there a need to acquire more self-confidence, more tact, more self-discipline—to become firmer with people— just what?"

k. Factors of job satisfaction? "What does a job have to have to give you satisfaction? Some people look for money, some for security, some want to manage, some want to create—what is important to you?"

l. Type of job desired?

(continued)

2. EDUCATION AND TRAINING

a. Best and poorest subjects?

b. Grades? "What about grades? Were they average, above average, or perhaps a little below average?"

c. College Boards? "What were your College Board scores?"

d. Extracurricular activities?

e. How much effort? "How conscientious a student were you? Did you work about as hard as the average person, a little harder, or perhaps not quite so hard?"

f. Special achievements?

g. Training beyond the undergraduate level?

h. How was education financed?

3. EARLY HOME BACKGROUND

a. Father's and mother's occupations? (socio-economic level)

b. Temperament of parents? "How would you describe your father at the time you were growing up? Was he calm or quick tempered, aggressive or unaggressive, extroverted or introverted? How would you describe your mother?"

c. Number of brothers and sisters? "Were you and your brother quite a lot alike in personality or perhaps somewhat different?"

d. How strictly raised? (parental guidance) "Would you say that you were raised fairly strictly or perhaps not quite so much so?"

e. Earliest age partially or wholly financially independent?

f. Effects of early home influences? "What effects do you think the early influences had on your early growth and development?"

(continued)

4. PRESENT SOCIAL ADJUSTMENT

a. Present interests and hobbies? Reading, sports, community participation, the arts.

b. Spouse's interests and personality? "Is your wife or husband quite like you as far as personality is concerned or perhaps somewhat different?"

c. Spouse's attitude toward relocating?

d. Attitude toward dependents?

e. Financial stability? (housing, insurance, etc.) "Has there been any opportunity to acquire a little financial reserve?"

f. Health status? (physical vigor and stamina) "What about health? Have you had a physical check-up recently?"

g. Energy level? "How would you describe your energy level—as average, above average, or perhaps a little below average?"

5. PERSONALITY, MOTIVATION, AND CHARACTER
   (+, A+, A, A−, −)

( ) a. Maturity
( ) b. Emotional
         adjustment
( ) c. Team worker
( ) d. Tact
( ) e. Adaptability

( ) f. Tough-mindedness
( ) g. Self-discipline
( ) h. Initiative
( ) i. Follow-through
( ) j. Self-confidence
( ) k. Personal forcefulness

( ) l. Conscientiousness

( ) m. Hard worker
( ) n. Honesty and
          sincerity

Interview Rating Form

INTERVIEW RATING FORM

Date_____

Interviewer_____

Name_____Age_____Position_____

1. WORK HISTORY

_____
Above avg. *Avg.* *Below avg.*

2. EDUCATION AND TRAINING

_____
Above avg. *Avg.* *Below avg.*

3. EARLY HOME BACKGROUND

_____
Above avg. *Avg.* *Below avg.*

(Front of form.)

4. PRESENT SOCIAL ADJUSTMENT _____

Above avg.   *Avg.*   *Below avg.*

5. PERSONALITY, MOTIVATION,
   AND CHARACTER
   (+, A+, A, A−, −)   *Above avg.*   *Avg.*   *Below avg.*

( ) a. Maturity   ( ) f. Tough-mindedness   ( ) l. Conscientious-
( ) b. Emotional   ( ) g. Self-discipline   ness
       adjustment   ( ) h. Initiative   ( ) m. Hard worker
                    ( ) i. Follow-through   ( ) n. Honesty and
( ) c. Teamworker   ( ) j. Self-confident   sincerity
( ) d. Tact   ( ) k. Personal
( ) e. Adaptability   Forcefulness

6. SUMMARY OF ASSETS	SUMMARY OF SHORTCOMINGS

7. OVERALL SUMMARY

8. OVERALL RATING _____

Excellent Above Average Average Below Average Poor

Illustrative Reports of Interview Findings

	Date _____
INTERVIEW RATING FORM	Interviewer W. Crocker

Name ___Mary Warden___ Age _22_ Position ___Engineering Design___

1. WORK HISTORY

	X	
Above avg.	*Avg.*	*Below avg.*

Took her first job at the age of 16 as a dishwasher in a restaurant owned by her father. This involved hard manual labor and sometimes as many as 60 hours a week. This represented good introduction to the "work-a-day world".

Worked every subsequent summer through high school and the first two years of college as a clerk in a supermarket. To her credit, she managed to save as much as $800 each summer. Mary enjoyed her people contacts and seemed to be motivated to do her work to the best of her ability—apparently has high work standards. The fact that the supermarket rehired her several summers in a row would seem to attest to the fact that she was a very satisfactory worker.

Last summer worked for Westinghouse as an expediter in the shop. Not very happy with this because it did not draw upon her engineering training. Admits, though, that she "did not show much initiative in trying to get a better assignment." She also felt that the job had "too much pressure for me," raising some question concerning her emotional adjustment. Again, evidently got along well with people but did not press hard enough in her expediting function, reflecting some lack of aggressiveness, self confidence and mental toughness.

The fact that Mary sees herself as managerial material in spite of her lack of leadership characteristics shows that she does not know herself and is somewhat immature.

Mary's work experience is of course rather limited but she is nevertheless conditioned to work.

2. EDUCATION AND TRAINING

	X	
Above avg.	*Avg.*	*Below avg.*

Did exceptionally well in high school, graduating third in a class of 458 and doing her best work in math and science. College Boards were 630 verbal (good) and 745 math (exceptional). Because she was very shy, Mary did not take part in extracurricular activities and did not date boys.

(continued)

Studied very hard at Swarthmore—a top school—and made outstanding grades (3.7 out of a possible 4.0), winning election to Tau Beta Pi during her junior year and graduating magna cum laude. Mary majored in electrical engineering and enjoyed all of the more theoretically oriented courses such as thermodynamics, circuitry, and higher math—a strong clue to her ability to think in the abstract. Also enjoyed and did well in her design courses. Began to "blossom out a bit" in college, becoming more social and beginning to date more frequently. But she almost left college one semester because she was "upset over a relationship with a boy," again raising some question concerning her emotional adjustment.

Mary made an exceptional record at a top school and hence is unusually well trained academically. Obviously, too, she has superior intelligence both with respect to quantity and quality (analytical, perceptive, critical).

3. EARLY HOME BACKGROUND

	X	
Above avg.	*Avg.*	*Below avg.*

Mary is a product of a small town, provincial early home background. Her father, a high school graduate, made good vocational progress in a glove manufacturing company, eventually becoming supervisor of the making department. He went on from there to develop his own restaurant business.

Mary thinks of her mother as "very dominant and possessive." She evidently raised her very strictly and made too many of her decisions for her.

Both parents expected a lot of Mary and fostered a deep-seated conscientiousness as well as good moral and ethical standards.

But the over-protected nature of her upbringing seems to have retarded her development in such areas as maturity, self-confidence, and personal forcefulness.

4. PRESENT SOCIAL ADJUSTMENT

	X	
Above avg.	*Avg.*	*Below avg.*

Mary seems gradually to be coming "out of her shell" now that she has been away from home for a few years. While working for Westinghouse last summer, for example, she shared an apartment with another engineering student, dated more often, and was even active on the company softball team.

As might be expected, Mary's interests are largely intellectual in nature. She reads 3 or 4 good books a month, enjoys classical music, and likes to play chess.

(continued)

Mary's physical health and energy level appear to be good. But she takes things too seriously and tends to worry more than she should. Happily, though, she seems to be improving in this area also. Things apparently no longer "get her down" to the extent that they used to.

It seems clear that Mary's social adjustment is improving but still needs further development.

5. PERSONALITY, MOTIVATION,
   AND CHARACTER
   (+, A+, A, A−, −)

	X	
Above avg.	*Avg.*	*Below avg.*

(A−) a. Maturity   (−) f. Tough-mindedness   (+) l. Conscientiousness

(A−) b. Emotional   (+) g. Self-discipline

       adjustment   (A) h. Initiative   (A+) m. Hard worker

(A+) c. Teamworker   (A+) i. Follow-through   (+) n. Honesty and

(+) d. Tact   (A−) j. Self-confidence   sincerity

(A) e. Adaptability   (−) k. Personal
                                forcefulness

6. SUMMARY OF ASSETS   SUMMARY OF SHORTCOMINGS

a. Excellent mental ability   a. Lacks leadership ability

b. Superior math aptitude   b. Somewhat immature for her age

c. Analytical and perceptive   c. Some question concerning her

d. Good intellectual depth   emotional adjustment

e. Generally good motivation

f. Exceptionally well trained technically

g. Gets along well with people

h. Good character

(continued)

7. OVERALL SUMMARY

Mary Warden has a great deal to recommend her. She is bright mentally, has a superior math aptitude, and is uncommonly well trained as an electrical engineer. Equipped with a high degree of analytical power, Mary is perceptive and has quite a lot of intellectual depth. She is capable of solving complex problems and shows some promise of being creative. Because of her tact and social sensitivity, she normally gets along with people very well. The kind of a person who has built-in high standards, Mary is very conscientious and likes to do things to the best of her ability.

On the negative side of the picture, Mary is somewhat immature, due in part to certain unfavorable factors in her early home background. As a consequence, for example, she aspires to a management position despite the fact that she is decidedly lacking in some of the most important management requisites—self-confidence, personal forcefulness, toughmindedness, and initiative. Because she is not quite as well adjusted emotionally as might be desired, moreover, there is some question as to how well she can stand up under pressure.

In summary, although Mary has little promise as a potential manager, she is very well qualified for the role of individual contributor—particularly in the engineering design area. She is definitely a "late bloomer" and now seems to be developing quite rapidly. Employment is definitely recommended.

8. OVERALL RATING   X

Excellent   Above Average   Average   Below Average   Poor

INTERVIEW RATING FORM	Date_____
	Interviewer R. Kelley

Name Harry Ritter_____ Age 28 Position Manufacturing Supervision_____

1. WORK HISTORY

	X_____
	Above avg. *Avg.* *Below avg.*

Started working for father at the age of 14 doing construction work and continued after school, Saturdays and summers until he was 17, by which time he "could lay 375 building blocks a day"—excellent conditioning to hard work.

Joined the Army at 19 when his money ran out at the end of his first year at Boston U. Motivated by a "burning desire to be best," he became top man in a basic training class of 380 men. Progressed rapidly from personnel specialist to head of administrative procedures, supervising 20 men. Apparently gained reputation as a "doer" but consistently disliked paper work, raising a question concerning his attention to detail. Had a "personality conflict" with his boss, perhaps because of some inflexibility and a desire to do things his own way. But he made a good record of accomplishment in the Army and got out in Feb. 1968 with the rank of Sgt.

Went to work for Elmer Electric in March 1968 in production control at $575 a month. Disliked the detail in this job and showed initiative in his efforts to get a transfer to asst. foreman. Now earning $800 a month as a foreman. Apparently has earned a reputation for getting things done but admits that he sometimes "pushes people too hard," thus reflecting some lack of tact and social sensitivity. Now looking for another job because Elmer Electric has lost a big government contract and will have to lay off 35% of its employees.

Has an impressive record of work accomplishment for a man of 28, having acquired some relevant experience with electrical hardware and some good supervisory exp. as well.

2. EDUCATION AND TRAINING

	X
	Above avg. *Avg.* *Below avg.*

Graduated in upper third of H.S. class. Liked math but had some difficulty with English and History. College Boards: math 675 (very good), verbal 550 (fair). No time for extracurricular activities because of after-school job.

Made 3.1 out of possible 4.0 during 1st yr. at Boston University, apparently studying very hard and devoting complete effort and attention to his studies.

(continued)

Deserves great credit for taking extension courses (Univ. of Maryland) during 5 of his six years in the Army, demonstrating initiative, maturity, and self discipline. Accumulated 40 hours of college credit in that way.

Now attending Northwestern at night, working on a degree in industrial mgt. Grades are "just over a B." Has accumulated 113 credits toward this degree.

Harry's academic record seems more a result of strong motivation than high-level intellect but his mental ability is undoubtedly somewhat above average for college-trained people.

Harry cannot be considered as well trained academically because he does not yet have a college degree but he must be given credit for having done the best he could with his opportunities.

3. EARLY HOME BACKGROUND   X

Above avg.   *Avg.*   *Below avg.*

Harry's father, a moderately successful small building contractor, is described as "dominant, hard-working, hard-nosed but extremely fair" while his mother is "more sympathetic, tactful, and strongly dedicated to helping others." Quite correctly, Harry believes his own personality is more like that of his father.

Both parents nurtured the concept that Harry must make something of himself and this is probably responsible in part for his strong motivation and competitive spirit.

There is every reason to believe that Harry was raised in such a way that he developed good standards of moral character as well as good emotional adjustment during the early, formative years.

4. PRESENT SOCIAL ADJUSTMENT   X

Above avg.   *Avg.*   *Below avg.*

Harry's outside interests are understandably limited because he has been going to school during the past three years. When time permits, he likes to participate in several sports—tennis, handball, swimming, and golf.

He seems to be profoundly influenced by his wife who already has her college degree and "pushes" him to get his. She is an avid reader and may conceivably be the brighter of the two. She may also be part of the motivating force that propels him in his strong desire to get ahead in management. They have three children and seem to have achieved a good marital adjustment.

(continued)

School expenses and raising a family have prevented Harry and his wife from saving much money but he seems to have quite a good insurance program.

Health seems good and energy-level is of course very high.

Harry's present social adjustment reflects a considerable amount of maturity—a willingness to put first things first and to make present sacrifices for future gains.

5. PERSONALITY, MOTIVATION, AND CHARACTER

$(+, A+, A, A-, -)$

	X		
	Above avg.	*Avg.*	*Below avg.*

(+) a. Maturity

(+) b. Emotional adjustment

(A) c. Teamworker

(A–) d. Tact

(A) e. Adaptability

(+) f. Tough-mindedness

(+) g. Self-discipline

(+) h. Initiative

(+) i. Follow-through

(+) j. Self-confidence

(+) k. Personal Forcefulness

(+) l. Conscientiousness

(+) m. Hard worker

(+) n. Honesty and sincerity

6. SUMMARY OF ASSETS

a. Outstanding motivation

b. Good record of job accomplishment

c. A genuine "doer"

d. High energy

e. Strong competitive spirit

f. Relevant experience with electrical hardware

g. Makes maximum use of his abilities

SUMMARY OF SHORTCOMINGS

a. Needs better "people skills"—tact and social sensitivity

b. Mental ability probably not much better than average

c. Not very analytical or perceptive

d. Needs better attention to detail

e. Not yet a college graduate

f. Slightly inflexible

(continued)

7. OVERALL SUMMARY

Harry Ritter deserves great credit for what he has been able to make of himself in view of what he has had to work with. Without much in the way of early financial, educational or cultural advantages, he has managed to attain a very good record of achievement both in the Army and at Elmer Electric. He has done this primarily as a result of his tremendous energy, his willingness to work hard and to put in long hours, and his ability to make maximum utilization of his abilities. In addition, Harry has some natural leadership ability as a result of his personal forcefulness, self confidence and tough-mindedness. Finally, his experience with Elmer Electric represents a strong plus in terms of his ability to fit in here.

Negatively, Harry is not especially gifted intellectually, although his intelligence probably falls within the average range of the college population. Nor does he have a great amount of intellectual depth or breadth. Hence, he is more of a "doer" than he is a "thinker." The kind of a person who tends to push people a bit too hard, Harry needs to develop more tact and social sensitivity.

Harry Ritter's assets clearly outweigh his shortcomings—to the point that he represents a very good candidate for the first level of supervision in the manufacturing function. Actually, he has a rather ideal personality for production supervision in the sense that he is at his best when he can "put out the day-to-day fires" and move the "pieces out the door." Harry should be able to progress to the middle management level without much difficulty but it is somewhat doubtful that his intellectual capacity will carry him much beyond that point.

8. OVERALL RATING _____X_____

Excellent   Above Average   Average   Below Average   Poor

| INTERVIEW RATING FORM | Date_____ |
| | Interviewer T. Hooker |

Name Edward Teller_____ Age 30 __Position Technical Sales_____

1. WORK HISTORY

		X
Above avg.	Avg.	Below avg.

Early jobs in a boy's camp probably did not do much for his development of maturity but he apparently did manifest good "people skills" and enjoyed working with the kids.

While attending college, worked three summers as quality control lab technician at Dow Chemical where he seems to have exhibited good work habits, attention to detail, and reliability.

Since graduating from college in 1963, has worked as a research assistant at Washburn Biological Institute where his salary has increased from $5,100 to only $8,200 a year. He is co-author of several publications but there is no real evidence of any great creativity on his part. Admits that his projects were always designed and closely supervised by his superior. But he does seem to have shown qualities of organization and attention to detail. Plans to leave because "there is no future for a non-Ph.D. in the lab." He says his company is now hiring Ph.D's for more than he is earning after eight years of experience. Ed's willingness to remain in what appears to be a dead-end job—and low-paying at that—would seem to reflect lack of initiative and an inclination to take the path of least resistance. Still somewhat unsure of himself, Ed says that he has always been reluctant to "press for a raise in pay or a different job."

That Ed now wants a job in sales despite the fact that he clearly does not have a sales personality reflects his immaturity. While Ed has acquired good lab experience, he has not demonstrated much vocational achievement for a man of 30. And he has no sales experience at all.

2. EDUCATION AND TRAINING

	X	
Above avg.	Avg.	Below avg.

Did poorly in H.S. "because I didn't study hard and ran around with the wrong crowd." Apparently quite easily influenced and dependent upon others.

Did much better at Central Witner College where he graduated with a 2.9 out of a possible 4.0. Despite his conscientious study (often until 1 or 2 A.M.) he could "never pull an A" in his chemistry major. Actually, he preferred some of the humanities—English and History—to his science subjects.

(continued)

Rather artistically inclined in college, Ed played first violin in the orchestra and sang in the Glee Club.

That Ed's grades were not higher in view of his consistent effort—particularly at a school where the academic standards are not considered particularly high—would seem to indicate that his intellectual level is not especially high. Ed knows that he is "not brilliant" and admits that his grades "came as a result of hard work."

Says that he has thought about doing graduate work but one gets the impression that he is not academically inclined and will probably never do any additional study.

Ed is not particularly well trained academically and is not strongly oriented technically.

3. EARLY HOME BACKGROUND

		X	
Above avg.		*Avg.*	*Below avg.*

Raised in above average socio-economic circumstances. Father, a well established artist, is evidently very bright and creative. His mother is also a college graduate but is "less bright."

Ed says that he takes after his mother while his brother and sister "got most of the brains in the family," and take after their father. Both have I.Q.'s over 140.

The experience of growing up with two much brighter siblings probably tended to undermine Ed's self-confidence. As the youngest child he was "somewhat overprotected" and this may account in part for the fact that he did not mature very rapidly. On the other hand, he apparently did develop many fine traits of character.

4. PRESENT SOCIAL ADJUSTMENT

	X		
Above avg.		*Avg.*	*Below avg.*

Ed's outside interests are neither broad nor intellectual in nature. In fact, they are pretty much confined to spectator sports, an occasional novel, and movies. Strangely enough, he is no longer very much interested in music, even though he was very much involved in music at the time he was in college.

Ed's wife, a non-college girl, does not have intellectual interests either. But both seem very fond of their two boys and appear to get along well together.

(continued)

Despite his relatively low salary and the demands of his growing family, Ed has managed to save a fair amount of money—enough to put a sizeable down payment on a home and to establish quite a good insurance program. This attests not only to his thrift but to his sense of responsibility as well.

The indications are that Ed is in good health (has only lost three days due to sickness in the last four years). Energy-level seems above average but not really high.

5. PERSONALITY, MOTIVATION, AND CHARACTER

(+, A+, A, A−, −)

	Above avg.	Avg.	Below avg.
			X

(A−) a. Maturity

(A+) b. Emotional adjustment

(A+) c. Teamworker

(+) d. Tact

(A) e. Adaptability

(−) f. Tough-mindedness

(A+) g. Self-discipline

(−) h. Initiative

(A+) i. Follow-through

(A−) j. Self-confidence

(A−) k. Personal Forcefulness

(+) l. Conscientiousness

(A+) m. Hard worker

(+) n. Honesty and sincerity

6. SUMMARY OF ASSETS

a. Good laboratory experience

b. Generally good motivation

c. Very responsible

d. Well organized

e. Excellent character

f. Able to get along well with people.

SUMMARY OF SHORTCOMINGS

a. Not very strong intellectually

b. No sales experience

c. Does not have a sales personality.

d. Not strongly oriented technically

e. Only moderately well trained academically.

f. Relatively immature for age.

(continued)

7. OVERALL SUMMARY

Edward Teller is in many ways a fine human being. He is honest; he is responsible; he is a good family man; and he is able to get along well with others. At this point in his life, he has accumulated eight years of solid experience in the laboratory. Ed works conscientiously, is well organized and gives good attention to detail.

Although very personable, Ed's personality is not suitable for sales. He does not have enough aggressiveness and self-confidence to persuade others to his point of view. Nor does he have enough mental toughness to take rebuffs in his stride. Moreover, he is not bright enough mentally or strong enough technically to handle the demands of the sales function as it exists in this company.

In summary, although Edward Teller has many fine assets, he does not qualify for a technical sales job in our company. He not only has no sales experience but does not have the necessary personality requirements for this field. Moreover, he has not demonstrated sufficient vocational achievement for his thirty years. Consequently, further consideration is not recommended.

8. OVERALL RATING _____ X_____

Excellent   Above Average   Average   Below Average   Poor

Index

Index